DEVELOPING AND MAINTAINING PRACTICAL ARCHIVES

A How-To-Do-It Manual

Gregory S. Hunter

**HOW-TO-DO-IT MANUALS
FOR LIBRARIANS**

NUMBER 71

NEAL-SCHUMAN PUBLISHERS, INC.
New York, London

Published by Neal-Schuman Publishers, Inc.
100 Varick Street
New York, NY 10013

Printed and bound in the United States of America.

Library of Congress Cataloging-in-Publication Data

Hunter, Gregory S.
 Developing and maintaining practical archives / Gregory S. Hunter.
  p. cm.—(A how-to-do-it manual ; no. 71)
 Includes bibliographical references and index.
 ISBN 1-55570-212-0
 1. Archives—Handbooks, manuals, etc. I. Title. II. Series : How-to-it
manuals for libraries ; no. 71.
CD950.H86 1996
027—dc20   96-43872

CONTENTS

FIGURES

ACKNOWLEDGMENTS

This book is the culmination of almost twenty years' education, experience, and professional activity. Therefore there are many people to thank.

I was introduced to archives in the mid-1970s while a graduate student in New York University's History Department. Tom Bender, Mike Lutzker, and Carl Prince were my first archives teachers and also role models for my own academic career. I benefited from a year of working with Linda Edgerly in the Chase Manhattan Archives in New York City. Linda was and is a consummate professional especially concerned with the ethical aspects of archival work.

I was very fortunate to have two remarkable professional working environments. In 1978, the United Negro College, Fund, Inc. (UNCF) hired me to establish an archives for its headquarters and to work with the forty-one UNCF member colleges in improving their archives. Chris Edley and Turner Battle were excellent superiors, always very supportive of the mission of the archives. Even more, I will forever be in UNCF's debt for offering the opportunity for an Irish kid from the Bronx to meet some of this century's legendary black educators; I have been forever touched by Frederick Patterson, Benjamin Mays, Hollis Price, Albert Dent, and Harry Richardson, to name just a few. As a first generation college graduate, I remain in awe of the accomplishments of the men and women who pursued higher education early in this century and founded UNCF in the 1940s.

In 1984, I left UNCF to become Manager of Corporate Records at ITT's World Headquarters. Phil Coombe and Barry Kalen encouraged my professional growth, made it easier for me to finish my doctorate, and permitted me to teach as an adjunct. God put no better boss on this earth than Barry Kalen – and he certainly is one of the world's top ten people as well!

It was Mildred Lowe, the director of the Division of Library and Information Science at St. John's University, who arranged for me to get bitten by the teaching bug. I can never thank her enough for opening up this new world to me. Lucienne Maillet, the Dean of the Palmer School of Library and Information Science at Long Island University in 1990, worked long and hard to add me to the full-time faculty. My current dean, Anne Woodsworth, has continued to make the Palmer School a hospitable place for the study of archives and records management.

In terms of this book, I want to thank Charles Harmon, the acquisitions editor at Neal-Schuman Publishers, for his patience with me and his persistence in seeing the project through. I also want to thank the external peer reviewer who sharpened several sections of the manuscript.

Above all else, I have been blessed with an extraordinary family. My mother, Isabelle Hunter, was a liberated woman before her time who always encouraged me to follow my dreams. My wife, JoAnn Heaney-Hunter, is a nationally-recognized scholar in her own right—and "Dr. Mom" in our house. Few men are blessed with a wife who is also a friend and colleague. Her energy and courage never cease to amaze me.

Finally, I have dedicated this book to my daughters, Beth and Kate. Both of them have grown up hearing about archives and other strange things. Years ago Beth, who now is almost ready for high school, took great pride in telling me a joke she heard on Mr. Rogers: "Where did Noah keep the bees? In the ark-hives!" Kate, who is in fourth grade, recently helped me design logos for my consulting firm. May you both always know how much I love you.

DEDICATION

To my wonderful daughters, Beth and Kate. May the past be a prologue to happy and healthy lives.

PREFACE

Last year, I visited my daughter's sixth grade classroom as part of "career week" to talk about what an archivist is and does. Lawyers they knew, doctors they knew; but only one child in the class had ever heard of an archivist—and you can guess whose child that was! What a challenge it was to talk about the value of the past to children consumed by the present and anxious for the promise of the future.

How could I make archives "practical" for them? It would not be enough to quote the inscription on the front of the National Archives Building in Washington, "What is past is prologue." That would probably make things worse. I needed a way to show them that the past was not something abstract, that the past was inhabited by real people not very different from themselves, and that archivists preserve the records left by those real people.

I chose to bring to class copies of some primary sources relating to Black History Month, which was then in progress. I selected part of a transcript from an oral history interview with a freed slave; the questionnaire used to keep blacks from voting in the South; and a flyer announcing a rally at which Dr. Martin Luther King, Jr. would be present. I could see in their faces that history had a different impact once we were talking about concrete evidence of the past. We then discussed the sources the students would preserve if they were their school's archivists—sources that future generations would use to understand their school in the mid-1990s.

The phrase "Practical Archives" in this book's title, therefore, has two meanings. First, it involves making people today aware of just how much their lives depend upon the existence of archives and the information they contain. This is what I tried to do in my daughter's school last year. This also is the reason for the numerous real-life examples of the value of records found throughout the book. Secondly, managing archives can never be an abstract process; every day archival work utilizes many of archival science's practical aspects. The latter point has been brought home to me again and again in my teaching career. While those professionals working with archives have a body of theory and methodology to guide them, it is the actual practice of the archival craft that enables society to benefit from the records preserved. I always am pleased when graduates tell me that the things we discussed in class really made a difference in their working lives—that class was not only theoretical but practical.

In writing this book, I have tried to achieve an optimum balance of theory and practice. In each chapter I summarize the best thinking on archival theory and methodology and combine it with practical advice for those who are working in archives at *any* level. *Practical Archives* covers developing and maintaining archives in ten chapters. These progress from Chapter One, "Introduction to Archives and Manuscripts" which discusses what an archive is and provides basic definitions to Chapter Two, "Conducting a Survey and Starting an Archives Program" which details the steps needed to plan for and begin implementing an archival program for any type of organization. Chapters Three through Eight cover the technical basics of day-to-day operations: "Selection and Appraisal," "Acquisitions and Accessioning," "Arrangement," "Description," "Preservation," and "Security and Disaster Planning." Once these basics are in place, an archive is ready to provide "Access, Reference, and Outreach," which is the topic of Chapter Nine. The final Chapter, "Electronic Records," is of ever-increasing importance in today's world as it explores aspects of archiving electronic records from policies to system dependence.

To help readers new to archives picture an archival operation, I use a case study throughout the book in which an archive is envisioned, planned, set up, and operations begun. Additionally, I have chosen short quotes from popular newspapers and magazines that illustrate the importance of archives in different walks of life. I intend them to illustrate why archives *are* practical. Readers should feel free to use these quotes to convince administrators and others (whose exposure to archives may not be much greater than the students in my daughter's sixth grade class) why they need archives, archivists, and librarians.

Responsibility for archival records can be a daunting task. *Developing and Maintaining Practical Archives: A How-To-Do-It Manual* is intended to be both a companion for the professional journey and a balm for the frazzled archival psyche. My hope is that you will find working with archives as satisfying and rewarding as I have.

1 INTRODUCTION TO ARCHIVES AND MANUSCRIPTS

"I have drove Fords exclusively when I could get away with one," wrote a satisfied customer to Henry Ford in 1934. "For sustained speed and freedom from trouble the Ford has got ever other car skinned." The Ford Motor Company has received thousands of similar letters over the years. Why was this one preserved? Because a trained eye caught the play on words above and associated it with a famous (or infamous) author: " . . . even if my business hasn't been strictly legal it don't hurt anything to tell you what a fine car you got in the V8. Yours truly, Clyde Champion Barrow." There is no record of whether or not Bonnie agreed with Clyde's judgment.[1]

Archivists and manuscript curators are the ones whose eyes are trained to recognize such hidden values. They work in many different settings: government agencies, colleges and universities, profit-making and nonprofit corporations, religious communities and institutions, labor unions, and fraternal and similar organizations. Though the settings may vary, the mission of the archivist is the same: to identify, preserve, and make available records and papers of enduring value.[2]

This book is intended as a one-volume introduction to archives and manuscripts—a first step in the training of an archival eye. It will cover all aspects of the archivist's work, combining theory with practice.[3] As will become clear, archival management is as much an art as a science.

BASIC DEFINITIONS

Before proceeding further, it is necessary to define some basic terms. In the past it was easier to understand the meaning of archives. There was a general sense that archives were items retained for a long period of time. The information age, however, has led to confusion. "Archiving" a word-processing document, for example, now means saving it on a floppy disk, perhaps only for a day or two. The distinction between long- and short-term retention has been blurred.

As used in this book, "archives" has three possible meanings:

- *Materials.* The noncurrent records of an organization or institution preserved because of their enduring value.
- *Place.* The building or part of a building where archival materials are located (also referred to as an archival repository).
- *Agency.* The program office or agency responsible for identifying, preserving, and making available records of enduring value (also referred to as an archival agency, archival institution, or archival program).[4]

Archives is a collective noun, correctly used in the plural, though one may see the singular form used by some repositories.

In common parlance, a manuscript is either a handwritten document or the first draft of a book or article. Though correct, there is a third meaning of the term in the context of this manual. While archives are generated by organizations or institutions, manuscripts are generated by individuals or families.

The holdings of an archival repository are called "records." An example would be the records of the Ford Motor Company. By contrast, the holdings of a manuscript repository are called "papers"—for example, the Papers of Thomas Jefferson, or the Rockefeller Family Papers. It is correct, however, to refer to both records and papers as "collections." Finally, the custodian of organizational records is called an archivist, while the custodian of personal papers is called a manuscript curator. Figure 1.1 summarizes these distinctions.

Figure 1.1 Distinctions Between Archives and Manuscripts		
Category	**Archives**	**Manuscripts**
Source	Organization or Institution	Individual or Family
Specific Terminology for Holdings	Records	Papers
General Terminology for Holdings	Collections	Collections
Title for Custodian	Archivist	Manuscript Curator

Almost all organizations have records of enduring value; many have a place for the storage of these records (the place may even be *suitable* for storage); fewer organizations, however, have a department or program to manage the records effectively. This book is intended for the librarian or other professional who is responsible for archival records and wants to do the correct thing for them, but must do so on a limited budget and with modest staffing. It presents as much defensive archives as practical archives.

THE ARCHIVAL MISSION

Let's look at the mission of the archivist in greater detail. It has three elements:

- to identify records and papers of enduring value
- to preserve them
- to make them available to patrons

Were you surprised that the definition of archives did not mention permanence? Why did I use enduring—rather than permanent—value as the mark of archival records?

This subtle change of wording is relatively recent. Archivists know that most records will not last forever, despite our best intentions. Fragile physical media, atmospheric pollutants, and improper handling all take their toll. More importantly, the research value of the records may change over time, making them expendable for historical purposes. If we define archival records as having permanent value, we have bestowed sainthood on them—and have limited our ability to condemn them later on. Records of enduring value are beatified—a state below sainthood. Archivists maintain future flexibility while still treating the records with reverential care.[5]

Archivists used to think of the elements of their mission in a linear fashion: from identification through preservation, to reference and access (see Figure 1.2). This reflects the order in which archival tasks usually are accomplished. Today, however, archivists increasingly are taking a cyclical view of their work, focusing more on the objective of their work (use of the collections) than on the progression of activities (see Figure 1.3).[6]

A cyclical model of the archival mission also permits one to locate the various archival functions and to relate them to one another. As part of *identifying* records and papers of enduring

Figure 1.2 Linear Expression of the Archival Mission

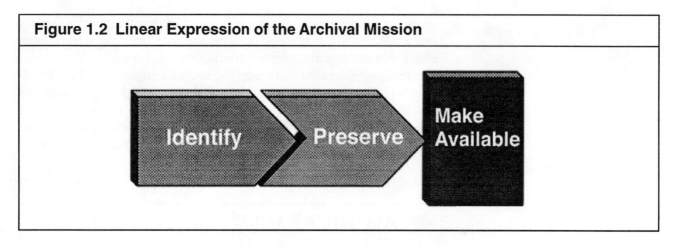

value, archivists conduct surveys and appraise records. A survey is a systematic procedure used to locate items of possible archival value. Appraisal is the process of determining the value, and thus the disposition (retention or destruction), of records.[7]

The bridge between identifying records of enduring value and preserving them is represented by two archival functions: acquisition and accessioning. Acquisition covers such areas as donor relations and contacts, and policies for collecting records and papers. Accessioning involves the actual transfer of records or papers to an archives or manuscript repository, along with the transfer of legal rights to the physical and intellectual property.

The mission of *preserving* historically valuable items encompasses three archival functions: arrangement, preservation, and security. Arrangement is the organization of archives or manuscripts in accordance with accepted professional principles. Preservation is both the protection of records from physical deterioration and damage, and the restoration of previously damaged items. Security is the safeguarding of records from natural and human disasters.

Description is the bridge between preserving records and making them available; it is the opportunity for the archivist to record what is known about the collection and its arrangement, in a way that will facilitate access by researchers. Description requires both clear and concise writing skills and a feel for the research questions archives patrons ask.

The third part of the archival mission, *making records available,* focuses on two archival functions: access and reference, and outreach and promotion. Access and reference involve more than just presenting a box of records to a researcher. Rather, archivists employ a number of policies and procedures to ensure that use of the records involves neither physical damage to the items nor vio-

Figure 1.3 Cyclical Expression of the Archival Mission

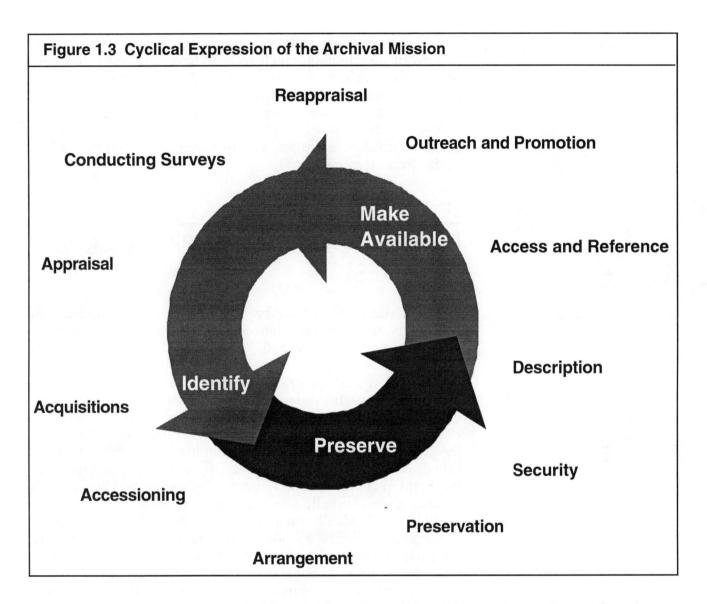

lations of copyright and the right to privacy. Outreach and promotion are attempts to make people aware of archival records and the valuable information they contain. To this end, archivists use exhibits and audiovisual presentations as well as the more traditional press releases and newspaper feature articles.

In a cyclical view, the archival mission does not end with making records available. On the contrary, archivists today use research trends and reference statistics when identifying additional records for preservation. And in a radical departure caused by the bulk and complexity of modern records, archivists are using past reference activity as a basis for *reappraising* records already in archival institutions.[8]

And so the archival mission comes full circle. It is a continuous process of determining which records have archival value, preserving them in a professional way, and making them available to a wide variety of researchers. As with a three-legged stool, no one part of the mission is more important than the other two—unless all three legs are in place, the stool will fall. A well-balanced archival program will rest firmly on the three strong legs of the archival mission.

DIFFERENCES BETWEEN LIBRARIES AND ARCHIVES

Libraries and archives have been closely related for decades. In fact, many archives collections are located within library structures, especially on college and university campuses. This does not mean, however, that libraries and archives are the same or that the theories and practices of one are transferable to the other. There are important differences that must be understood in order to manage an archives or manuscript repository properly.[9]

The nature of the items in a library and those in archives differs. The fundamental difference is that library materials are published, while archival materials are, by and large, unpublished. Furthermore, libraries collect discrete items—books, journals, videotapes, slides—usually one at a time. The books or other items are judged individually, on a case-by-case basis. In addition, most of the items collected by one library are also collected by other libraries. Therefore a particular book usually is available in more than one location. In contrast, archives collect groups of related items: the records of a particular company or institution, for example. These items do not stand alone; they gain significance and importance from their relationship to other items. Archival and manuscript collections also are unique. While occasionally two or more archival institutions may have parts of the same collection, seldom do they completely duplicate one another.[10]

There is also a difference in the creators or originators of the items collected by libraries and archives. The books, journals, videotapes, and other items acquired by a library are created by many different individuals and organizations, ranging from a lone novelist to agencies of the federal government. Archives, on the other hand, usually collect only the records generated by the parent organization or institution; there is one creator as opposed to thousands.

Figure 1.4 Differences Between Materials in Libraries and Archives		
Category	**Libraries**	**Archives**
Nature	Published	Unpublished
	Discrete items	Groups of related items
	Independent signifcance	Significance from relationship to other items
	Available elsewhere	Unique
Creator	Many different individuals or organizations	Parent organization or institution
Method of creation	Separate, independent actions	Organic—normal course of business
Method of receipt	Selected as single items	Appraised in aggregate
	Decisions revocable	Decisions irrevocable (destruction is forever)
Arrangement	Predetermined subject classification	Provenance and original order (relation to structure and function)
Level of description	Individual items	Aggregate (record group or series)
Descriptive media	Built into the published item (title page, table of contents, index)	Must be prepared by the archivist
	Card catalog, online public access system (OPAC)	Guides and inventories, online systems
Access	Open stacks	Closed stacks
	Items circulate	Items do not circulate

"In April 1945, more than 30 years before Love Canal became a synonym for toxic-chemical disaster, a manufacturing analyst at the Hooker Chemical Company wrote in an internal report that he worried about a 'potential future hazard' and a 'quagmire at Love Canal which will be a potential source of lawsuits.'

"In a Buffalo courtroom this week, R. H. Van Horne's prophetic memorandum, along with other yellowing documents from the company's archives, will be at the center of a $250 million trial of Hooker Chemical that lawyers on both sides agree will measure the company's conduct for history."—*New York Times,* October 22, 1990.

The method of creation similarly varies. Library materials are created as the result of separate independent actions by a wide variety of authors or compilers. Archival materials, however, are never explicitly created—no one in an institution says, "Today I think I'll create some archival records." Archives grow organically as part of the creation of records in the normal course of an institution's business. Only at a later date are records judged to be of archival interest and properly preserved for future generations.

"Wells Fargo & Co. was once confronted with a $480 million suit alleging that it had misappropriated an idea to start a credit-card operation. Using materials from the bank's archives dating back to the 1960s, lawyers were able to prove that Wells Fargo had developed the idea itself."—*Wall Street Journal,* December 21, 1987.

There is a difference as well in the receipt of items. Libraries usually select items one at a time, though they may buy a number of books at once from a single source. Library acquisition decisions usually are revocable—if a book is not purchased this year, it often will be available next year. An archivist appraises materials in aggregate and adds them to the collection—accessions them—in a group. Archival decisions are irrevocable—destruction is forever. The appraisal of materials is thus one of the most important duties an archivist performs.

Library materials are arranged according to a predetermined subject classification system. The Library of Congress classification system is the most widely used today, replacing such earlier classification schemes as the Dewey Decimal system. The bases for archival arrangement are two closely-related principles, provenance and original order. Since Chapter 5 defines and explains these terms, suffice it to say at this point that archival principles stipulate that records created by different organizations or entities not be mingled and that the order given the records by their creators be preserved as much as possible.

Description is different in libraries and archives. First of all, the published nature of library books and periodicals means that they come with built-in descriptive media: title pages, tables of contents, indexes, and other bibliographic access points. In contrast, archivists must build their own descriptive media for the unpublished materials under their control. Second, since library materials are acquired one at a time it is logical that they are also described.

"On any given day, a dozen or so people can be found huddled over vintage metal table lamps in the hushed reading room of the Communist Party's main archive, . . . culling the millions of files for pieces to the vast puzzle of Soviet history.

"Now called the Storage Center for Contemporary Documentation, the building in the old Central Committee complex on Staraya Square is only one depository for 204 million separate files now controlled by the Russian Government.

In the 18 months since President Boris N. Yeltsin placed all K.G.B. and Communist archives under Russia's control, a steady stream of revelations large and small has already come out. . . . Yet for every piece fitted into the puzzle, another gap becomes more glaring. . . . Many answers may never be known. Untold volumes of files have been destroyed."—*New York Times,* February 8, 1993.

"When Mount St. Helens erupted in Washington in 1980, Weyerhaeuser was faced with the enormous task of salvaging downed timber. The extent of the damage reminded old-timers at Weyerhaeuser of Typhoon Frieda in 1962, when even more timber was downed.

"Fortunately, the company had established archives in 1974, and documents relating to the earlier disaster's salvage operations were readily available. Weyerhaeuser based its Mount St. Helens operations on this information, and employed 650 loggers and 600 trucks over three years to complete the job." *Wall Street Journal,* January 16, 1989.

Since library materials are acquired one at a time, it is logical that they also are described individually. Most often this is done with a catalog, whether it be a manual or computerized system. In keeping with their nature, archival materials are not described individually, but rather in the aggregate. Archival description explains the particular group of records, their relationship to other records, and their significance for research. Though many archives use a catalog as a secondary index, the principal descriptive devices are inventories of specific collections and guides to the general holdings of a repository.

Access is also different for library and archival materials. Library materials (except for very rare, fragile, or expensive items) are stored on open shelves. Researchers locate the items they require and often are permitted to borrow them from the library. Because of their uniqueness, archival stack areas are closed to researchers. Staff members retrieve requested items and carefully observe researchers while they use the items. Archival materials do not circulate, but some repositories will provide copies (either paper, microfilm, or digital) for the private use of researchers.

Figure 1.4 summarizes the differences between libraries and archives in the area of the materials they contain. As subsequent chapters will indicate, these core differences affect all aspects of institutional administration.

Despite these many differences, it would be wrong to assume that libraries and archives have nothing in common. They share the mission of making knowledge available to a wide variety of patrons. They share a concern about the preservation of existing materials, especially those produced on paper in the last 100 years. They share a belief that what has gone before can benefit generations still to come.

And, curiously enough, they also share a saint. Lawrence the Librarian was a Church archives official in Rome. In the year 258, as part of persecution of the Church, imperial guards searching for membership lists demanded the surrender of the Church's archives. Lawrence previously had hidden the archives and refused to divulge their location. The guards tied him to a grid iron over a charcoal fire, but Lawrence still refused to relinquish the archives, telling his tormentors, "I am roasted enough on this side, turn me over and eat." In subsequent years, a cult grew up around Lawrence. Numerous churches were dedicated to him and he was the subject of artwork by Rubens, Titian, Ribera, and Fra Angelico. Even today, pilgrims still visit the basilica over the tomb of this librarian who died to defend the archives in his custody.[11]

A BRIEF HISTORY OF ARCHIVES

Archives are as old as civilization. As long as there have been records to preserve, people have preserved them. A brief history of archives will highlight this fact.

The ancient world preserved records on a variety of media. Clay tablets have survived from 690 B.C. documenting the Egibi family of Babylon's trade in slaves and real estate. Records exist on papyrus from Elephantine, a Persian military post on the Egyptian frontier garrisoned by Jewish mercenaries. These records document all aspects of community life and financial dealings.

The foundations of Western civilization, Athens and Rome, also preserved records. In Athens, valuable papyrus documents were kept in the temple of the mother of the gods. In addition to such official records as treaties, laws, and minutes, important cultural documents—what we would call manuscripts—were also maintained. Among these cultural documents were the statement Socrates wrote in his defense, plays by Sophocles and Euripides, and the lists of victors in the Olympic games. Since ancient times, then, archives and manuscripts have often gone hand-in-hand.

Rome had no official archives until the time of Cicero (first century B.C.). Catallus built the *tabularium*, the state archives of Rome, between 121 and 60 B.C.; however not all official records reached the archives. Magistrates kept *commentarii* which they took with them when they left office. Archivists today still face this problem of separating official records from personal papers.

Archives in Rome went beyond government records. Business people kept daybooks, called *adversaria*, in which they recorded daily transactions. Many prominent Roman families went so far as to keep their own "house archives," called *tablinum*. For example, the papers of the Flavius family document their own prisons, postal service, racing stables, public baths, counting houses, and Nile boats. By modern standards, the Flavius family would have been a conglomerate.[12]

Modern archives began in 1543 at Simancas in Spain. In fact, the rules developed at Simancas still remain useful to this day. Modern archives really developed, however, as a by-product of the French Revolution. France established the first of the modern national archives in order to document newly won freedoms and to protect the rights of citizens. Though some radicals wanted to destroy the records of the old order, calmer heads saw the value of these records for documenting the shortcomings of the monarchy and the need for revolution. France also was the first nation to pass a law guaranteeing citizens the right of access to archival records. After the French Revolution, government archives were considered public, not private, property.

In 1838, 50 years after the French Revolution, England established its first central archives, the Public Records Office. At that time England's badly decaying archival records were scattered in 50 repositories all over London. The historical community, in particular, pushed for the recognition of the importance of archival records and the establishment of a repository that reflected this importance. In contrast to the situation in France, the Public

Records Office was a separate department, not part of a larger ministry. This independence of the archival function was later to become a key part of archival development in the United States.

The United States did not have a national archival repository until 1934, 100 years after England. This does not mean, however, that there was no lobbying before this time. President Rutherford B. Hayes recommended a national archives in his annual messages of 1878 and 1879. The American Historical Association began pushing for a national archives in 1884. While Congress authorized the building of the National Archives in 1913, there was no construction for 20 years. For its first few years, the National Archives was an independent agency. After World War II, however, the National Archives was made a part of the General Services Administration, the agency responsible for the government's buildings and supplies. Historians and archivists fought a long battle to restore the independence of the National Archives, only achieving success in 1984.

Archives in the United States, however, go far beyond the government setting. As mentioned at the beginning of this chapter, there are archives in a wide variety of institutions and organizations. The first business archives, for example, was started in 1943 at the Firestone Tire and Rubber Company.[13] Each institutional setting will also have a story of its archives development.

A BRIEF HISTORY OF MANUSCRIPT COLLECTING

As with archives, manuscript collecting has been pursued since antiquity. In Rome, both Cicero and Pliny had collections. Caesar kept his personal papers, called *sacrarium*, separate from the state archives. His successors followed suit. Constantine moved the *sacrarium* to Constantinople in 300 A.D., where it was destroyed by fire during the reign of Justinian, 250 years later.[14]

During the medieval period, manuscripts were seldom collected except by religious groups. The efforts of monks in carefully copying and preserving key documents and books helped to preserve and document Western civilization.

The modern era of manuscript collecting began in the fifteenth century with the founding of such institutions as the Vatican Library and the Bibliothèque Nationale in France. Autograph collecting by individuals began around 1600; in England by the 1800s it was an avidly pursued, middle-class hobby.

In the United States, there were four strains of manuscript collectors: historians, institutions, editors, and autograph seekers. The earliest of the historian-collectors were Harvard-educated ministers. Their love of history led them to identify and preserve items of enduring value. Thomas Prince (1687–1758) collected the records of Plymouth plantation and the Increase Mather papers. One of Prince's students, Jeremy Belknap, was an aggressive collector. He also was instrumental in the founding in 1791 of the first collecting institution, the Massachusetts Historical Society. In Belknap's view, "There is nothing like having a *good repository*, and keeping a *good look-out*, not waiting at home for things to fall into the lap, but prowling about like a wolf for the prey." Except for the rapacious analogy, this view has endured.[15]

The Massachusetts Historical Society began the era of the institutional collector. Other states gradually followed Massachusetts's lead. Between 1830 and 1850, 35 state and local historical societies were founded. It was in the Midwest, however, that the historical society movement flourished. Lyman Draper, a private collector turned institutional collector, started the program in Wisconsin by collecting the papers of Revolutionary War heroes and trans-Allegheny pioneers. By the mid-1880s there were more than 200 state, local, and regional historical societies, though few were as active as those in Massachusetts or Wisconsin.

After 1880 there was a shift in collecting focus spurred by a new type of researcher—even then, responding to the changing needs of researchers and modifying collecting programs to meet those needs was part of the archival mission. The end of the nineteenth century saw the rise of academic historians trained in the German tradition at such institutions as Johns Hopkins and Harvard. The German method, which is still in use today in graduate schools, relied heavily on seminars and the "scientific" use of evidence found in original records. This new breed of historian criticized the local collecting focus of most historical societies. The result was the growth of manuscript collections on university campuses for educational and research purposes.

The third major strain of manuscript collecting was that of the editor-collector. These individuals acquired papers with the intention of publishing them, thereby making historical items more widely available to the public. The first of the great editor-collectors was Peter Force, who began to collect state papers in 1822. By 1853 he had published over a dozen volumes of documents in series called *American Archives* and *Tracts and Other Papers*. In 1867 Force sold to the Library of Congress for $100,000 his collection of 429 volumes of original manuscripts and 360 volumes of transcriptions. Jared Sparks, another editor-collector and future president of Harvard, published 12 volumes of diplomatic correspondence. He also devoted seven years to a multivolume biography and writings of George Washington.

The last manuscript tradition is that of the autograph collector. Yale graduate William B. Sprague was America's first major autograph collector. He was fascinated by the European hobby of collecting signatures of royalty. He decided to collect the signatures of "American royalty": the signers of the Declaration of Independence and the Constitution. After Sprague, autograph collecting grew in popularity in the United States. The first sale of a major autograph collection was in 1867 in Savannah, Georgia. This strain of autograph collecting reached its peak in the United States and Britain in the 1890s. While autograph collecting still continues, most manuscript curators today are more interested in the contents and research value of an acquisition rather than just its signature value.

THE ARCHIVAL PROFESSION TODAY

Today's archivists draw upon their professional tradition to meet the challenges posed by new records media and new institutional settings. Archival education takes place at the graduate level, which is the case with most professions. Archival education programs are found in history departments and schools of library and information science. The Society of American Archivists (SAA), the national association of archivists, has established education guidelines for the profession. The most current guidelines endorse the concept of a Master of Archival Studies (MAS), a separate degree already found in Canada. Unlike library education, there is no accreditation of archival education programs.

In addition to SAA, archivists have numerous regional and local professional organizations. Meeting several times each year, these organizations offer professional discourse in smaller settings.

In 1989, archivists established a separate national organization to certify individual practitioners. The Academy of Certified Archivists (ACA) administers a certification examination that tests the full range of archival knowledge, skills, and attitudes. There also is a national organization for government archivists—

NAGARA, the National Association of Government Archives and Records Administrators.

Befitting the electronic age, archival professional community and discourse also happen on the Internet. There is more than one discussion group or "listserv," for people interested in recordkeeping issues. There are separate forums for archives, records management, electronic records, and imaging. Using these discussion groups, archivists can get almost immediate answers to work-related questions as well as insights into professional issues.[16]

CONCLUSION

Archives and manuscripts are not something of value only in the past. Archives are important for many aspects of contemporary life; they affect us on a daily basis. Without archival records, both business transactions and personal endeavors would be more difficult, if not impossible, to complete. A young couple would not be able to close on their first home unless a search of government records confirmed a clear title to the property. A mid-career professional enrolling for an advanced degree would be rejected without a transcript of twenty-year-old grades from an undergraduate institution. A recent senior citizen awaiting a pension check from a long-term employer would wait a long time if the corporation did not maintain adequate payroll records.

Sometimes, however, we do not realize or appreciate the centrality of records. This book reinforces the centrality of records through a series of stories drawn from the news media over the past ten years. These real-world examples have a common theme—each situation would have been very different had relevant records not existed. Today's archivists help guarantee that future generations will have the records they need to function in society.[17]

Building upon a long tradition and using the strengths of such related disciplines as library science and history, archivists and manuscript curators daily try to fulfill their mission of identifying, preserving, and making available records and papers of enduring value. The rest of this book will discuss in greater detail how this is done.

NOTES

1. Letter dated April 10, 1934, from the collections of the Archives and Research Library, Henry Ford Museum, reprinted in the *American Archivist* 45 (summer 1982): 283. Authentification of documents also was a traditional duty of early archivists and remains part of the basic training for European archivists today. If Clyde Champion Barrow did not actually write this letter, its historical value would be greatly diminished.

2. This statement of the archivist's mission is adapted from *Planning for the Archival Profession: A Report of the SAA Task Force on Goals and Priorities* (Chicago: Society of American Archivists, 1986).

3. For readability, I often will use "archivist" when referring to both archivists and curators of manuscripts. While there are important distinctions, archivists and curators have enough in common to permit the use of a single term.

4. This and subsequent definitions are adapted from two archival glossaries: Lewis J. Bellardo and Lynn Lady Bellardo, *A Glossary for Archivists, Manuscript Curators, and Records Managers* (Chicago: Society of American Archivists, 1992); Frank B. Evans, et al., *A Basic Glossary for Archivists, Manuscript Curators, and Records Managers* (Chicago: Society of American Archivists, 1974).

5. See Leonard Rapport, "No Grandfather Clause: Reappraising Accessioned Records," *American Archivist* 44 (spring 1981): 143–150; James M. O'Toole, "On the Idea of Permanence," *American Archivist* 52 (winter 1989): 10–25.

6. For an example, see Elsie T. Freeman, "In the Eye of the Beholder: Archives Administration from the User's Point of View," *American Archivist*, 47 (spring 1984), 111–123.

7. Again, for convenience throughout this book I often will use the term "records" in place of the more cumbersome "records and papers." I will, however, use both terms when manuscript practice differs from archival practice.

8. The best expression of this view is found in Rapport, "No Grandfather Clause."

9. A fuller discussion of these issues is found in Lawrence J. McCrank, ed., *Archives and Library Administration: Divergent Traditions and Common Concerns* (New York: Haworth Press, 1986). See also Theodore R. Schellenberg, *Modern Archives: Principles and Techniques* (Chicago: University of Chicago Press, 1956): 17–25.

10. The best discussion of the nature of archival materials is found in James M. O'Toole, *Understanding Archives and Manuscripts* (Chicago: Society of American Archivists, 1992).

11. *SAA Newsletter* (September 1984): 6. Not all sources confirm this legend. *Butler's Lives of the Saints* has the story of St. Lawrence being roasted but does not mention that it was because of archival records. Michael Walsh, *Butler's Lives of the Saints, Concise Edition Revised and Updated* (New York: Harper Collins, 1991), 245–246.

12. For more on ancient archives, see Hilary Jenkinson, *Archives in the Ancient World* (Cambridge, Mass.: Harvard University Press, 1972); and Luciana Duranti, "The Odyssey of the Records Managers" (two parts), *ARMA Records Management Quarterly* 23 (July 1989): 3–11, and 23 (October 1989): 3–11.

13. For more on the history of business archives, see David R. Smith, "An Historical Look at Business Archives," *American Archivist* 45 (summer 1982): 273–278; and Gary D. Saretzky, "North American Business Archives: A Developmental Perspective" (unpublished paper delivered at the annual meeting of the Society of American Archivists, August 30, 1986).

14. Most of this discussion is taken from Kenneth W. Duckett, *Modern Manuscripts: A Practical Manual for Their Management, Care and Use* (Nashville, Tenn.: American Association for State and Local History, 1975).

15. See, for example, the influential article by F. Gerald Ham, "The Archival Edge," *American Archivist*, 38 (January 1975): 5–13. Kenneth W. Duckett, *Modern Manuscripts: A Practical Manual for Their Management, Care, and Use* (Nashville: AASLH, 1975), 8–9.

16. The easiest way to learn more about national and regional archival associations, archival education programs, and Internet discussion groups is to contact the Society of American Archivists, 600 S. Federal, Suite 504, Chicago, IL 60605 (312) 922-0140.

17. I am indebted to my students over the past ten years at Long Island University and St. John's University for many of these stories. The discussion of "archives in the news" is a regular part of my introductory archives class.

2 CONDUCTING A SURVEY AND STARTING AN ARCHIVES PROGRAM

Starting an archives program involves two related functions: conducting a survey of the universe of records available within an organization or institution, and establishing basic policies and structures for the nascent archives. These activities usually happen simultaneously; while conducting a records survey, the archivist is also drafting basic policies and shepherding them through the administrative hierarchy.[1] Therefore the topics could be discussed in any order. This chapter, however, will look first at the records and then turn to the structure of the archives. This order reflects the situations in the real world where archivists must often begin the work for which they were hired even when the niceties of policy statements and other organizational basics are not yet in place.

INSTITUTIONAL CONTEXT

The real-world nature of archival work makes it difficult to discuss conducting a survey—and indeed any of the topics in this book—in the abstract. To help make concepts more concrete, I will use a fictitious institution, North Fork University (NFU), for many of the examples.

NFU is a private institution that collects both university archives and nonuniversity papers and records in a department of Archives and Special Collections. Since the department was recently created, much remains to be done. Appendix A provides background information on NFU.

SURVEYS: AN INTRODUCTION

A survey is formally defined as a systematic procedure used by archivists, manuscript curators, and records managers to gather information about records and papers not in their immediate custody.[2] The key points are that a survey is *systematic* rather than haphazard or piecemeal, and that a survey is for records *not under the immediate control* of the archivist. Depending on the type of survey, the records might be elsewhere in the organization or they might be in another archival repository.

Surveying records is an important archival skill, but one which does not currently receive enough emphasis within the profession. Everything else an archivist does—appraisal, arrangement, description, reference, and outreach—presupposes the ability to locate and identify records. Informed appraisal decisions, in particular, require detailed knowledge of all relevant records.

Perhaps surveys lost their glamour when they lost their grant funds. During the 1970s and early 1980s, a number of large surveys were conducted under federal and other grants. An example is the Women's History Sources Survey, funded by the National Endowment for the Humanities. While such large-scale projects may be less likely in the present economic climate, surveying needs to be reemphasized as a basic skill applicable to and essential for any archival situation.

Surveys can be a key part of the archivist's active role of consciously choosing records and papers for preservation, rather than waiting for the fallout from the modern paper explosion to land upon the archival repository. Any survey, large or small, enlarges the archivist's vision beyond the walls of the archives office and beyond the present holdings of the repository.

TYPES OF SURVEYS

There are four types of surveys in which an archivist may be involved:

- records management survey (single repository)
- archival records survey (single repository)
- multirepository survey
- nonrepository survey

Though there are differences among these types of surveys, many of the skills required to conduct them are interchangeable.[3]

RECORDS MANAGEMENT SURVEY

A records management survey covers a well-defined body of records—those for which the surveyor has administrative respon-

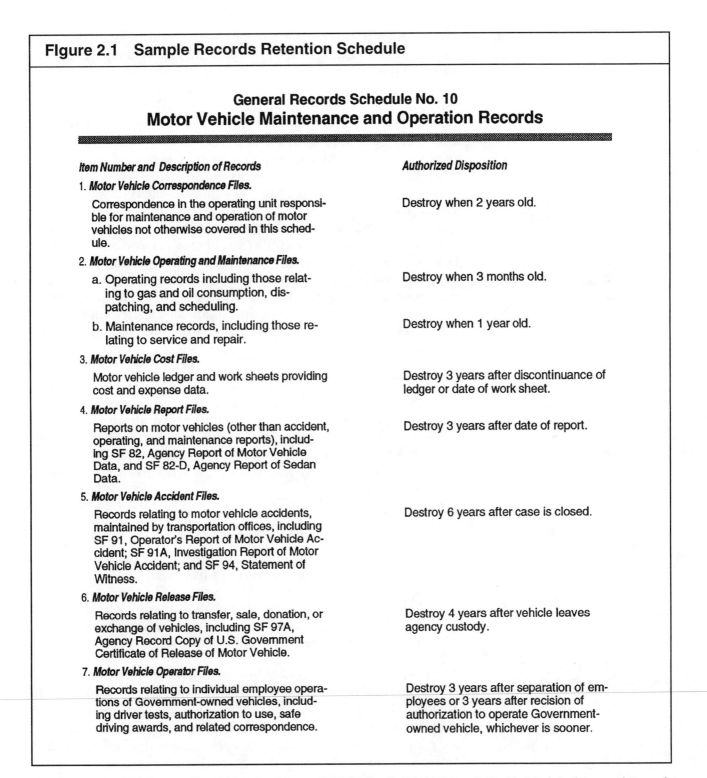

Figure 2.1   Sample Records Retention Schedule

General Records Schedule No. 10
Motor Vehicle Maintenance and Operation Records

Item Number and Description of Records	Authorized Disposition
1. Motor Vehicle Correspondence Files.	
Correspondence in the operating unit responsible for maintenance and operation of motor vehicles not otherwise covered in this schedule.	Destroy when 2 years old.
2. Motor Vehicle Operating and Maintenance Files.	
a. Operating records including those relating to gas and oil consumption, dispatching, and scheduling.	Destroy when 3 months old.
b. Maintenance records, including those relating to service and repair.	Destroy when 1 year old.
3. Motor Vehicle Cost Files.	
Motor vehicle ledger and work sheets providing cost and expense data.	Destroy 3 years after discontinuance of ledger or date of work sheet.
4. Motor Vehicle Report Files.	
Reports on motor vehicles (other than accident, operating, and maintenance reports), including SF 82, Agency Report of Motor Vehicle Data, and SF 82-D, Agency Report of Sedan Data.	Destroy 3 years after date of report.
5. Motor Vehicle Accident Files.	
Records relating to motor vehicle accidents, maintained by transportation offices, including SF 91, Operator's Report of Motor Vehicle Accident; SF 91A, Investigation Report of Motor Vehicle Accident; and SF 94, Statement of Witness.	Destroy 6 years after case is closed.
6. Motor Vehicle Release Files.	
Records relating to transfer, sale, donation, or exchange of vehicles, including SF 97A, Agency Record Copy of U.S. Government Certificate of Release of Motor Vehicle.	Destroy 4 years after vehicle leaves agency custody.
7. Motor Vehicle Operator Files.	
Records relating to individual employee operations of Government-owned vehicles, including driver tests, authorization to use, safe driving awards, and related correspondence.	Destroy 3 years after separation of employees or 3 years after recision of authorization to operate Government-owned vehicle, whichever is sooner.

Disposition of Federal Records: A Records Management Handbook (Washington, D.C.: National Archives and Records Admininstration, 1992).

sibility and authority. Such a survey is intended to identify *all* the records of an organization or institution, usually the parent institution of the archives. This kind of all-inclusive survey is a basic part of any records management program.

Records managers are interested in records from the time of their creation through their ultimate disposition (either permanent preservation or destruction). Therefore a records management survey tries to be as complete as possible—including active as well as inactive records, records in the offices as well as those in storage, and records of enduring value as well as those of short-term value.

A records management survey usually results in the creation of "records retention schedules." (See Figure 2.1 for an example.) These documents list all the records of an organization and assign retention periods and storage locations for each. The schedules are signed by all affected parties (the department that created the records, legal counsel, tax and financial experts, and the archivist) and become the approved plan for the maintenance of the organization's records.[4]

ARCHIVAL RECORDS SURVEY

An archival records survey also deals with records for which the surveyor has administrative responsibility and authority. Unlike a full-scale records management survey, however, this is a quick-fix approach when faced with severe time constraints. The object of this type of survey is to separate archival from nonarchival records quickly.

An example may clarify the situation. Very often an archivist beginning a program faces a challenge similar to the one at NFU:

> The new archivist received a call from Plant Operations one morning. A crew renovating a basement boiler room discovered some boxes of old records. The space must be cleared immediately so that the renovation can continue. The archivist must select the historically valuable records quickly; the rest will be destroyed.

Clearly it is not possible to prepare detailed retention schedules in the brief time allotted—this will have to wait until later in the life of the archival program. All that is possible now is a quick sort of the inactive records.[5] It is best, however, not to destroy any records until all records have been surveyed. Until the archivist has a thorough grasp of the entire universe of available records, it will be difficult to determine, for example, if these are duplicate copies. Records discovered later in the survey may af-

"Hundreds of unpublished songs, some previously unknown, by George Gershwin, Jerome Kern, Victor Herbert, Richard Rodgers and other composers have been identified in a treasure-trove of musical manuscripts stored in a Warner Brothers warehouse in Manhattan.

"The music—80 crates of it—was discovered in Secaucus, N.J., nearly five years ago. But because of the value of the material and the copyrights involved, the manuscripts were immediately moved to a vault in Manhattan, where they have remained virtually inaccessible ever since.

"Now the music has finally been examined and an inventory has been prepared. The contents are more bountiful than anybody had dared dream."—*New York Times,* March 10, 1987.

fect the appraisal decisions: remember that archivists appraise records in groups.

There are two final points about an archival records survey. First, a quick sort is not necessarily haphazard. The survey should still be systematic, keeping, at a minimum, detailed lists of records saved and destroyed. Second, an archival records survey should have a conservative bias. Though the archivist at NFU will attempt to reduce volume quickly, it should not be done at the expense of records of possible enduring value. If in doubt, it is better to retain a particular record until it can be appraised in detail at a later date. With a smaller volume of records and less time constraint, a final decision can be reached.

MULTIREPOSITORY SURVEY

A multirepository survey, the third major type of survey, deals with materials in more than one archival agency or institution. Unlike the previous two types of surveys, this one involves records or papers over which the surveyor does not have administrative control. The survey usually is intended to identify materials united in some way: by subject, type of record, or geographical region, for example. Very often these surveys are funded with outside grants and result in a published guide to aid researchers—the previously mentioned Women's History Sources Survey is an example. Beginning archivists usually will not be involved in administering this type of survey, although they may be asked to participate by completing questionnaires about their repositories.

NONREPOSITORY SURVEY

Beginning archivists also may have little involvement with the fourth type of survey, the nonrepository survey. This survey is directed at records outside archival custody. The survey usually has one or more of the following objectives:

- to make the creators and custodians of records more aware of the historical value of materials
- to improve access to materials not in archives
- to identify records or papers for possible acquisition by the surveying institution

An example of a nonrepository survey is the "Brooklyn Rediscovery" project of the Brooklyn Educational and Cultural Alliance. This grant-funded project identified records of historical value not already in archival custody.

A nonrepository survey can be tricky, especially if it is intended as a precursor to acquisitions. The surveyor must tread a fine line: a records custodian who fears loss of the records may choose not to participate in the survey at all. The ill will created may even have the undesired effect of *reducing* access to the records in the future. As the next section will discuss, it is important to define the goals of a survey and to design the survey to meet these goals.

SURVEY GOALS

Any survey, even a small one, is a complex task. It will require a great deal of time and effort, resulting in the diversion of staff time from other activities. In order to have an effective survey, it is necessary to define the survey's goals—what it is intended to accomplish.

There is a difference between an *efficient* and an *effective* survey. An efficient survey gets the work done: there are procedures to smoothly report and summarize information about records. An effective survey, however, gets the *right* work done: it collects information to meet the survey's goals. It is possible to have an efficient survey without having an effective one—it is similar to an airline baggage operation that safely and smoothly delivers your suitcase to the wrong continent.[6]

The way to ensure effectiveness is to focus on the goals of the survey and to monitor constantly the progress toward these goals. There are six possible goals of a records survey, each of which will be discussed in detail. While many surveys will have more than one goal from the following list, usually one goal predominates:

- to aid researchers
- to foster administrative efficiency
- to promote preservation of archival materials
- to further a collecting program
- to improve planning for archival programs
- to educate and train

TO AID RESEARCHERS

The goal to aid researchers is a natural extension of the archivist's mission of identifying, preserving, and *making available* for research records of enduring value. This goal usually applies to all types of records surveys, with the possible exception of a records management survey. A good example is the New York Historical Documents Inventory (HDI), which produced county-by-county guides to historical records across the state.

If a survey is intended to aid research, it should be designed for the broad benefit of as many researchers as possible. However as Chapter 9 shows, identifying "the researcher" in archives is not as easy as it sounds. Researchers come from a broad range of backgrounds and interests: academics, genealogists, lawyers, students, and reporters, to name a few. In many cases archivists and manuscript curators have incorrectly assumed that they understood the needs of researchers. This has led to surveys of questionable value.[7]

TO FOSTER ADMINISTRATIVE EFFICIENCY

The goal to foster administrative efficiency applies particularly to a records management survey—economy and efficiency are basic goals of any records management program. The records manager tries to reduce the use of expensive office space and equipment, substituting lower-cost options like storage in a records center or microfilming.

But administrative efficiency will also benefit the archivist. Better administration of current and noncurrent records permits easier identification and transfer of archival records. Microfilming also can be of value by substituting a more permanent storage medium for modern, highly acidic papers. A survey is the important first step toward improving the efficiency of records administration.

TO PROMOTE PRESERVATION OF ARCHIVAL MATERIALS

The immediate result of many surveys is the transfer of valuable materials to better storage conditions, if not to a formal archives collection. Sometimes, by carefully documenting through a sur-

"New York City has faced urban crises, fiscal crises, even crises of confidence. But today, says Cooper Union architecture professor Kevin Bone, it faces an archival crisis.

"The city, he says, has hundreds of thousands of historical documents crammed in warehouses, closets, and basements—and many are in peril. Bone's own students helped discover an enormous cache of rare drawings, maps, and blueprints of the city's waterfront tucked away in the leaky, rodent-infested ground floor of the Battery Maritime Building on South Street...."—*New York,* January 17, 1994.

vey the poor quality of records storage, it is possible to build institutional support for improvement. If the survey report is combined with reasonable suggestions for action (those which take into account such factors as institutional budget, staffing levels, and physical facilities), it is possible to get quite a bit done. But without a well-designed and well-managed survey, there will be insufficient data upon which to base recommendations for action.

TO FURTHER A COLLECTING PROGRAM

Very often the goal to further a collecting program is part of a nonrepository survey. After surveying and identifying records, the archivist tries to convince records creators to transfer them to archival control. Sometimes records creators are relieved that the records for which they have cared will now be properly preserved and made more widely available. Also, the creator often is flattered that an archival or manuscript repository thinks the records are of enduring value.

As mentioned previously, it requires a great deal of tact to balance surveying and acquisitions in such a way that the records creator is not threatened. The archivist must realize at the outset that most of the records identified in a nonrepository survey will *not* be potential donations. Overzealousness for acquisitions may endanger the openness of respondents toward the survey.

TO IMPROVE PLANNING FOR ARCHIVAL PROGRAMS

Perhaps the key goal in any survey is to improve planning for archival programs, but it is a goal that does not receive enough emphasis. Even if a survey does not result in the immediate transfer of any records, it can be a valuable means of identifying priorities for the future and of marshaling resources to meet those priorities. To spend time on a survey, without using the results for institutional planning, is a squandering of resources. Similarly, to plan for an archival program without having an accurate survey of existing records and storage conditions is to risk failure of the entire effort.

An example of using a survey as a planning tool is a project undertaken in 1982 by the United Negro College Fund (UNCF), a fund-raising consortium for 41 private, predominantly black colleges and universities. With a grant from the National Historical Publications and Records Commission, UNCF developed a program to help its member colleges and universities establish or improve archival programs. The program consisted of a six-day training institute on the basics of archives followed by a survey of member institutions. Each college surveyed both archival records and institutional resources available to care for the records. After the survey, UNCF member institutions were eligible for consultant visits from recognized archival experts to help develop plans. Several UNCF institutions have built upon these plans in the intervening years to improve archival preservation.[8]

TO EDUCATE AND TRAIN

Education and training can be an important part of any survey. As part of the UNCF survey, for example, at least one person from each college was trained in the basics of archives. Not only can the survey educate the surveyors, but it can also educate the administrators within an institution. Reporting survey results can offer an entrée for the discussion of archival topics and issues. The firm foundation laid here can support the entire future archival program.

Figure 2.2 summarizes the above discussion. It shows the connection between survey types and survey goals.

PLANNING A SURVEY

Since most beginning archivists will be involved first in surveying the records of their own institutions, this section and the next focus on planning and implementing such an in-house survey. Many of the techniques apply to both a records management and an archival records survey; therefore they will be discussed together.[9]

In addition to defining the goals of a records survey, planning requires answering five basic questions:

- Who will coordinate the survey?
- Who will conduct the survey?

Figure 2.2 A Comparison of Survey Types and Survey Goals				
	Survey Types			
SURVEY GOALS	Records Management Survey	Archival Records Survey	Multirepository Survey	Nonrepository Survey
Aid Researchers		X	X	X
Foster Efficiency	X	X		
Promote Preservation		X		X
Further Collecting	X	X		X
Improve Planning	X	X		
Educate and Train	X	X	X	X

- How will you gather the information?
- What information will you collect?
- What will you do with the information gathered?

WHO WILL COORDINATE THE SURVEY?

The first order of business is to determine who will have administrative responsibility for the survey. Usually one person is the "project director" who will coordinate the day-to-day effort. Many projects also use an advisory board or committee to provide additional expertise, to involve those people being surveyed, and to receive guidance from researchers and other users of the survey results. The archival advisory committee is covered later in this chapter.

WHO WILL CONDUCT THE SURVEY?

Will your staff conduct the survey, or will you expect the staff of the surveyed departments to complete the assignment in addition to their regular duties? There will be more consistent results if a specialized project staff conducts the survey—because there are fewer people to train and monitor. Budgetary constraints, however, may not permit hiring additional staff. When that is the case, the archives will have to use the staff of the surveyed departments and design effective controls to ensure usable results. Another way to reduce costs—one which should not be overlooked—is to use archival students or volunteers to conduct the survey.

HOW WILL YOU GATHER THE INFORMATION?

This question is directly related to the previous one. The principal options are

- to use field workers to visit each department or institution
- to send a questionnaire to the departments for completion

Among the factors to consider in making this decision are the complexity of the survey, the strain on the surveyed institution or department, the skill of the people in the surveyed institution or department, and the project budget.

If at all possible, it usually is better to have field workers visit all survey sites. The people in the surveyed institutions or departments have many other responsibilities; a questionnaire to complete independently will be low on their list of priorities. The best way to get good consistent data—data on which one can base future decisions—is to have regular project staff conduct the survey through on-site visits. This consistency becomes even more important if a computer will be used to compile, summarize, and analyze data.

WHAT INFORMATION WILL YOU COLLECT?

The project director must select the appropriate level of detail for the survey. As Chapter 5 on "Arrangement" discusses in much greater depth, archivists usually think in terms of five levels of detail. The levels and an example of each are as follows (terminology is defined in Chapter 5):

Level of Detail	Example
Repository	North Fork University
Record Group	Comptrollers Department
Series	Check Vouchers
File Unit	Vouchers 9600-9625
Item	Voucher 9617

The series is the most common level for a records survey. A records series is defined as materials used or filed together as a unit because of a relationship among them resulting from their creation, receipt, or use. In the earlier example, the NFU Comptrollers Department would contain many records series: accounts payable check vouchers, general and subsidiary ledgers, journal vouchers, financial statements, audit reports, and debit and credit advices, for example. A survey done at the series level would generate one survey form for each of these categories.

The survey form is the first link between the series and the researcher. The success or failure of the survey will depend in large measure upon the survey form used. Careful survey design is especially important if the survey takes the form of a questionnaire completed by the staff of the surveyed institution.

The general rule for survey forms is to *keep them as brief as possible:* the longer the survey form, the lower the response rate and the poorer the quality of the responses one receives. While there are numerous pieces of information that would be nice to collect about a records series, the person designing the form must determine which pieces of information are *essential* to the survey. Is the information so important that it merits inclusion on the form even if it lowers the response rate? Unless the answer is a resounding "yes," the question probably should be omitted. The ideal is a one-page survey form that follows a logical order and is easy to complete. An example appears in Figure 2.3.

Another advantage of using a one-page form is that instructions or guidelines for completion can be placed on the back of the form for easy reference. The inclusion of "check offs" for the most common responses will speed form completion; the use of such boxes also makes it easier to compile survey results. Most database software packages permit the creation of electronic

Figure 2.3 Survey Form

SERIES INVENTORY FORM

1. DATE PREPARED	2. OFFICE MAINTAINING THE FILES *(Name and symbol)*

3. PERSON DOING INVENTORY *(Name, office, phone number)*	4. SERIES LOCATION

5. SERIES TITLE	6. INCLUSIVE DATES

7. SERIES DESCRIPTION

8. MEDIUM *(check all that apply)*
- ❏ Paper
- ❏ Microform
- ❏ Electronic *(use information system form)*
- ❏ Audiovisual *(use audiovisual form)*

9. ARRANGEMENT
- ❏ Subject file classification system
- ❏ Alphabetical by name
- ❏ Alphabetical by subject
- ❏ Geographical by *(specify)*
- ❏ Numerical by *(specify)*
- ❏ Chronological
- ❏ Other*(specify)*

10. VOLUME *(in cubic feet)*

11. ANNUAL ACCUMULATION *(in cubic feet or inches)*

12. CUTOFF *(e.g., end of FY)*

13. REFERENCE ACTIVITY *(after cutoff)*
- ❏ Current *(At least once a month per file unit)*
  For how long after cutoff?_____
- ❏ Semicurrent *(Less than once a month per file unit)*
- ❏ Noncurrent *(Not used for current agency business)*

14. VITAL RECORDS STATUS: ❏ Yes ❏ No
(If yes, indicate type here; use entry 15 to show any duplication.)
____ Emergency-operating ____ Rights-and-interests ____ Both

15. DUPLICATION: Are documents in this series available in another place or medium? ❏ Yes ❏ No
(If yes, explain where and in what medium.)

16. FINDING AIDS *(if any)*

17. RESTRICTIONS ON ACCESS AND USE

18. CONDITION OF PERMANENT RECORDS
❏ Good ❏ Fair ❏ Poor
Comment:

19. DISPOSITION AUTHORITY: Does the series have an approved disposition authority?
❏ Yes *(List the schedule and item number, give the current disposition instructions, and justify any proposed change.)*

❏ No *(Propose an appropriate retention period.)*

Disposition of Federal Records: A Records Management Handbook (Washington, D.C.: National Archives and Records Admininstration, 1992) III-11.

forms: as each form is completed on the computer, responses are automatically entered into a database.

Most forms collect the following information for each records series:

- *Creator*. The department or individual that originated the records.
- *Title*. Both the formal title of the record series and any "slang" or abbreviated title. For example, audit reports might also be known as "red binder studies."
- *Location*. Where the records are now located. Some survey forms have several lines for listing records both in office areas and in storage. This permits completion of only one form per record series, no matter where the records are found.
- *Quantity*. What is the total volume of records found in each location? Quantity can be expressed by number of file drawers, number of boxes, or filing inches on open shelves, for example. Most forms, however, include space for conversion to the standard archival measure of cubic feet. This standard permits easier planning and better space management. The most common conversions are found in Figure 2.4.
- *Inclusive dates*. The beginning and ending dates for the records in each location. In addition to the span dates, it also is helpful to note the dates of greatest concentration. For example, the survey may uncover records dated from 1926 to 1985, with the bulk of the records dated from 1980 to 1985.
- *Description*. What the records series contains. Some examples are correspondence, minutes, photographs, bound volumes, and forms.
- *Current use*. A brief explanation of the purpose of the records series. Why was it created? What function or activity does it facilitate? How does the originating department use the records series? This information is important in assessing the value of the records series for preservation purposes.
- *Arrangement*. How the originating department organized the records. Typical arrangements are numerical, chronological, and alphabetical.
- *Form*. An assessment of such things as the size of the paper (letter or legal), its color, and whether or not both sides of the paper are used.
- *Medium*. Are the records on paper, microfilm, photographic media, or computer tape or disk?

- *Physical condition.* Is the paper torn or brittle? Is it badly yellowed? Are the records so far beyond salvaging that they are not worth saving?
- *Relationship to other records.* An important aspect of appraisal is whether or not the records are "unique." Is there an exact physical duplicate of the records stored elsewhere? (For example, is a second copy of the form filed by another department?) Is the intellectual content of the records series summarized elsewhere?
- *Frequency of use.* Usage is often difficult to gauge in a quick survey. People usually overestimate their use of a particular record. Short of a detailed user study, the best that may be possible is a range of reference: Do you use the records every day? Once a week? Once a month? Once a lifetime?
- *Annual accumulation.* How fast is the records series growing? This information is important for planning space in a records center.

A form that gathers the above information will enable the archivist to meet the specific goals of the records survey.

Figure 2.4 Cubic Foot Equivalents[10]	
Item	**Equivalent (expressed in cubic feet)**
One letter-size file drawer	1.50
One legal-size file drawer	2.00
Seven reels of standard digital computer tape (2400 feet long, $1/2$ inch wide)	1.00
One standard records center carton	1.00
Fifty 100-foot 35mm microfilm reels	1.00
One hundred 100-foot 16mm microfilm reels	1.00
One letter-size archives box	0.35
One legal-size archives box	0.43

WHAT WILL YOU DO WITH THE INFORMATION GATHERED?

The last consideration in planning a survey is to determine what you will do with the results. It is foolish to conduct a survey without planning for the dissemination of the findings; the survey form and procedures should be designed to facilitate reporting of the results.

The principal options for the product of a survey are

- to compile and file information
- to produce an internal report for management
- to publish a guide for external distribution

While the first option may seem facetious, it is the end product of too many surveys. After all the time and expense involved in a records survey, very often nothing is done with the results. The survey forms are filed away and quickly forgotten; in a few years it is necessary to conduct another survey to reassess the mess. The effort required for a survey is only justified if it leads to some action—a survey should be a means, not an end.

Most surveys result in internal reports to management recommending actions to improve the present situation. As stated before, a carefully crafted survey followed by reasonable recommendations for action often can achieve quite a bit. It is important to keep in mind, however, that years of neglect probably will take years to correct. Therefore the survey results may lead to a plan of action for the next five or ten years, rather than just for the next six months.

Survey projects intended to promote research usually publish a guide at the end of the project. A guide can take many forms: an elaborate hardcover volume; an inexpensively produced, offset pamphlet; a computer printout; a computer tape or disk; a roll of microfilm; or a page on the World Wide Web. Whatever its form, the guide should meet the needs of the target audience of researchers. This is possible only if the design and format of the guide are considered at the earliest stages of planning the survey and if they are reconsidered and revised as necessary throughout the project.

IMPLEMENTING A SURVEY

The bridge between planning and implementing a survey is a realistic action agenda. This document should list all the various activities of the survey along with target completion dates. It should divide big projects into smaller units, in order to make them easier to understand and achieve. The action plan becomes the basic control document for monitoring the progress of the survey. Figure 2.5 is an example of an action plan.

Figure 2.5 Action Plan for North Fork University's Records Survey	
Activity	**Completion Date**
Select departmental liaisons	June 1
Train department liaisons	July 1
Design and test survey form	August 15

Survey departments
    Accounting
    Public Relations
    Personnel
	
	August 30
	September 15
	September 30

Issue report to management
    First draft
    Final copy
	
	October 31
	December 31

The activities involved in implementing a survey can be divided into two broad categories: activities before visiting departments and activities during the actual visits.

Before visiting the departments, it is important to have the project personnel structure in place—the project director, advisory committee (if any), and departmental liaisons. It is also important to have visible evidence of top management support in the form of an authorizing policy statement, which is discussed later in this chapter, or a management memorandum.

The management memorandum directs each department head to appoint a contact person, or liaison, to work with the survey team. The liaison should be someone with a thorough knowledge of the department files. While the liaison will not do the actual survey, he or she will be expected to be available to clarify the purposes of file series and to explain the various uses of the files. If the survey results in the transfer of records to lower-cost, inactive storage, the liaison will be the one to box and ship records and to request retrieval of the records as necessary.

Before conducting the full survey, it is a good idea to test the form on one or two departments. The time spent at this point may save a great deal of time later in the project. Since so much of the success of the survey depends upon the quality of the survey form, it is not unreasonable to review as many as four drafts of the form.

Both before and during the survey it is desirable to publicize the project using whatever internal media are available. Employee newsletters, in particular, can help build interest in the project. Articles in such publications should stress the value of the project to the surveyed departments, rather than focus on the intricacies of the survey. Orientation sessions, especially for departmental liaisons, are another common way of promoting the project.

When one is ready to begin the actual survey, it is crucial to consider the order in which to visit the departments. Careful selection of the first department to be surveyed is especially important, since the organizational grapevine will quickly spread word of your success or failure.

It is best to begin the survey with a visible, mid-level department. The archivist should avoid beginning with the highest administrative levels for two reasons. First, since the survey staff will be new to the game, it is best to make mistakes with someone other than the president. Second, beginning at such a high level may build unreasonable expectations for the completion time of the survey: it will take time to survey all other departments.

On the other hand, beginning with a department too low in the administrative hierarchy, such as the mail room, can affect the "word of mouth" about the project. It may also reduce the "clout" carried to the next department on the survey schedule.

An example of a visible, mid-level department is public relations. This department often has valuable records; more important, however, are the organizational contacts of the department. Doing a good job with a department such as this will help with surveying other departments.

This is not to say that every survey should begin with public relations. Another item to consider is the "resistance factor." All things being equal, one should follow the path of least resistance. In terms of a records survey, this means beginning with friends or supporters, those enthusiastic about the project. Why begin with the reluctant and unenthusiastic? After all, you may be seen as a threat by some long-term custodians of records. It is better to save these people until the end of the survey, when you have built up momentum and have a track record for successfully surveying other departments. If necessary, you can then have senior management back up their authorizing memorandum with a friendly follow-up memo.

No matter where one begins the survey, it is important to pay an early visit to the big records creators. In most organizations, this means the accounting department. Though such a large department may seem daunting, it really is quite manageable. While accounting records series are large, they usually are straightforward: check vouchers, general ledgers, journal vouchers, and expense accounts. Also, guidelines often exist for the retention of such records. In this regard, the Internal Revenue Service has been very helpful. Because of these factors, it usually is easier to survey accounting records than to survey convoluted subject files in other departments.

There is another reason for visiting the large records creators early in the survey. If one of the survey goals is to save space by shifting inactive records to lower-cost storage, the transfer of accounting records may produce sufficient savings to justify the entire program. Studies have shown that the ten largest records series in an organization account for over 50 percent of the storage requirement. Several of these series may be found in the accounting department.

SURVEYING INDIVIDUAL DEPARTMENTS

Once the order of the departments has been set, it is time to develop a strategy for the actual survey of each department. The following strategy has proven successful:

1. Contact the department head in advance to schedule the visit. Send a copy of the authorizing memorandum and any other background materials you may have.
2. On the day of the survey, make a courtesy call on the department head, but plan on spending most of your time with the liaison.
3. First survey the active records still in the office files. This will make best use of the liaison. Later, when surveying the storage areas, you can try to match inactive records series with the active ones. To begin by plunging into an inactive storage area would take a great deal more time and lead to a considerable amount of confusion.

4. Sketch a floor plan of the department before beginning the survey. Identify and number all filing equipment. This will help with the subsequent transfer or destruction of records.

5. Systematically proceed around the department until you have surveyed all the files. Except for badly disorganized "miscellaneous" files, you will not need to review in detail individual files. A series of questions and answers with the liaison will identify the files, their arrangement, and purpose.

6. Because of this give-and-take approach, some experienced records surveyors prefer not to attempt to complete forms while walking around the department. They prefer to jot down notes on a pad as the liaison speaks, saving until later the distillation of these notes onto the survey instrument. These surveyors find that the form sometimes constrains them and discourages rather than encourages an open exchange. It is best to use whatever style makes you most comfortable, as long as you get the information necessary for the form.

7. After completing the survey, send a draft copy of the floor plan and survey results to the liaison. The draft copy will serve as a future reference for answering questions and clarifying the nature of the records series. It is also an important statement of the partnership between you and the liaison. Remember that a survey is not just something you do *to* a department; a successful survey must be done *with* them. This partnership will be particularly valuable when you develop retention schedules for the various departments.

8. Throughout the survey project, issue regular reports to management. These reports should be frank and truthful. It is best not to wait until the end of the project to surprise management with problems. This can ruin your credibility and endanger the entire emerging archival program. Management is used to problems—every project has them. Hiding problems will not solve them. Often the opposite happens: a submerged problem gets worse. Reports should be easy and quick to read. In particular, a graphic presentation is helpful for giving an overview of progress to date. The report need not be elaborate: it could just be a restatement of your action plan along with an accounting of what has been accomplished.

9. Finally, be certain to thank both the department head and the liaison at the conclusion of the survey. Thank-yous are especially important if you will be working with the liaison to draft retention schedules and transfer records.

STARTING AN ARCHIVES PROGRAM

While a well-designed and carefully implemented survey is a basic part of a beginning archival program, it is not the only part. There are a number of basic issues that the archivist must consider in establishing the program. As the previous sections of this chapter imply, many of these issues can be addressed as part of the records survey, especially at the planning stage. By way of summary, three items that a nascent archival program should consider are:

- issuance of an authorizing policy statement
- placement of the archives within the administrative hierarchy
- use of an advisory committee

AUTHORIZING POLICY STATEMENT

An authorizing policy statement, sometimes called a mission statement, is the foundation for all actions undertaken by the archivist. If possible, it should be approved by the highest governing body of the organization—the board of directors or the president—to make it clear that the archival program has the support of top management.

There are two strategies for getting a policy statement approved:

- Take a long time to work out every eventuality in writing before seeking administrative approval of the statement.
- Develop a very brief (one paragraph) statement that can be approved quickly. Revise and expand upon this statement at a later date as circumstances require.

The choice of strategy will depend upon the situation within the parent institution. Are you likely to be able to go to the governing body only once for approval? If so, it is better to take a longer time to develop a more detailed policy statement. Do you have an immediate need for a sign of top management support? If so, then a brief policy statement that meets the present need may be preferable to a more detailed—but delayed—document.

Federal grants agencies have been instrumental in encouraging the development of archival policy statements. One factor in evaluating grant applications is to assess the level of institutional commitment to and support for the project. A policy statement approved by the highest governing body is one indication of such support. It some cases, the granting agency may require (rather than just recommend) the issuance of a policy statement.

Policy statements for archival programs typically cover the following points:

- purpose or mission
- responsibilities and duties of the archivist
- responsibilities of others throughout the institution
- scope of items the archives or manuscript repository will collect
- prohibition against the removal or destruction of records without prior approval of the archivist

Longer or more detailed policy statements may also discuss other areas. Some of the more common areas are:

- access to records
- records management
- copying or reproducing records[11]

Figure 2.6 is an example of a policy statement, one for the NFU Department of Archives and Special Collections.

A good policy statement also can serve a public relations or outreach function. This brief statement can make both other staff members and the outside world aware of what the archives collection is and what it does. The policy statement can answer repetitive questions in a minimum amount of space. It can provide the clout necessary to back up a policy decision the archivist makes. And, most important, it can provide a context for all the detailed, day-to-day archival work.

PLACEMENT OF THE ARCHIVES

The placement of the archives within the administrative structure of the institution is another key consideration. The most common options in use today are:

- *Corporate Secretary.* The charters of most corporations assign responsibility for the "official records" to the secretary of the corporation. It is natural, therefore, for ar-

---

Figure 2.6   Policy Statement: NFU Department of Archives and Special Collections

The North Fork University Department of Archives and Special Collections exists to identify, preserve, and make available records and papers of enduring value. Its mission is twofold:

- *University Archives.* To collect and maintain records of enduring value created or received by the university and its employees.
- *Special Collections.* To collect and maintain nonuniversity records and papers that support the academic mission of the university. Areas of collecting interest are specified in a separate Collection Development Policy.

On behalf of the President and Board of Trustees, the Director of the Department of Archives and Special Collections is authorized to review all university records to identify those of enduring value. All university employees are directed to cooperate with the Director in the performance of this responsibility.

The Department of Archives and Special Collections provides access to its collections under a separate access policy that is available from the Director.

---

chives to be part of this department. Also, the corporate secretary usually creates a number of records series of permanent value, such as minutes of board of directors meetings. Making the archives part of the secretary's function may make it easier to transfer these valuable records to archival custody.

- *Public Relations.* Businesses, in particular, favor this placement. One of the major values of an archives collection for a business is in projecting a positive image of the corporation—for example as a leader or innovator. Some businesses reproduce artifacts preserved in their archives and make them available to the public. In the absence of an archives collection, the public relations library might have preserved records of permanent value in order to answer questions and to provide background for speeches by executives; placing the archives within public relations may increase the visibility and influence of the archives program.
- *Office of the Chief Executive.* Since many archival programs owe their establishment and continued existence to the support of the chief executive of the institution, it is common to place the archives within that office. Naturally, this placement offers the ultimate in clout and vis-

ibility for the program. The disadvantage is that the archives may be seen as a personal project of the chief executive rather than as an integral part of the institution—the program may be endangered if the next chief executive does not support archival activities or wants to change the policies of a predecessor.

- *Administration.* Some archival programs, especially those involved with records management, are placed within the administrative services hierarchy. The rationale for this placement is that the records program improves efficiency and saves space. Depending on the organization, this placement may offer less clout than some of the options outlined above. The advantage is the integration of active and inactive records within one program.

- *Library.* This is the most common administrative placement for college and university archives and manuscript repositories. The library is also the most common site for the physical placement of an archives collection on a college campus. Among the advantages are the following: researchers need only visit one building, archival finding aids can be integrated into the main library catalog, and it is possible to interchange library staff members to meet peak demands in the various areas. The major disadvantage is that many library administrators do not understand archival functions and how they differ from library fuctions. This factor can lead to tension, misunderstanding, and the possible underfunding of the archival program.

Usually the archivist will not have a choice in selecting administrative placement of the program. The archivist who does have a choice, however, should look beyond the structure to the individuals involved. The archives may do better as part of a lower-prestige department where the executive-in-charge believes in archives, actively promotes the program, and fights for the necessary organizational resources—such a placement is preferable to having the archives wither higher up on the organizational vine.[12]

ADVISORY COMMITTEE

An archival advisory committee may be one way to overcome some of the problems of organizational placement and visibility. An advisory committee can give the archival program added credibility and assist the archivist who lacks experience in specific areas.

An advisory committee differs from a governing board. The

former has no real authority over the archival program, whereas the latter exercises administrative control. In order to avoid misunderstandings, it is important to understand which kind of body is present and to define clearly its purpose and scope of operations.

Therefore the first step in creating an advisory committee is to draft a mission statement for the body. (See Figure 2.7 for an example.) The statement should cover the following points:

- purpose of committee
- areas of responsibility (many organizations exclude such matters as personnel and budgets from the advisory committee's domain)
- composition of committee
- frequency of meetings (probably a minimum of one meeting per year)
- reporting relationship (where does the "advice" go?)

The archivist usually coordinates the meetings of the advisory committee, decides which topics will be discussed (in consultation with the chair of the advisory committee, if there is one), sets the agenda, prepares background materials for the committee members, keeps the discussion moving, and prepares minutes of the meeting. The archivist also makes certain that the recommendations of the advisory committee reach the proper ears.

The composition of the advisory committee can take several forms. One approach is to represent certain interests, such as outside researchers and community leaders. A second approach is to form a committee composed entirely of professional archivists with expertise in areas where the archives collection is heading, such as acquisitions, grant writing, and oral history. A third approach, especially in an institutional setting, is to involve administrators from key departments with which the archives must work, for example the legal and tax departments, public relations, and accounting.

Whatever the composition of the committee, the archivist must make certain that it accomplishes what he or she has in mind. While some authors have urged an almost Machiavellian approach, I do not believe this extreme is necessary. In fact, it may be counterproductive. The members of an advisory committee will soon be able to tell if they are being manipulated or if their only role is to rubber-stamp decisions that the archivist has already made.

The most successful advisory committees are those where there is a feeling of openness and cooperation. The archivist must sincerely want the advice of the committee, and must be willing to listen to what they have to say and be open to changing plans and policies to reflect the thinking of the advisors. Anything less makes the advisory committee a waste of time for all concerned.

A final consideration in establishing an advisory committee is the matter of financial reimbursement for committee members. In most cases, the archives should pay travel and a per diem for out of town members. Many archivists use local people in order to avoid such costs.

Honoraria are a different matter. If honoraria are paid, they should go to all members, no matter where they live. Small, non-profit institutions may not be able to pay honoraria. There is no shame in this. It just means that the archivist has another factor to consider in selecting advisory committee members—those who are committed enough to the goals of the institution that they will be willing to donate time. Larger, better-funded institutions probably will want to offer honoraria in order to attract the people they desire. The size of the honorarium will depend on the qualifications and reputation of the person sought. It should be noted, however, that some granting agencies have an upward limit on the size of honorarium that may be paid with their funds. As with other aspects of the advisory committee, it is best to spell out the financial aspects at the beginning in order to avoid misunderstandings later.[13]

Figure 2.7 Mission Statement: NFU Advisory Committee

The Advisory Committee for the NFU Department of Archives and Special Collections was formed to assist the department in its mission of identifying, preserving, and making available records and papers of enduring value.

The committee will offer advice in all areas of departmental operations, as requested by the Director of the Department of Archives and Special Collections. Excluded from the committee's deliberations are matters of personnel and budget.

The committee is composed of six members—three from the university community and three from outside the university. All nominees to the committee must be approved by the President of the University, who also selects the chair of the committee. The Director of the Department of Archives and Special Collections will serve as secretary of the Advisory Committee.

The committee will meet at least twice per year and at other times by call of the chair. The committee will submit an annual report to the President of the University.

CONCLUSION

With a structure for the archives in place and the results of a records survey in hand, the archivist is ready to tackle one of the most difficult—and most important—aspects of the archival mission: deciding which records to keep and which to destroy. The items discussed in this chapter provide the context and background for appraisal decisions.

NOTES

1. A records survey is also called an "inventory," especially in government settings. I will not use this term, however, since I will use the term inventory when discussing an archival finding aid.

2. Records management is a closely related profession that grew out of archival work at the end of World War II. Records managers are responsible for the systematic control of all records of an organization, not just those of enduring value. Records managers control records throughout their "life cycle": creation or receipt, active use, semiactive use, and ultimate disposition (destruction or transfer to an archives).

3. The best source on surveys remains John Fleckner, *Archives and Manuscripts: Surveys* (Chicago: Society of American Archivists, 1977). Much of the discussion in this chapter is adapted from Fleckner.

4. For more on records management, see Gregory S. Hunter, "Thinking Small to Think Big: Archives, Micrographics and the Life Cycle of Records," *American Archivist* 49 (summer 1986): 315–320; and Mary F. Robek, et al., *Information and Records Management,* 4th ed. (Encino, CA: Glencoe Publishing, 1995).

5. One must be extremely careful, however, in making certain that the records are old enough that all fiscal and legal requirements are met. If there is any doubt, the archivist should not destroy the records without checking with professionals competent to make judgments in these areas.

6. This distinction between efficient and effective is taken from Peter F. Drucker, *The Effective Executive* (New York: Harper & Row, 1966). 1–24.

7. For more on this point, see Elsie T. Freeman, "In the Eye of the Beholder: Archives Administration from the User's Point of View," *American Archivist* 47 (spring 1984): 111–123.

8. For more on planning, see Gregory S. Hunter, "Filling the GAP: Planning on the Local and Individual Levels," *American Archivist* 50 (winter 1987): 110–115; and Thomas Wilsted and William Nolte, *Managing Archival and Manuscript Repositories* (Chicago: Society of American Archivists, 1991), 27–33.

9. This section also relies heavily on Fleckner, *Archives and Manuscripts*.

10. This table is taken from *Disposition of Federal Records* (Washington, D.C.: National Archives and Records Administration, 1992), III-10.

11. For more on policy statements, see Wilsted and Nolte, *Managing Archival and Manuscript Repositories*, 15–16.

12. See Wilsted and Nolte, *Managing Archival and Manuscript Repositories*, 16–18.

13. For more on advisory committees, see Linda Henry, "Archival Advisory Committees: Why?" *American Archivist* 48 (summer 1985): 315–319; and Wilsted and Nolte, *Managing Archival and Manuscript Repositories*, 19–20.

3 SELECTION AND APPRAISAL

Appraisal is at the heart of archival work. To emphasize the point, some archivists call apraisal the profession's first responsibility. Unless archivists do appraisal well, everything else is meaningless. While careful arrangement and expansive description are laudable goals, they are wasted effort on a collection with no enduring value. Because of the huge volume of modern records, appraisal currently is receiving much attention within the archival profession.[1]

In terms of a formal definition, appraisal is the process of determining the value, and thus the disposition, of records based upon

- their operating, administrative, legal, and fiscal values
- their evidential and informational value (research or historical value)
- their arrangement and physical condition
- their intrinsic value
- their relationship to other records[2]

The elements of this definition will be discussed at appropriate places throughout this chapter. Suffice it to say at this point that the archivist tries to determine if the records in question have sufficient "value" to justify their continued retention in the archives.

This process of determining value is similar to triage in medicine. In triage, a medical professional sorts patients, and allocates treatment based on the resources at hand and the number of patients to treat. As anyone who has watched the "M*A*S*H" television program will recall, triage separates patients into three categories:

- those requiring immediate attention
- those who will not survive, even if treated
- those whose treatment will be second priority as resources permit

The archival professional also uses three categories, sorting records into

- those definitely having enduring value
- those definitely not worth preserving

- those whose preservation will be a second priority if resources permit

---

"There is history and there is junk in Senator Robert T. Stafford's cartons of letters, newsletters, speeches, memorandums, reports, schedules, notes, statements, photographs, and press clippings. It is Connell B. Gallagher's job to decide which is which.

"Mr. Gallagher's mission is to spare Senator Stafford the burden that befalls most senators and their states: how to deal with senatorial records collected over years of public service. . . ."—*New York Times,* August 16, 1988.

Appraisal decisions are so difficult because all records have *some* conceivable value. If one names any record series, it is possible to think of a person who might have some use for the records. The archivist's job, however, is to select those records with *sufficient* value to justify the costs of storage, arrangement, description, preservation, and reference. The scarcer the institution's resources, the more difficult the appraisal decisions.

In judging value, possible research use is a key consideration. To quote Philip Bauer, one of the early leaders of the profession, "Prophecy is the essence of archival evaluation." The archivist must be aware of current research trends and interests, using this information to extrapolate what may be of interest to future researchers. This is a weighty responsibility: a wrong appraisal decision means always having to say you're sorry. The nature of the responsibility has led in the past to a conservative bias, with archivists keeping many records of limited value "just in case" someone might want to see them. The exploding volume of modern records combined with the imploding resources of many archives collections has forced a reevaluation of this conservative bias and even a reappraisal of records previously accepted into archival custody.

The appraisal (and reappraisal) process ends with a number of possible dispositions for noncurrent records. The options are

- transfer to a records center for low-cost, temporary storage
- transfer to an archives collection within the agency or institution
- donation to a suitable outside repository
- reproduction on microfilm or other alternate media
- destruction

"Richard Nixon had a one-line retort on Monday when asked about the lesson of Watergate: 'Just destroy all the tapes.' That's what he told the annual luncheon of The Associated Press when asked what his presidential successors could learn from his experience."— *Newsday,* April 22, 1986.

Many times, records managers use "disposition" as a synonym for "destruction." But this is only one choice, albeit the choice for the great majority of institutional or organizational records. In a typical business, only one or two percent of the records are worthy of archival preservation. In some government settings, the figure might approach five percent. And in a nonprofit institution very conscious of its history, eight to ten percent of the records might reach the archives. These figures contradict the view that we must keep "everything." Similarly, they also provide an argument against the view that nothing merits archival preservation.

THE VALUES OF RECORDS

Basic to the appraisal process is an understanding of the values of records. Value, in this sense, is not a monetary term, even though records may be bought and sold. Rather, value refers to the underlying reasons for retaining a record series. There are five reasons, or values, for retaining records:

- operating value
- administrative value
- fiscal value
- legal value
- archival value

The first four of these reasons are considered primary values, in that they are important mainly for the agency that originated the records. The concept of primary value reflects the fact that an organization creates records to accomplish some purpose—to pay bills, to sell products, or to care for patients, for example. At a later date, some records may have secondary value for others outside of the originating agency—scholars, genealogists, and lawyers, for example. This secondary, or archival, value continues indefinitely, thus justifying preservation in a specialized facility.[3] Margaret Cross Norton, the former Illinois State Archivist, said it well: "The difference between a file clerk and an archivist is that an archivist has a sense of perspective. He knows that these documents have two phases of use: their present day legalistic use, and their potential historical value."[4]

Let us now turn to a more detailed discussion of the five values of records. It should be noted that the retention period generally lengthens as records move through these five values.

OPERATING VALUE

Operating value is the value of the records for the current work of the organization or institution. To use an example, check vouchers have an operating value in paying bills and documenting payment when questioned by the vendor. Most operating value is short-term: in the case of check vouchers (and, indeed, most records of transactions), items have operating value for only a few weeks. If the records have no other value, they can be destroyed after that time.

ADMINISTRATIVE VALUE

After the records no longer are needed for current operations, they still may be valuable for some administrative reason. Perhaps management will use them to summarize operations or as the basis for a speech or written report. Administrative value often is difficult to judge, since "management" includes a wide variety of individuals with differing needs. In general, administrative values are in the range of one to two years.

FISCAL VALUE

It may be necessary to keep certain records as an "audit trail" to document transactions. The Internal Revenue Service and other agencies usually specify how long records must be retained for audit purposes. Once the originating organization clears the audit for the year in question, records being retained solely for their fiscal value may be destroyed. Most organizations destroy the check vouchers, for example, after satisfying all audit requirements.

LEGAL VALUE

There are two distinct kinds of legal value:

- The organization may be required by statute or regulation to retain certain records for a set period of time. For example, the Occupational Safety and Health Administration (OSHA) specifies how long organizations must retain records of employee exposure to hazardous materials.

- The records in question might document the legal rights of individuals or corporate bodies. If so, the records need to be retained as long as the legal right must be protected. An example is a patent or trademark file.

Unless there also is archival value, usually both categories of records are destroyed once the legal value has expired.

ARCHIVAL VALUE

The determination that records are worthy of "permanent" preservation in an archival repository is an assessment of archival value. Archival value is also known by other terms: historical, continuing, research, or enduring value. The remainder of this chapter further defines and applies archival value.

Figure 3.1 summarizes these five values of records and shows how they apply to three sample records series.

Figure 3.1 Five Values of Records as Applied to Three Sample Series					
Series	**Operating**	**Administrative**	**Fiscal**	**Legal**	**Historical**
Check Vouchers	Yes, 30–60 days	Yes, year-end summary reports	Yes, hold for audits	Yes, in case of claims	No, except perhaps for prominent individuals
Press Releases	Yes, 30 days	Yes, annual reports	No	No	Yes, important source of information
Employee Personnel Folders	Yes, while an active employee	Yes, summary reports	No	Yes, in case of legal actions	No, too confidential to open

ARCHIVAL VALUE: CLASSIC APPRAISAL THEORY

It should not be surprising that archivists have spent a great deal of time developing and refining appraisal theory. While appraisal theory undoubtedly dates back to antiquity, most discussions of appraisal theory in the United States begin with Theodore R. Schellenberg, a former staff member at the National Archives.

Schellenberg developed the concepts of "evidential" and "informational" value and made them the core of appraisal theory. He wrote extensively on appraisal, thereby influencing an entire generation of archivists. As this chapter shows, subsequent authors have further refined Schellenberg's elements and applied them to new situations and types of records.[5]

EVIDENTIAL VALUE

By referring to items with evidential value, Schellenberg meant those records necessary to document the organization and functioning of the institution or department. The archivist, therefore, would preserve records of

- The origin of each entity. Background on the problems or conditions that led to the establishment of the entity, as well as the actual documentation for its establishment, such as a charter.
- The substantive programs of each entity. Documentation for the development and execution of major programs, including such items as summary narrative accounts, policy documents, publications and publicity materials, and internal management records.

Before determining evidential value, it is important to do some preliminary research into the structure and function of the institution. What is the position of each office in the administrative hierarchy? What functions does each office perform? What types of decisions do the people in each office make?

In this regard, there is an important distinction between "substantive" and "facilitative" records. Substantive records are just what the name implies: the substance or core of the department's function. Facilitative records are those supporting records necessary to carry out the main activity. Most modern records fall into the facilitative category.

Preserving evidence of a department's activities most often will involve substantive rather than facilitative records. Very few petty cash forms will be of enduring value—except, perhaps, those that George Washington submitted to the Continental Congress. Facilitative records usually are of short-term value.

Figure 3.2 illustrates the differences between substantive and facilitative records.

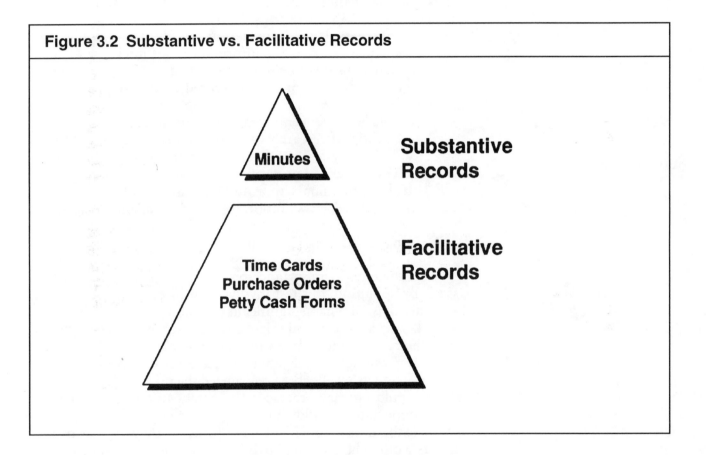

Figure 3.2 Substantive vs. Facilitative Records

Minutes — **Substantive Records**

Time Cards
Purchase Orders
Petty Cash Forms — **Facilitative Records**

INFORMATIONAL VALUE

The second part of Schellenberg's formulation, informational value, shifts the appraisal emphasis. Instead of focusing on evidence about the organization itself, the archivist now considers the extent to which the records shed light upon

- persons (both individuals and corporate bodies)
- things (places, buildings, and other objects)
- events (the interaction between persons and things)

The satisfied customer letter from Clyde Barrow to Henry Ford, which appeared at the beginning of this book, is an example of a record retained for its informational value. The letter was associated with a famous person; it was not retained because of the evidence it provided about how the Ford Motor Company dealt with customers.

Informational value can be difficult to determine. In order to help with the appraisal decision, Schellenberg provided three "tests" of informational value.

- *Uniqueness.* Is the information not physically duplicated elsewhere? Also, is the information not intellectually duplicated—is this the most complete and usable version of the information, or is it presented or summarized better elsewhere?
- *Form.* How concentrated is the information—is there a high ratio of research value to volume of the collection? Will the physical condition and arrangement lend themselves to archival preservation, or will they require a great deal of preliminary time and expense?
- *Importance.* How important are the persons, places, or events dealt with in the records? Are they likely to be the subject of future research?

Of the three tests, importance probably is the most difficult to assess. By definition, this test involves a subjective determination by the archivist of what is significant or noteworthy. Furthermore, recent historical and social science research, with their emphasis on ordinary men and women instead of such "Great White Fathers" as Washington and Jefferson, have turned importance on its head. Though Schellenberg recognized the difficulty of this third test, he could not have foreseen the extent to which the definition of importance would change.[6]

Schellenberg also could not have foreseen the way electronic records would change the above formulations. He assumed that concentrated information would be more desirable for research. With electronic records, however, raw data often have the greatest research value: they can be sorted and manipulated to answer new questions. This issue is addressed again in Chapter 10.

Very often informational value is either not recognized or not considered important by the creators of the records. This is often the case in private organizations or businesses that do not want to keep records "just to support research." The archivist in such a situation must be prepared to spend a great deal of time educating records creators about the secondary values of records.

CASE STUDY

In the previous chapter, I mentioned a situation where the NFU archivist had to survey records quickly and decide which had enduring value. The details of the situation are as follows:

> One day you receive a call from NFU's Director of Plant Operations. He tells you that you "really should come down to the boiler room because there are a lot of boxes of old files down there." You ask if he mentioned this to your predecessor as archivist. He replies, "Naw, because space never was a problem. But now we need to move those boxes out in a week, because we're gonna replace the old boiler."
>
> You immediately send your Assistant Archivist to the boiler room to make a list of records. When she returns, you decide what to save and what to destroy, using the concepts of evidential and informational value. Figure 3.3 summarizes your decisions.

BEYOND SCHELLENBERG: REFINEMENTS OF APPRAISAL THEORY

As this case study indicated, even with Schellenberg's framework as a guide, appraisal decisions still are difficult to make. While evidential and informational value may be good starting points, they sometimes are inadequate as ending points. To borrow a concept from logic, evidential and informational value are necessary but often are not sufficient for making a sound appraisal judgment.

Furthermore, there are two major problems with Schellenberg's approach.[7] The first problem stems from Schellenberg's background in government archives. In this setting, evidential value may assume greater importance than it would in the private sector: there is a desire to document for the citizenry how the government functioned. In effect, Schellenberg equated the records appraisal mandate with the statutory requirements of the National Archives.[8]

The second problem flows from the first. Schellenberg advo-

Figure 3.3 Evidential and Informational Value at NFU			
Record Series	**Evidential Value**	**Informational Value**	**Retain? (Yes/No)**
Employee time cards, 1960–72, 5 cubic feet	While the series provides evidence of how employees received pay checks, this part of the function does not have enduring value	Would only be present if NFU had a famous employee	No
Minutes of the Board of Trustees (official copy signed by the University Secretary), 1939–50, 2 cubic feet	Evidence of decisions and key actions	Might also contain information about key persons, things, or events	Yes. May need preservation work
Vice President for Academic Affairs, Curriculum Development Files, 1925–40, 23 cubic feet	Documentation for changes to the curriculum as well as the curriculum development process	Might be present, but is not the main reason for retention	Yes
Applications for employment, 1953–58, 6 cubic feet	As with time cards, evidence not worth preserving	Unlikely to be present; it would be too time-consuming to review all applications for fame of sender	No
Development Office, daily reports of contributions received, 1940–53, 18 cubic feet	While these provide detailed evidence of fundraising activities, the summary in the annual report should be sufficient	Same as previous series	No
University Bookstore, annual reports, 1976–80, 1 cubic foot	There is evidence elsewhere of how the bookstore operated	None	No. With space at a premium in the archives, there are higher priorities for preservation
Library daily circulation records (by student), 1966–69, 50 cubic feet	Documents a major activity of the library	Shows what individual students were reading during the Vietnam War era	No. Privacy concerns would prevent the records from being opened for research

cated that archivists preserve a completeness of documentation for all government functions and activities. In the private sector, it is impossible to preserve evidence about every entity and substantive program in a large organization. Even if it were possible, would this be the best use of limited archival resources? Is it better to try to preserve evidence about everything rather than commit additional resources to the more significant entities or programs? As previously stated, archivists must consider the potential uses of records, as well as their evidential value, in making appraisal decisions.

A lot has been written on appraisal, especially in the last ten years. Much of this literature has direct application for the working archivist facing appraisal decisions on a daily basis. To illustrate this, I will discuss four refinements of appraisal theory and show how their insights would help with the NFU case study presented above. The refinements are

- the "black box" concept
- intrinsic value
- sampling
- functional approach[9]

THE BLACK BOX CONCEPT

To Frank Boles and Julia Marks Young, appraisal of modern records sometimes seemed to be derived from a "black box": archivists mixing together a variety of considerations and pulling as from a box the determination of the record's value. Boles and Young analyzed university administrative records and developed an integrated system for their appraisal, one that made explicit the many factors archivists consider in making an appraisal judgment. The system is flexible enough, however, to apply to nonuniversity settings. A grant from the National Historical Publications and Records Commission (NHPRC) enabled Boles and Young to test their system in other types of institutions.[10]

The core of the Boles and Young system is three closely-related modules:

- the value of the information
- the cost of retention
- the implications of the appraisal recommendation

These three elements are considered together in reaching an appraisal decision. Depending on the repository, one element may be given greater weight than the others. But neither one of the three should be ignored. This comprehensive scheme incorporates in a logical form all the significant parts of the appraisal process. The scheme includes both elements traditionally acknowledged by archivists (like evidential and informational value) and those often left unspoken (like the implications of the appraisal decision). An overview of the modules will illustrate this.

The value of information module contains much of Schellenberg's theory. It has three major subsections:

- *Circumstances of creation.* What is the position of the creating department within the organizational hierarchy? What are the principal functions and activities of the unit? To what extent do the records document these principal functions?

- *Analysis of content.* Are there practical limitations with the materials in terms of legibility and understandability? Does an exact physical duplicate exist elsewhere? Is there an intellectual duplication, with the information contained elsewhere? What topics do the records cover? What was the creator's relationship to the topic—a participant or an observer? What is the quality of the information about the topic?

- *Use of the records.* What is the extent of user interest in the records? Will the records be of interest to the repository's regular clientele? How do the records relate to present and future research trends and methodologies? Are there any restrictions on access imposed by either the donor or the repository?

The second module, cost of retention, raises a number of practical questions. It helps the repository determine if it has the staff and other resources to preserve and make available the collection. By giving these monetary concerns equal consideration with the value of the records, Boles and Young acknowledge that archivists exist in a world of limited resources. Boles and Young identify costs in four areas:

- *Storage.* How much space will the records require? What type of storage is required? Are there any special environmental concerns? Are the present facility and shelving adequate?

- *Processing.* How much time and effort will it take to arrange and describe the records? Does the institution have sufficient expertise (both archival and subject area) to process the collection? How much will boxes, folders, and other supplies cost?

- *Preservation.* What quantity of preservation work will the collection require? Does the institution have, or can it acquire, the necessary preservation expertise? How much will preservation supplies cost?
- *Reference.* Can the institution provide adequate reference service for the collection? Is there sufficient staff and researcher space? Does the institution's staff have sufficient expertise in the subject matter to be able to answer researcher questions?

The third module, implications of the appraisal decision, is the area often left unarticulated by archivists and manuscript curators. Archivists like to think that they are serving posterity or scholarship, and therefore are above politics. But as anyone who works in an institution knows, programs of any type—not just archives—can be made or broken on this point.

Boles and Young do a great service by specifically making two elements—political considerations and procedural precedents—part of the appraisal decision. Usually these elements come into play when an archivist believes the records do not have sufficient value to justify preservation, but he or she is worried that a person with "clout" might be offended by the decision. Specific questions to consider are

- *Political considerations.* How important is the donor of the records? What kind of authority and influence does the donor have over the archival program? If the donor disagrees with the archivist's appraisal decision, is it because of a factual dispute or just an emotional attachment to the records? What kind of authority and influence do others such as potential users and affected third parties have? Do they carry sufficient weight to affect the appraisal decision?
- *Procedural precedents.* If the repository accepts the records, what precedent is it setting? In the future, will it have to accept records of similar value? Will the repository also have to commit itself to similar costs of storage, processing, preservation, and reference?

Let's apply the black box scheme to one of the records series that the NFU archivist is in the process of appraising. To do this, it is necessary to provide additional information about the series (see Figure 3.4).

The NFU archivist can use the black box scheme to make certain that all appraisal factors receive consideration. In their sub-

---

Figure 3.4 Additional Detail on NFU Record Series

Vice President for Academic Affairs, Curriculum Development Files, 1925–40, 23 cubic feet.

The records in this series document changes made to the curricula of the various schools and departments at NFU. Changes in curricula originate with the faculty of the school or department. The proposed change, along with detailed supporting documentation, is sent to the Vice President (VP) for Academic Affairs. The VP submits copies to all departmental chairpersons for their comments. The VP weighs these comments and decides whether or not to recommend approval by the President and Board of Trustees. In the case of programs approved by New York State, the VP is responsible for submitting copies to the state and following through with state approval.

The records are in letter-size file folders. All documents are typed, though some also have margin comments handwritten by the VP, departmental chairpersons, or others. Some of the older records are yellowed and brittle, ultimately requiring some preservation work.

The records series is arranged as follows: first, by department or school; second, by specific program within the department; and third, by date of change to the program. Copies of each proposed change are retained by the originating department. The state retains a copy of each change it considers.

Since the records contain detailed comments submitted to the VP, the current VP wants to consider this part of the collection "confidential" and to close it forever to outside researchers. You don't believe that these comments are as confidential as the VP believes—but you don't know if you'll be able to convince her of this.

In terms of the politics of the university, the library director (your boss) reports to the VP for Academic Affairs. There are three other vice presidents (Student Affairs, Financial Affairs, and Development), all of whom have similar types and volumes of program files that you might be asked to add to the archives. Accepting the records of the VP for Academic Affairs clearly would establish a precedent.

---

sequent NHPRC-funded project, Boles and Young attempt to develop weights and other measurements of the relative importance of the various factors. Even used qualitatively rather than quantitatively, the black box approach can be very helpful, as Figure 3.5 illustrates.

Taken as a whole, the Boles and Young framework provides a good working guide for appraisal decisions. It forces archivists to consider in a systematic way the many factors that should be a part of the decision. It also facilitates the creation of written appraisal documents explaining the decision (for future reference by archivists and researchers). This may be its greatest practical benefit for the working archivist.

Figure 3.5 Application of the Boles and Young Scheme

Module	Element	Comments
Value of the information	Circumstances of creation	The creating department is high in the organizational hierarchy (vice president). The records document a substantive function of the department: the development of academic programs.
	Analysis of content	The records are legible and understandable. While some parts of the records are duplicated elsewhere (originating departments and New York State), no other copy is as complete as this one. The vice president was a participant in the development of the programs. The information is of high quality.
	Use of the records	The records will be useful for university administrators. They also may be of interest to researchers of educational history or the development of the North Fork. If the restrictions on access stand, however, access to the records by outside researchers will be severely limited.
Cost of retention	Storage	The archives has space at the moment for the records, although 23 cubic feet is a sizable commitment. There are no special environmental concerns.
	Processing	The archives has sufficient expertise to process the collection. It is not in a specialized subject area unfamiliar to the staff.
	Preservation	The collection will require the usual acid-free boxes and folders. Some brittle items may require some additional preservation work.
	Reference	The archives should be able to provide reference service for the collection.

Figure 3.5 (cont.)		
Implications of the appraisal recommendation	Political considerations	The donor of the records is very important to the archives (the archivist's boss's boss). The vice president has great influence over the archival program. She may have an emotional attachment to the records (she may think that her area of responsibility is a natural for archival preservation). Other parties (such as researchers) do not have the same kind of weight to influence the appraisal decision.
	Procedural precedents	Accepting the records would set a precedent for the value of vice presidential program records. The other three vice presidents will expect their records to be preserved as well.

INTRINSIC VALUE

As part of the appraisal decision, archivists must address the following question: even if the records have sufficient value to justify retention, must we preserve the records in their original form? The U.S. National Archives, in particular, grappled with this issue of "intrinsic value"—some records have physical qualities that make the original form of the records the only archivally acceptable one. For example, one would not microfilm the original Declaration of Independence and then throw out the document as a space-saving measure.

As facetious as this may sound, it is not that far removed from the situation faced by the National Archives in the late 1970s. At that time the head of the General Services Administration, then the parent body of the National Archives, advocated the microfilming of all records in the National Archives and the destruction of the original documents. The need to rebut the argument that all records were disposable forced the National Archives to articulate more clearly which records fell into the following categories:

- records that could be destroyed if an adequate copy were made
- records possessing qualities that would make disposal undesirable even if an adequate copy existed

At the heart of this distinction is that fact that records are composed of both "medium" and "message," to use Marshall McLuhan's terms. With records of intrinsic value, both the message and the medium merit preservation. By way of contrast, archival records without intrinsic value may have their message preserved in another medium: microfilm, optical disk, magnetic tape, or photographic film, for example. The decision to reformat is based on such factors as space savings, improved access, and permanence of the medium.

The National Archives published the results of its study in 1982 as a staff information paper. This paper identified nine qualities or characteristics of records with intrinsic value.[11] Figure 3.6 summarizes these characteristics.

Figure 3.6 Characteristics of Records with Intrinsic Value	
Characteristic	**Example**
Example of a physical form that may be the subject of study	Glass plate photographic negatives
Aesthetic or artistic quality	Architectural drawings, watercolor sketches
Unique or curious physical features	Watermark, unusual binding
Age that provides a quality of uniqueness	Anything from before the Civil War
Value for use in exhibits	The first ledger book of a company
Questionable authenticity requiring physical examination	The Hitler diaries
Substantial public interest because of direct association with prominent people, things, or events	Anything connected with where George Washington slept
Documentation for legal status	Original corporate charter, signed copy of minutes
Documentation of the formulation of policy at the highest level	Cuban Missile Crisis memoranda

Using these categories as a basis, the staff of the National Archives surveyed the holdings in the main building in Washington, D.C. They concluded that only 20 percent of the textual records in the building held intrinsic value—the rest could be microfilmed and destroyed. The percentage would probably be lower in many other archival repositories across the country.[12] At NFU, only one of the records series under consideration has intrinsic value: the official, signed copy of the trustees' minutes should be retained for documentation of legal status.

The obvious conclusion is that archivists can be more aggressive than they have been in the past about microfilming records and destroying the paper. All too often, archivists microfilm documents and still keep the originals even though they have no intrinsic value. As the bulk of records increases faster than the space and resources available for preservation, archivists must seriously rethink this practice.[13]

SAMPLING

Archivists have known about sampling techniques for decades, but such techiques have not been used to the fullest extent possible. This is due to two factors: confusion about the mathematics used in social science sampling, and fear of discarding a piece of paper crucial for future research. A more thorough understanding of sampling theory and practice should lead to its wider use by archivists in the future.[14]

As the name implies, sampling involves selecting only some of the records in question for preservation. It works best when the record series is homogeneous: for example, hundreds of boxes of invoices to customers. Sampling works less well when there is great variation within the record series, as with subject files or general reference files. It is important, therefore, for the archivist to analyze and understand the record series before deciding that sampling is the best solution.

Experience has shown that sampling is a viable option for record series with the following general characteristics:

- some research value, but not sufficient value to preserve the entire series
- too large a volume of records for the archives to store in hard copy
- prohibitively high cost to microfilm the entire series

These characteristics are very common in records series created by modern organizations and institutions.

Depending on the type of information the archivist seeks to preserve, there are a number of different sampling techniques.

- probability or statistical sampling
  - random
  - systematic
- purposive or judgmental sampling
  - exemplary
  - exceptional[15]

In statistical sampling, the archivist selects a small portion of records with the intention of accurately reflecting all important characteristics of the larger series. Mathematical formulas are used to determine the number of records required for a representative (statistically valid) sample. Social science researchers, in particular, favor statistical sampling because conclusions about the sample can be applied to the entire records series. In order to make such conclusions, the sample must be chosen in a rigorous way. The following paragraphs focus on reasons and theory, rather than mathematical formulas. Detailed discussions and explanations of such concepts as validity and sample size can be found in any of the statistics textbooks used in the social sciences.

There are two types of statistical sampling. The first, random sampling, has been considered the purest form of sampling because it is the freest of biases. To obtain a random sample, an archivist uses a random number table to identify which records to save. If the records are arranged numerically, this may be a relatively easy sample to pull. If the files are arranged alphabetically or in some other nonnumerical sequence, however, they can be very difficult to pull—it first will be necessary to number the files. This is a slow, labor-intensive activity.

Systematic sampling, also a type of statistical sampling, is considerably faster and easier to manage. As the name implies, it involves selecting files according to some system—for example, every twentieth file, all files for years ending in 8, or all files for surnames beginning with M. Most authorities agree that if care is taken in obtaining the systematic sample, there is little mathematical difference between it and a random sample. A systematic sample, therefore, is the favored option among archivists for files which are not already numbered.

Either type of statistical sampling has a major disadvantage: while it is possible to preserve a microcosm of the entire records series, it is not possible to preserve the "unique" or "important" case (unless by chance it falls within the sample pulled).

Purposive sampling is used when the archivist is not concerned with obtaining a representative sample. Rather, the archivist makes a judgment about which individual items or cases merit retention. Such subjective sampling is very familiar to archivists; in fact, it is very similar to a standard archival appraisal decision.

The danger with any type of purposive sampling is that it is susceptible to bias. The judgment of a fallible human being is at the heart of the decision to retain or destroy an item. In order to make an informed decision, the archivist must have some expertise in the subject area and a familiarity with present research trends in the discipline. But no matter how careful the selection, there always will be some researcher upset that the files needed for a particular study were destroyed years before. Keeping this caveat in mind, let's turn to the two principal types of purposive samples.

With exemplary sampling, the archivist selects all items conforming to a particular "type." The goal of the sample is to document some characteristic, activity, or time period. A few examples will clarify this point:

- all files from one region to show how a typical field office operated
- all court cases of a particular type (e.g., felony convictions)
- all files from the years immediately before and after reorganization to show its impact on actual operations
- all files for faculty members reaching the rank of associate professor or above

In contrast, exceptional sampling seeks to identify and retain files on significant individuals and events, precedent-setting programs, and landmark cases. This type of sampling requires the greatest subject expertise on the part of the archivist. It also is the method most subject to second-guessing by researchers: they may not all consider the same items to be important.

One common way of selecting an exceptional sample, especially if the archivist is not confident of his or her expertise in a particular area, is the so-called fat file method. In this case, the archivist will retain all files measuring more than an agreed-upon thickness—one inch, or two inches, for example. The underlying assumption is that important or problem files are larger in volume than ordinary files. In fact this is often the case; "fat" files often are the ones most in demand by researchers.

There is a problem, however, with the fat file method. Keeping all the thick files makes it extremely difficult to control the size of the sample and to plan space for the collection. In fact, depending on the record series, the fat file method may not even save very much space.

One of the records series discussed earlier at NFU might be a candidate for sampling. The library's daily circulation records (by student) totaled 50 cubic feet. They were dated 1966–1969, during the era of student protests and the Vietnam War. The records consist of call slips submitted by students to request books—at that time the NFU library stacks were closed to everyone but staff members. A request was given the next sequential number at the time the request was made. The slips are filed by request number. While it might not be worth keeping the entire series, a sample could be valuable for future researchers. Figure 3.7 compares the four sampling types as related to this records series.

Figure 3.7 Sampling Possibilities: Library Daily Circulation Records	
Sampling Method	**Comments**
Random	It would be easy to use a random number table to pull a statistically valid sample. Any analysis of this sample would represent the entire population.
Systematic	It also would be easy to pull a systematic sample of every 10th or 20th call slip.
Exemplary	This method seems less applicable, unless one wants to keep only the call slips of a particular type of student (graduate students, for example).
Exceptional	To identify "significant" students (however defined) and locate their call slips would take a great deal of time. It also would raise the greatest privacy concerns.

Perhaps the most interesting example of sampling deals with records from the Federal Bureau of Investigation. In 1979 a group of social action organizations, historians, journalists, and others filed suit in U.S. District Court to stop the destruction of FBI field office records and to challenge the archival appraisal decision upon which the destruction was based. At the heart of the dispute was a National Archives practice dating back to 1945 that permitted the destruction of FBI field office records. The National Archives had not reviewed the files in question, originally because FBI director J. Edgar Hoover refused to permit anyone to see raw FBI files. As a result, archivists relied on FBI assurances that the field office files either were duplicated at FBI headquarters or were summarized in reports submitted to headquarters. At issue were a huge and steadily increasing volume of records. In 1979 it was estimated that the FBI field offices contained 300,000 cubic feet of records, even after destroying 710,000 cubic feet in the previous two years.

After a five-day trial in October 1979, Judge Harold H. Greene ruled in favor of the plaintiffs. He imposed a moratorium on the destruction of FBI files and ordered the National Archives to prepare a plan for handling the FBI's voluminous records.

The National Archives first undertook a lengthy and intensive study of FBI field office and headquarters records. Central to this study was the use of a stratified statistical sample to select items for appraisal. With stratification, some parts of the universe to be sampled are weighted differently from others, thereby increasing their odds of being selected. This differs from a straight statistical sample in which theoretically all parts of the universe have an equal chance of being selected. A stratified sample would be used when some parts of the universe are considered to be more valuable than others.

"A worker watches as about 15 tons of security files that had been kept on Greek citizens go up in flames in a blast furnace of a steel mill near Athens. The files were destroyed in a symbolic act marking the 40th anniversary of the end of the Greek civil war. Dossiers on the activities and political leanings of millions of Greeks considered threats to the state since 1944 were dropped into the furnace."—*Newsday,* September 2, 1989.

At the conclusion of this study, the National Archives prepared a new retention schedule for the FBI's investigative case files. The schedule is a convenient summary for this section on sampling, since it incorporates many of the sampling types previously discussed. The schedule calls for:

- retaining all exceptional cases (a list of which was developed in conjunction with researchers)
- retaining all files more than one folder thick
- judging remaining files by individual case type, such as auto theft, kidnapping, or espionage
  - In some case types, where the informational content is low, a small random sample will be retained.
  - In case types with greater informational content, a larger sample will be retained.[16]

While most archival situations will not be as complex as the FBI investigative case files, sampling still is a viable appraisal option in numerous settings.

FUNCTIONAL APPROACH

Archivists continue to search for new tools to assist with appraisal. A recent work by Helen Willa Samuels of the Massachusetts Institute of Technology argues that archivists must start their selection activities not with a consideration of specific sets of records, but with an understanding of the context in which records are created. She recommends a functional approach to provide an understanding of the institution and its documentation. The emphasis would be on what organizations do, rather than who does it.[17]

Samuels believes that a functional approach can best achieve adequate documentation of an institution. Such documentation requires both official and nonofficial materials, as well as published, visual, and artifact materials. The basic approach is that analysis and planning must precede collecting.

Samuels identifies seven functions of colleges and universities that certainly apply to NFU:

- confer credentials
- convey knowledge
- foster socialization
- conduct research
- sustain the institution
- provide public service
- promote culture

For some of these functions, like sustaining the institution, the archivist's problem is an abundance of records—reams of accounting records, financial aid applications, and check vouchers. For some functions, like fostering socialization, the problem is a scarcity of records—there is little documentation for how students develop socially. Finally, in some areas we have plenty of documentation, but not of the proper type. For example, under conveying knowledge, we may know what courses were taught, but have few details of the educational experience—what actually happened in the classroom.

In the last section of her book, Samuels presents a model for developing an institutional documentation plan. Figure 3.8 outlines the steps required to develop the plan. This is a promising methodology that likely will be tested in a number of archival settings over the next few years.

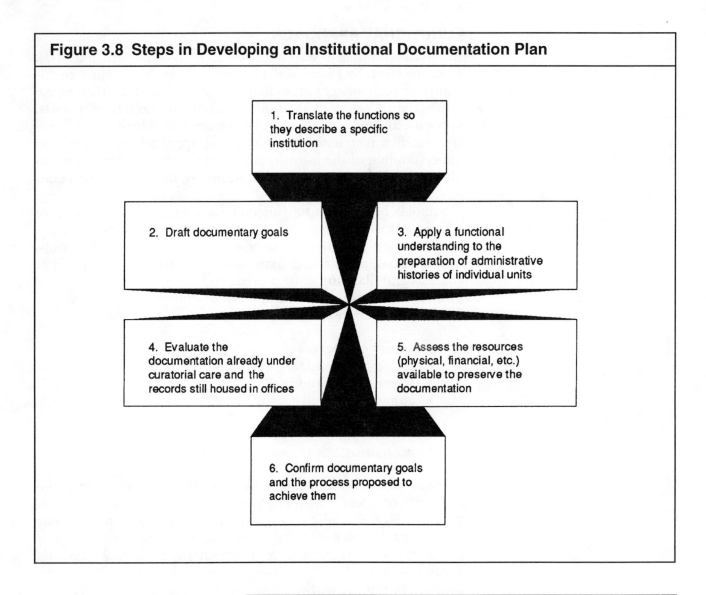

Figure 3.8 Steps in Developing an Institutional Documentation Plan

1. Translate the functions so they describe a specific institution

2. Draft documentary goals

3. Apply a functional understanding to the preparation of administrative histories of individual units

4. Evaluate the documentation already under curatorial care and the records still housed in offices

5. Assess the resources (physical, financial, etc.) available to preserve the documentation

6. Confirm documentary goals and the process proposed to achieve them

CONCLUSION

In 1951 an ad hoc committee of the American Historical Association issued a report on the problems associated with large, modern manuscript collections. The committee addressed the issue of how one locates the valuable information so often buried deep within these collections.

It is not surprising that they realized "practically any paper may conceivably be of some use, to somebody, at some time." This is what we would expect researchers to say. What is surprising is their sympathy for the task of the archivist and their encouragement for making hard choices. In the words of the committee, "the archivist must be wise enough, and bold enough, to take a calculated risk, and the historian and the biographer must recognize the difficulties, assist with conference and advice whenever possible, and finally, accept the situation."[18]

Appraisal decisions are not for the faint of heart. These decisions will shape the scholarship of the future and the view that subsequent generations have of our society. While they involve risk, however, they also offer opportunity: the exciting chance to apply archival theory, historical knowledge, and awareness of research trends in a way that will have a true impact on the future. No wonder appraisal is at the heart of all archival work.

NOTES

1. Richard J. Cox and Helen W. Samuels, "The Archivist's First Responsibility: A Research Agenda to Improve the Identification and Retention of Records of Enduring Value," *American Archivist* 51 (winter/spring 1988): 28–42. The best one-volume work on archival appraisal is F. Gerald Ham, *Selecting and Appraising Archives and Manuscripts* (Chicago: Society of American Archivists, 1993).

2. Lewis J. Bellardo and Lynn Lady Bellardo, *A Glossary for Archivists, Manuscript Curators, and Records Managers* (Chicago: Society of American Archivists, 1992).

3. This distinction between primary and secondary values, as well as the fuller hierarchy of five values, is taken from Theodore R. Schellenberg. For a statement of his views, see *The Appraisal of Modern Public Records, National Archives Bulletin* 8 (Washington, D.C.: National Archives and Records Service, 1956).

4. Margaret Cross Norton, "The Scope and Function of Archives," in Thornton W. Mitchell, ed., *Norton on Archives: The Writings of Margaret Cross Norton on Archival and Records Management* (Chicago: Society of American Archivists, 1975), 9.

5. Among Schellenberg's most influential works were *The Appraisal of Modern Public Records, National Archives Bulletin* 8 (Washington: National Archives and Records Service, 1956); and *Modern Archives: Principles and Techniques* (Chicago: University of Chicago Press, 1956).

6. For more on subjectivity versus objectivity in archival appraisal decisions and the entire concept of value, see Hans Booms, "Society and the Formation of a Documentary Heritage: Issues

in the Appraisal of Archival Sources," *Archivaria* 24 (summer 1987): 69–107.

7. These views on Schellenberg are taken from Frank Boles and Julia Marks Young, "Exploring the Black Box: The Appraisal of University Administrative Records," *American Archivist* 48 (spring 1985): 121–140.

8. This emphasis on evidence continues even today at the National Archives. John W. Carlin, the new archivist of the United States, recently shared with the archival profession his vision for the National Archives and Records Administration: "It enables people to inspect for themselves the record of what government has done. It enables officials and agencies to review their actions and helps citizens hold them accountable. It ensures continuing access to essential evidence that documents the rights of American citizens, the actions of federal officials, and the national experience." *Archival Outlook* (the newsletter of the Society of American Archivists), November 1995, 26.

9. I will save another influential concept, documentation strategies, for the next chapter.

10. For the original article, see Frank Boles and Julia Marks Young, "Exploring the Black Box." For a report on the NHPRC project, see Frank Boles in association with Julia Marks Young, *Archival Appraisal* (New York: Neal-Schuman, 1991).

11. *Intrinsic Value,* Staff Information Paper 21 (Washington: National Archives and Records Service, 1982). Reprinted in Maygene F. Daniels and Timothy Walch, eds., *A Modern Archives Reader: Basic Readings on Archival Theory and Practice* (Washington, D.C.: National Archives, 1984).

12. Trudy Huskamp Peterson, "The National Archives and the Archival Theorist Revisited," *American Archivist* 49 (spring 1986): 125–133.

13. Gregory S. Hunter, "Thinking Small to Think Big: Archives, Micrographics and the Life Cycle of Records," *American Archivist* 49 (summer 1986): 315–320.

14. See Frank Boles, "Sampling in Archives," *American Archivist* 44 (spring 1981): 125–130; David R. Kepley, "Sampling in Archives: A Review," *American Archivist* 47 (summer 1984): 237–242; Paul Lewinson, "Archival Sampling," *American Archivist* 20 (October 1957): 291–312; Felix Hall, *The Use of Sampling Techniques in the Retention of Records: A RAMP Study With Guidelines* (Paris: UNESCO, 1981); and Ham, *Selecting and Appraising Archives and Manuscripts,* 75–79.

15. This categorization of sampling techniques is taken from an SAA case study prepared by Trudy Huskamp Peterson.

16. For more on this case, see James Gregory Bradsher, "The

FBI Records Appraisal," *Midwestern Archivist* 13 (1988): 51–66; and Susan D. Steinwall, "Appraisal and the FBI Case Files: For Whom Do Archivists Retain Records?" *American Archivist* 49 (winter 1986): 52–63.

17. Helen Willa Samuels, *Varsity Letters: Documenting Modern Colleges and Universities* (Metuchen, N.J.: Scarecrow Press, 1992). Hans Booms discusses the functional approach in "Society and the Formation of a Documentary Heritage."

18. "Report of the Ad Hoc Committee on Manuscripts Set Up by the American Historical Association in December 1948," *American Archivist* 14 (July 1951): 229–232.

4 ACQUISITIONS AND ACCESSIONING

The previous chapter discussed appraisal mainly from the context of selecting records generated by the parent agency or institution. This chapter adds two closely related concepts:

- acquisition of records and papers not generated by one's parent institution
- accessioning records or papers, from whatever source, in order to establish control over them.

An archival repository need not acquire records or papers from other institutions or individuals. The decision to do so must be made with the consent of the governing body of the archival repository. All institutions, however, must establish control over their holdings through a process that begins with accessioning.

ACQUISITIONS

In reality, both this and the previous chapter deal with acquisitions, and the distinction between the chapters is somewhat artificial. An acquisition is nothing more than an addition to the holdings of an archives collection, manuscript repository, or records center.

An acquisition of records or papers includes two elements: physical custody and legal title. Archives must deal with both of these elements.

- *Physical custody* involves *possession* of the records or papers. Usually the custody shifts from the creator or recipient of the item to the archives or manuscript repository. Custody, however, may not change. In the electronic environment, for example, several government archives are advising creating agencies about the long-term preservation of databases and other electronic records without ever transferring them into the archives. To these government archivists, the only alternative is for the archives to become a museum of computer hardware and software.

- *Legal title* involves *ownership* of the records. As with most things legal, there are further distinctions under this general heading. Legal title includes two elements reminiscent of Marshall McLuhan. Figure 4.1 summarizes these elements.

Figure 4.1 Elements of Legal Title

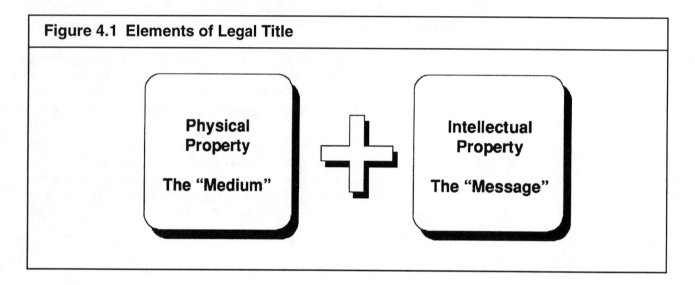

For an archives collection to "own" a record or paper completely, it must have title to both the physical and the intellectual property. Ownership of the "message" involves the archives in the area of copyright: the right vested by law in the author of a document and his or her heirs or assignees to publish or reproduce the document or to authorize publication or reproduction of it.[1] Copyright later becomes a key issue in archival reference services—the archives must be careful not to violate the rights of the owners of the intellectual property.[2]

Transfers of both kinds of title must be stated explicitly—they cannot be presumed or assumed. A subsequent section will describe instruments that archives use to transfer title to the physical and intellectual property.

FIVE BASES FOR ACQUISITIONS

Archival institutions typically use five bases to justify the acquisition of materials.

- *Statute.* In many government settings, a statute passed by the legislature and signed by the chief executive of the jurisdiction forms the basis for the acquisition of records. This is the case with the U.S. federal government where the Federal Records Act and other statutes not only define a record, but empower the National Archives and Records Administration to acquire them on behalf of the people of the United States.

- *Administrative regulation.* Also in the government setting, there may be an administrative regulation rather than a statute, that empowers an agency to acquire records. Regulations are issued by executive branch agencies or independent regulatory agencies in the discharge of their responsibilities authorized by statute.
- *Records retention schedule.* In both government and private sectors, many archives acquire records as the end result of a records retention program. Key to such a program is a records retention schedule, a listing of all series identified during an inventory along with the retention period for each series. Items identified as "permanent" are transferred to an archives collection, perhaps with an intermediate stop in a records center for more efficient retrieval during their semi-active life.
- *Permissive policy statement.* As noted previously, an archives policy statement usually authorizes the archives to acquire the records of the organization. The policy statement also may authorize the archives to acquire "other records and papers" related to the organization but not generated by it. While this gives permission, it often does not sufficiently focus the collecting energies of the archivist.
- *Acquisition policy approved by a governing body.* If an archives or manuscript repository wishes to acquire records or papers systematically, it is best to develop an acquisition policy and have it approved by the governing body of the institution. This is discussed at some length below.

THREE METHODS OF ACQUISITION

Whatever the basis for the acquisition, there are three principal methods for acquiring records or papers: transfer within an agency or institution, purchase, and gift. The type of institution will dictate which of these three methods is used most often. Figure 4.2 relates the three methods of acquisition to the previous discussion of custody and legal title.

For *transfers within an institution*, physical custody usually changes since the archives takes possession of the records. The ownership, however, does not change: it is the institution itself—

Figure 4.2 Relationship of Acquisition Type to Custody and Title		
Acquisition Type	**Transfer of Custody?**	**Transfer of Title?**
Transfer within agency	Yes	No
Purchase	Yes	Yes
Gift	Yes	Yes

rather than the various departments—that owns both the physical and intellectual property, a concept called "dominion." As long as the records being preserved are from the parent institution, there is no change in ownership.[3]

Having said this, transfer to an archives collection involves different thinking from transfer to a records center. Once in archives, records are governed by the access policies in place for the archives (see Chapter 9). By contrast, a records center has responsibility for the physical safety of the materials but no control over use of the records, especially by outside researchers. Access to items in a records center is determined by the originating department. The records center, in effect, is nothing more than an extension of the filing equipment of the department; a records center is established for administrative efficiency rather than scholarly research.

For *purchases and gifts*, one transfers legal title as well as physical custody. Ideally, the title to both the physical item and the intellectual content of the documents passes from one party to the other.

A *purchase* is the transfer of title for financial consideration. The primary concern of the archives should be with the legitimacy of the seller: does he or she have clear title to the property? If not, the archives may be forced to surrender the items at a later date to someone with a claim to the title.

While some manuscript repositories have built extensive collections through purchases, this method has several disadvantages, especially for the small archives. First and foremost, it is expensive. Most archives have limited budgets to begin with; using that small budget to purchase collections further limits the resources for essential archival activities. Secondly, once a repository begins purchasing manuscripts, there is a strong tendency to focus on individual items rather than entire collections. While isolated manuscripts containing autographs of prominent people may have monetary value, they may have little or no research value because

"Stanford University is getting hip—and hip-deep in Beat Generation memorabilia—after buying poet Allen Ginsberg's archives. Stanford wouldn't say yesterday how much it paid for the roughly 300,000 items in the Beat Generation poet's exhaustive and eclectic collection that ranges from original manuscripts to old electric bills."—*Washington Post,* September 8, 1994.

they exist out of context. Finally, once money is involved, fraud rears its ugly head. While most autograph and manuscript dealers are honest, there still will be individuals willing to sell an unsuspecting repository the manuscript equivalent of the Brooklyn Bridge. The less knowledgeable an institution is about the ins and outs of the autograph business, the more it should heed the words of P.T. Barnum that a sucker is born every minute. Anyone want to buy the "authentic" Hitler diary?[4]

A *gift* is a transfer of ownership without financial consideration. As with a purchase, the key question is: does the person really own what he or she is giving to the archives? If not, someone with a better claim to ownership may be able to force its return. Any gift has three characteristics:

- a clear offer
- acceptance of the offer
- delivery

Whether we are talking about a birthday present or the donation of historical manuscripts, these three elements apply. A deed of gift agreement, discussed below, attempts to document all three elements of the gift as well as the transfer of title to the physical and intellectual property.

Soliciting manuscript gifts requires patience and diplomacy. It sometimes takes years for a manuscript repository to receive a donation from a prospect. The repository must be interested but not obtrusive, solicitous but not sycophantic. Finding people who can achieve the right balance may be the key requirement for a successful manuscript gift program.

As important as interpersonal skills are, the best manuscript repositories do not rely on them alone. Repositories generate leads by keeping in touch with their constituents: researchers, benefactors, patrons, and previous donors. Staff members make the public aware of the repositories through speeches to community groups and interviews with the media. Brochures and flyers ensure that those contacted can review information about the repository at a later date.

Perhaps most important, successful manuscript repositories

maintain good records of potential donors and the development of the prospect. While this practice should not be surprising in a profession that deals with records, it still is something that a repository can take for granted. Most curators establish "lead files" into which they place correspondence, notes on telephone conversations, and field reports. If a gift is made, transfer agreements and publicity about the donation become part of the "collection file" that may or may not be the same as the lead file.[5]

Potential donors often inquire about the monetary value of their collection and whether or not they can take a deduction for their donation. In the past, donors could take a tax deduction for the appraised value of the papers. The Tax Reform Act of 1969, however, changed this. To be a tax deductible contribution for an individual, the donated property must be a "capital asset" for the donor. Normally the papers cannot be a capital asset for the creator of the papers. The allowable deduction, therefore, is limited to the out-of-pocket costs of the creation of the material—such as the cost of paper and ink, typewriter ribbons, and floppy disks.

A second common donor question involves monetary appraisals. The Deficit Reduction Act of 1984 requires donors of property valued in excess of $5,000 to obtain a qualified appraisal of the property. The law prohibits the recipient of the donation, such as an archives, from providing the appraisal. As a general rule of thumb, it is safest for an archivist to refer all monetary appraisal questions to those best able to handle them—professional appraisers. Even better, the archivist should refer the donor to a professional association of appraisers—and not to an individual appraiser—so there is no hint of favoritism or collusion.[6]

DEVELOPING AN ACQUISITION POLICY

While an institutional archives documents the organization of which it is a part, a manuscript repository must establish a collecting focus or theme to guide its efforts. To use a formal definition, an acquisition policy is a written statement prepared by a specific repository to define the scope of its collection and to specify the subjects and formats of materials to be collected. Without such a focus, the repository runs several risks:

- The collection might be so scattered as to have no internal unity.

- There might not be a critical mass of information in any one area to support research.
- The repository might squander scarce resources on collections it probably should not have acquired in the first place.
- Several repositories might compete in one collecting area while neglecting other aspects of the human experience.

An acquisition policy, however, must achieve a balance; while one wants definition, one also wants some flexibility—so the collection has room to grow and evolve.

Maynard Brichford has outlined five ideals to guide the development of an acquisition policy. According to Brichford, an institution should collect in areas that:

- extend research strengths, interests, and needs in a logical manner
- anticipate future research needs
- support the institution's extensive holdings of published or unpublished materials
- show a high ratio of use to volume and processing costs (high research value)
- do not directly compete with another major collector in the same region

Focusing on these ideals enables an institution to maximize research interest in its collections while minimizing the inappropriate use of scarce resources.[7]

How does an institution actually draft an acquisition policy? It is best to involve the various constituencies of the repository, such as staff, administrators, researchers, donors, and volunteers. While the governing body will decide the ultimate policy, the input of all constituents guarantees that the acquisition policy will not lose touch with the people who care the most about the repository. A helpful discussion starter is to have the assembled group answer questions in the following areas:

- *What are the financial resources of the institution?* What budget does it have for staff salaries, supplies, and other items? Based upon the financial resources, will the collecting program be modest or extensive? Some archivists consider it unethical to collect more materials than one can process and make available in a reasonable time.
- *How much space is available?* Are the shelves full or empty? Are you likely to collect in an area that will over-

whelm storage capacity? Is there sufficient space for staff to process records and for researchers to access them?

- *What is the quality of the staff?* For example, if the repository decides to collect items dealing with quantum physics, will it have staff members competent to process the materials and help researchers? If the repository is using volunteers, will they be able to handle the complexity of the anticipated collections?

- *Who are the patrons of the repository, both present and anticipated?* What types of collections interest them? If the repository is moving away from its traditional researcher base, how will it attract the new researchers to use the new collections?

- *What formats or types of materials would the institution like to collect?* Is the institution able to preserve and provide access to the items in question? Most repositories collect unpublished materials on paper; some also collect published materials. In addition to paper, there are other record media: photographs, video and audio tapes, microfilm, magnetic disks and tapes, and optical disks. All of these media require special storage and handling that may be beyond the financial resources of some repositories.

- *What collecting themes or focuses would the institution like to pursue?* Should the institution concentrate on a particular geographic area? This often makes sense for a local historical society. Should the focus be a particular time period? Most often, a repository will collect around one or more subjects: people, things, or events. There usually are more possible subjects than any one repository can reasonably collect, so it becomes a question of priorities and selectivity.

This approach to developing an acquisition policy forces the institution to address resource issues before embarking on grandiose collecting projects. There usually is no shortage of collecting ideas; there often is a shortage of institutional resources.

APPLYING AN ACQUISITION POLICY

The staff at NFU developed an acquisition policy by following the above suggestions. They assembled an advisory group composed of administrators, faculty, students, current researchers, and members of the local community. After several group meetings and numerous drafts, they agreed on an acquisition policy which they forwarded to the university administration. The president and board of trustees made a couple of minor changes before approving the statement found in Figure 4.3.

Figure 4.3   NFU Department of Archives and Special Collections Acquisition Policy

In addition to University records, the Department of Archives and Special Collections wishes to identify, preserve, and make available for research materials relating to the following major areas of life on the North Fork of Long Island:

- *The environment.* This area of interest includes the waters surrounding Long Island as well as the land use in the region. The department is particularly interested in documenting the impact of environmental changes on such industries as fishing, farming, and winemaking.
- *Social welfare.* The department seeks to document human and social conditions on the North Fork, particularly the life of the migrant worker.

The department will acquire unpublished records and papers, books, pamphlets, periodicals, maps, photographs, audiotapes, videotapes, microfilm, and magnetic disks and tapes related to the above areas.

The University wishes to work cooperatively with historical societies and local community groups to gather and preserve the history of the region without duplication or competition.

Materials may be added by gift, bequest, purchase, or any other transaction by which title passes to the University. In order to maintain and improve the quality of the collection, materials may be deaccessioned due to irrelevance, lack of space, duplication, or irreparable condition. This will be done only with the approval of the Director of the Library.[8]

With this acquisition policy in hand, the director of the Department of Archives and Special Collections opened a folder left by the previous director: "Offers to Donate Materials." Apparently, as soon as the previous director started interviewing for a job elsewhere, he suspended all acquisition decisions. A note in the front of the file said, "I wanted to give you a free hand to decide which collections to accept. Some of these may be difficult decisions. Good luck."

The new director decided to compare each of the possible donations with the recently approved acquisition policy. Figure 4.4 is the worksheet used for this comparison.

COOPERATIVE COLLECTING AND DOCUMENTATION STRATEGIES

As the above case study shows, North Fork University came to realize that it could not document the North Fork of Long Island by itself. The university had limited staff and other resources to devote to the task. But even with unlimited resources, the task would be too complex for any one institution to do well.

Some institutions work around resource shortages and other limitations by developing cooperative collecting programs. Such arrangements minimize wasteful competition while guaranteeing everyone a well-defined piece of the historical pie. For example, NFU might refer collections dealing with the arts and culture to another repository specializing in those areas.

Some archivists believe that even cooperative collecting programs do not go far enough. The focus, they say, is incorrect, because it still begins with the universe of records that exist rather than with the aspects of society that should be documented. This new approach, called a documentation strategy, attempts to channel energies into the *documentation of society* rather than into the *collection of existing records*. A diverse group of individuals—archivists, researchers, records creators, and community members— would determine the aspects of society that need documenting, identify institutions that may have records shedding light on these aspects, and work with those institutions to preserve and even create records, if necessary.[9]

For example, if one wished to document the AIDS epidemic in a particular community, one might identify several institutions whose records might have historical value. One organization targeted for preservation might be an advocacy and counseling group for gay men and lesbians. What if this organization purposely avoided creating records in order to guarantee the confidentiality of its clients? Should the archivist encourage the creation of records so they can be preserved? Once the records are in the archives,

Figure 4.4 Comparison of Possible Acquisitions to the New Policy		
Collection Title	**Collection Description**	**Acquisition Notes**
Peconic Bay Yachting Association, 1899–1960, 30 cubic feet	A voluntary association of people interested in boating. Collection contains minutes of meetings, membership rosters, photographs of members and events, general correspondence, and racing programs and publicity.	Fits acquisition policy. We are interested in uses of the water surrounding the North Fork.
Florence Kelly Papers, 1917–1989, 6 cubic feet	Ms. Kelly was a teacher in the Orient Public Schools, a leader in the preservation of the Orient Point Lighthouse, and a local community activist. The collection includes correspondence, diaries, press clippings, and memorabilia.	Does not fit acquisition policy. Not primarily concerned with the environment, though it does relate tangentially. This collection is more appropriate for a local historical society.
South Shore Environmental Coalition, 1978–1988, 15 cubic feet	A new group concerned especially with preservation of the pine barrens watershed recharge area. The collection contains lobbying records, press releases and clippings, correspondence with other environmental groups, records of contributions, and other financial information.	Fits acquisition policy, especially if we want to establish a strong regional collection. It is virtually impossible to separate the groups interested in the environment into "North" and "South" Fork.
Dr. Andrew Seligman Papers, 1906-1968, 13 cubic feet	Dr. Seligman was a graduate of NFU and a prominent social worker living in Riverhead. He was instrumental in establishing many of Suffolk County's social work programs. The collection includes correspondence, patient case files, reference files, and photographs.	Fits acquisition policy. A prominent person in the social welfare field as well as an alumnus.
Greenport Bakery, 1927–1980, 6 cubic feet	A "Mom and Pop" bake shop, a fixture in Greenport until it closed in 1980. The collection contains financial data, letters from customers (some quite famous) and recipes.	Does not fit acquisition policy. While it would be heartbreaking to destroy the records of this piece of North . Fork life, we have no other choice. Try to interest a local historical society in the collection.

Figure 4.4 (cont.)		
Collection Title	**Collection Description**	**Acquisition Notes**
Nancy Smith Papers, 1923–1980, 4 cubic feet	Ms. Smith was president of the North Fork Gardening Association and vice president of the Southold Historical Society. Her main interest was historic houses. The collection includes correspondence, diaries, and records of both organizations.	Does not fit acquisition policy. More appropriate for a local historical society.
Nassau County Friends of the Environment, 1969–1980, 40 cubic feet	The leading organization promoting environmental awareness on Long Island. The collection includes correspondence, financial information, membership data, reference files about environmental issues, and publications of the organization.	Fits acquisition policy, but only if we broaden our geographical focus to all of Long Island. Otherwise, we would not take the collection.
North Shore Literary Guild, 1955–1976, 18 cubic feet	An association of authors, publishers, and other interested individuals who live on the North Fork. Collection includes correspondence with local and national authors, reviews of books, minutes of meetings, photographs of monthly meetings, and audio tapes of important lectures.	Does not fit acquisition policy. The arts are outside of our collecting focus.
Mary Winthrop Papers, 1919–1986, 29 cubic feet	Ms. Winthrop was a prominent local politician who served two terms in the state Senate. The collection includes constituent case files, legislative bill files, campaign materials, financial data, and personal correspondence.	Does not fit acquisition policy. Politics is outside of our collecting focus.
Long Island Winegrowers Association, 1975–1988, 15 cubic feet	The trade association of Long Island vineyard owners. Collection includes correspondence, financial data, membership applications, and general reference materials about wines and vineyards.	Fits acquisition policy. Wine growing is one of the current uses of the land.
Jonathan Redburn Papers, 1909–1975, 8 cubic feet	Mr. Redburn was a prominent environmental leader from the Baltimore area. He made two speeches at NFU in the early 1970s. The collection includes correspondence, financial data, and reference files.	Does not fit acquisition policy, unless we broaden our interest in the environment into a national collecting focus. To do so would require more shelf space than we have.

Figure 4.4 (cont.)		
Collection Title	**Collection Description**	**Acquisition Notes**
James Anderson Papers, 1899–1972, 18 cubic feet	Mr. Anderson owned one of the largest potato farms on Eastern Long Island. In addition to personal papers, the collection contains records from the farm itself.	Fits acquisition policy. Not only does it deal with the environment, but the collection might document farm workers (social welfare).

how will the archivist protect the rights and interests of the people who now—perhaps unbeknownst to them—have been made part of the historical record?

If embraced fully, the documentation strategy concept would change the nature of the archivist from impartial evaluator of existing documents to empowered advocate for a consciously shaped historical record. Some would look at this change and say, "It's about time. If we're not more active, all we'll have is a disjointed series of historical artifacts that tell a partial story." I call this alternative the "Sleeper" syndrome, after the Woody Allen film of the same title. In this film, Woody Allen is cryogenically preserved and thawed out in the future. He is then asked to comment on the few artifacts that have survived from the twentieth century. Scribes anxiously record his comments, for now they know the significance of the items they have been preserving. Unfortunately, the historical record as shaped by chance preservation and one person's interpretation, includes Richard Nixon as an obscure person who "did something wrong" and a pair of chattering novelty teeth as an indication of what Americans thought was funny.

Whether we are collecting or documenting, the responsibility is great. We owe it to our repositories to expend their resources effectively. We owe it to present and future researchers to preserve a historical record that helps them understand our times. And we owe it to ourselves to fulfill this responsibility as professionally as possible.

ACCESSIONS AND ACCESSIONING

Accessioning is defined as the act and procedures involved in a transfer of legal title and taking records or papers into the physical custody of an archival agency, records center, or manuscript repository. It is an attempt to establish three types of control over a collection: legal, physical, and intellectual.

LEGAL CONTROL

As noted earlier in this chapter, legal control of archives and manuscripts involves both intellectual and physical aspects—the medium and the message. The objective is to clearly and unambiguously document the transfer of both aspects. This can be done using one of six transfer instruments, some of which offer superior documentation to others. The six transfer instruments are:

- oral agreement
- purchase agreement
- letter
- will
- deposit agreement
- deed of gift agreement (or contract)[10]

Oral Agreement

Though an oral agreement can be legally binding, it offers the poorest documentation of the six transfer instruments. For this reason, it can be a dangerous way of securing collections. If challenged in the future, especially by someone other than the donor, how will the archivist document the offer, acceptance, and actual transfer of the historical materials? Archivists should avoid oral agreements by using one of the five other options below.

Even if an archivist or manuscript curator is painstaking in not entering into new oral agreements, there often is an invisible elephant in the middle of the repository: all the collections now on the shelves (for which there are no transfer instruments except oral agreements with parties long deceased). What does an archivist or manuscript curator do about these "undocumented gifts"?

The best the archivist may be able to do is to document the collections as they now exist before memory dims any more. What is in the collection? As best we can determine, where did the collection come from and when? A systematic way to capture this information is by using an accession form as described in the following section on intellectual control.

Purchase Agreement

As discussed earlier, a purchase involves a transfer of title for financial consideration. As long as the person offering the item has clear title, that person can enter into a sale. The documentation for a purchase may be as simple as a bill of sale or as complex as a formal contract. As with this and the following instruments, it is essential that they be reviewed by legal counsel before signing, to protect the interests of the repository.

Letter

Often a repository uses a letter to document the transfer of historical materials. It really is the *exchange* of letters, however, that is the key—the exchange documents the offer by the donor and the acceptance by the repository. While an exchange of letters is perfectly acceptable, the problem is that letters often do not go into enough detail. This can lead to problems later, especially in the areas of copyright and access. Did the donor want the repository to own the copyright—the intellectual property? Did the donor wish the collection or part of it to be restricted, and for how long? Can we discard duplicates or other items from the collection that do not interest us? Letters seldom go into such detail.

Will

A will transfers title upon the death of the donor. For prominent people, a lawyer usually consults with a repository while preparing the will, so the donation is to everybody's satisfaction. If a manuscript repository has been soliciting a collection for a number of years, a call from a lawyer preparing a will may be the first indication that the repository's persistence may pay off.

Sometimes an archives collection has no advance warning—it may just receive notice that it has been bequeathed a collection. If the collection does not relate to present holdings, or if there are serious restrictions on access, the archives can always refuse the donation. There is no obligation to accept the legacy.

Deposit Agreement

A deposit is the placement of records or papers in the physical custody of a repository without transfer of title. This is similar to what we do with a bank account—the bank does not have legal title to our money, only physical custody. We control the money and how it is dispersed.

The deposit agreement is a statement of intent to transfer title at some (usually unspecified) date. In the meantime, the prospective donor deposits the physical property with the archives for

> "The widow of the Rev. Dr. Martin Luther King, Jr., is in Superior Court here [Boston] this week, fighting Boston University for possession of more than 83,000 of her husband's papers, including his letters, manuscripts and correspondence from American presidents.
>
> "The papers, which Dr. King deposited at his alma mater in 1964 and 1965, at the height of the civil rights movement, are the crown jewel of the university's archives.
>
> "But Coretta Scott King wants them turned over to the Martin Luther King, Jr., Center for Nonviolent Social Change in Atlanta. She maintains that this is in keeping with her husband's wishes that the papers find a permanent home in the South. The King Center houses the rest of Dr. King's work."—*New York Times,* April 30, 1993.

safekeeping. Most archives try to avoid deposit arrangements unless the collection has great value and there is no other way to guarantee its preservation. With a deposit, there always is the chance that archives will use its resources to process the collection, only to have the creator change his or her mind and demand the return of the items. In terms of individuals, it is best to try to have title pass to the archives upon the individual's death, if not sooner.

If a repository chooses to enter into a deposit arrangement, it should be certain that the agreement answers the following questions:

- Is the archives responsible for accidental damage?
- Who insures the records from loss?
- What type of archival or preservation work may the repository undertake and who pays for this work?
- Is access permitted to the collection and, if so, who may grant access?
- If the depositor removes the records before transferring title, must he or she reimburse the repository for direct or indirect costs previously incurred?

Deed of Gift Agreement

A deed of gift is a signed, written instrument containing a *voluntary* transfer of title to real or personal property *without a financial consideration*. This is the preferred method of documenting gifts to archives or manuscript repositories. The deed of gift should be a written contract governing the transfer of title and specifying any restrictions on access or use. It need not be verbose, nor does it require any magic legal words—but it should be clear and unambiguous, to avoid future problems. The repository's legal counsel also should review it in advance.

Many repositories use a standard deed of gift that they can

modify to meet special situations. Using a standard form helps reassure donors that their materials are part of a professionally run repository and will be administered in the same way as other donations.

The elements of a typical deed of gift agreement are

- Name of donor as well as the donor's relationship to the creator of the records, if different.
- Name of recipient. For example, the receiving archives may be housed in a library on the campus of a branch of the state university. Is the donation to the archives, the library, the branch campus, the state university system, or the state?
- Date of the transfer of title.
- Detail on the materials conveyed by the deed of gift (such as the creator of the items, the volume, inclusive dates, and general description).
- Transfer of rights to the physical and intellectual property. In terms of copyright, it is important to detail the name of the person or institution holding copyright as well as the time period covered under copyright.
- Statement of restrictions on use. Typically there is a time restriction ("the entire collection is closed for ten years") or a content restriction ("confidential materials are closed"). The deed should specify who can impose restrictions, to whom the restrictions apply, who can lift restrictions, and how someone requests a temporary waiver of restrictions. Restrictions are discussed further in Chapter 9.
- Disposal criteria and authority. Under what circumstances can the repository dispose of materials if they are duplicates; if they do not have historical value; if they do not fit the acquisition policy or interests? If the repository does not want part of the collection, what are the options (return items to the donor, transfer them to other repositories, or destroy them)?
- Signatures of both the donor and the recipient.

Inclusion of all of these items may make the deed of gift appear very formal. This is precisely the point! The deed of gift agreement is a contract freely entered into by two parties and binding upon them. If the archives fails to meet its obligations, the contract can be voided and the items reclaimed by the donor. Also, the donor can sue for damages. Both parties must understand all parts of the agreement before committing to its provisions.

PHYSICAL CONTROL

Once legal control is established, the archives or manuscript repository can turn to physical control, especially shipping arrangements and the actual receipt of the collection.[11]

Shipping Arrangements

The most secure shipping arrangement is for the repository to pick up and transport the items itself. This will work for local collections, especially small ones. If small collections must be shipped, it is best to use one of the air express or parcel services known for their attention to detail. With large collections, there may be no choice but to use a freight handler or moving company. If possible, have the repository staff box and label materials, carefully maintaining original order and preparing a packing list. Care at this stage will make later processing of the collection easier (see Chapter 5). When transporting fragile materials, especially photographic or magnetic media, the repository should try to avoid sizable temperature fluctuations inside shipping vehicles. If, for example, a company is shipping a photograph collection in the summer from Florida, they should not be left on a siding for a week in a boxcar without air-conditioning.

Documenting Receipt of Collections

Once a collection is received, the repository should document the matter. An acknowledgment letter or memorandum usually suffices for statutory or regulatory transfers. For gifts, a thank-you letter from the staff member who had the most contact with the donor should be the minimum acknowledgment. For particularly important collections, a second letter from the head of the repository is appropriate.

At this point, the collection is on the repository's loading dock (or the archivist's desk). The archivist must know where to place the collection as well as what is in it. The archivist uses an "accession form" for this purpose. Since an accession form is the beginning of intellectual control, it is discussed below.

INTELLECTUAL CONTROL

An archivist must establish intellectual control—control over the contents of a collection—before researcher needs can be met. Accession records are an essential first step in this process for the following reasons:

- They provide a form of inventory control over total holdings by noting where each collection is located.
- They serve as temporary finding aids, providing intellectual control over collections until more-detailed arrangement and description are completed.
- They provide worksheets for the control of work activities and help to establish priorities.

Accession records can be kept manually on paper or electronically in a database. If at all possible, it makes sense to establish a new accessioning system on a database since this will permit easier searching and updating as the collection grows in size.

Whether paper or electronic, an accession form or log should contain the following information for each collection:

- accession number
- record group number (defined in chapter 5) and name
- title of collection
- name and address of source/donor
- date of receipt
- description of collection (approximate volume, inclusive dates, and general subject matter)
- comments on restrictions
- temporary location
- preliminary plans for processing (identification of divisions within the collection, recommendations about arrangement and description, recommendations about scheduling, time and staff requirements, and preservation considerations)

The accession record is the first part of a repository's intellectual control system. This is probably its most important role. A descriptive system should take a building block approach. There should be no wasted effort and no need ever again to begin from scratch.[12] What an archivist learns about a collection at the accessioning stage should help with later arrangement and description. Until that arrangement and description are completed, the accession register will serve as the primary finding aid. Archives have too much to do with too few resources to squander any information about a collection.

CONCLUSION

To fulfill its mandate, an archives collection or manuscript repository requires focus and organization. The focus comes from a mission statement and acquisition policy. The organization comes from establishing legal, physical, and intellectual control over the materials added to the archives. Both of these elements enable an archives collection to begin to preserve and make available the records and papers of enduring value in its possession. Only then can an archives collection turn its energies outward, to the researchers that it serves.

NOTES

1. Lewis J. Bellardo and Lynn Lady Bellardo, *A Glossary for Archivists, Manuscript Curators, and Records Managers* (Chicago: Society of American Archivists, 1992).

2. For more on copyright, see Gary M. Peterson and Trudy Huskamp Peterson, *Archives and Manuscripts: Law* (Chicago: Society of American Archivists, 1985), 81–89.

3. Peterson and Peterson, *Archives and Manuscripts: Law*, 20. Much of the following discussion is based upon this book. The U.S. National Archives and Records Administration (NARA) defines custody in a slightly different manner: "Guardianship, or control, of records including both physical possession (physical custody) and legal responsibility (legal custody), unless one or the other is specified." While legal ownership still does not change, in NARA usage legal responsibility does change. *Disposition of Federal Records: A Records Management Handbook* (Washington, D.C.: NARA, 1992), D-4.

4. A few years ago, the world was surprised by the discovery of Adolf Hitler's diaries. Several experts identified the diaries as authentic, only to be publicly humiliated when other experts proved the diaries to be fakes.

5. For more on this topic, see F. Gerald Ham, *Selecting and Appraising Archives and Manuscripts* (Chicago: Society of American Archivists, 1993), 37–50.

6. Peterson and Peterson, *Archives and Manuscripts: Law*, 35–37.

7. Maynard J. Brichford, *Archives and Manuscripts: Appraisal and Accessioning* (Chicago: Society of American Archivists, 1977), 18–19. See also Ham, *Selecting and Appraising*, 15–24.

8.   This acquisition policy is a modified version of one prepared by Candace Shuluk, a graduate student at the Palmer School of Library and Information Science, Long Island University, 1996.

9.   For more on documentation strategies, see: Ham, *Selecting and Appraising,* 95–97; Philip N. Alexander and Helen W. Samuels, "The Roots of 128: A Hypothetical Documentation Strategy," *American Archivist* 50 (fall 1987): 518–531; Helen W. Samuels, "Who Controls the Past," *American Archivist* 49 (spring 1986): 109–124; and Larry J. Hackman and Joan Warnow-Blewett, "The Documentation Strategy Process: A Model and Case Study," *American Archivist* 50 (winter 1987): 12–47. Not everyone thinks that the archivist should be shaping the historical record. For a view of the archivist as keeper rather than selector, see Sir Hilary Jenkinson, *A Manual of Archive Administration,* rev. 2d ed. (London: Percy, Lund, Humphries & Co., 1965).

10.   The following discussion is drawn from Peterson and Peterson, *Archives and Manuscripts: Law,* 24–38. See especially the model deed of gift on pages 28–34.

11.   See Ham, *Selecting and Appraising,* 84–90.

12.   Lydia Lucas, "Efficient Finding Aids: Developing a System for Control of Archives and Manuscripts," *American Archivist* 41 (winter 1981), 21–26.

5 ARRANGEMENT

Arrangement is the process of organizing records and papers to reveal their contents and significance. The process usually includes packing, labeling, and shelving archives and manuscripts, and is intended to achieve physical or administrative control and basic identification of the holdings. The key point is that arrangement (and, later, description) is a *process*, not a product. We should never think of arrangement and description as ends in themselves. Rather, they are the means to an end—the ready accessibility of information for researchers.[1]

BASIC PRINCIPLES

Any discussion of archival arrangement usually begins with the terms *provenance* and *original order*. Not only are these important archival principles, they are essential terms to master before one's first archival cocktail party. An aspiring archivist on a buffet line is always safe talking about the weather, sports, and original order.

PROVENANCE

The principle of provenance first was articulated by French archivists in the 1840s. According to this principle, archives of a given records creator must not be intermingled with those of other records creators. Archivists always try to keep separate the records of different creating individuals or agencies. Provenance also is referred to by the French expression *respect des fonds*, especially at more prestigious archival cocktail parties.

The French did not immediately develop the principle of provenance upon their archival epiphany. Rather, after the French Revolution, the French archivists spent almost half a century arranging records primarily by subject. Only after trial and error did the French take the idea of provenance and elevate it to a guiding principle.

Someone from a library background might say "a subject arrangement sounds pretty good to me." What archivists have found, however, is that while a subject arrangement makes it easier to answer *some* questions, it makes other equally valid questions almost impossible to answer. An example may make this clearer. Suppose a multinational bank decided to organize its archives by subject. Records received from the president, the public relations department, and the international finance department would all be broken apart by subject and intermingled with the records of other departments. This would make it easy for the bank's archivist to answer subject questions like "I need everything about our China branches." Other questions, however, would be difficult or impossible to answer: How did the public relations department function? What did the president know about the problems in Europe? How did information flow across departments? Archivists try to arrange collections in a way that answers the widest variety of potential questions.

ORIGINAL ORDER

Original order, the second fundamental principle of archival arrangement, was promulgated by the Prussian State Archives in the 1880s. Original order means that records should be maintained in the order in which they were placed by the organization, individual, or family that created them. Archivists restore and present to researchers, insofar as possible, the original order of the records as evidence of how the records were used by the creator.

There also is a practical reason why archivists respect original order: it is the only way to gain control over large, modern collections. When collections were small, archivists had the luxury of rearranging received collections in order to have them organizationally perfect. Archivists no longer have this luxury, for modern organizations create records far faster than archivists can rearrange them. Original order also is referred to by the French expression *respect pour l'ordre primitif*.

As with provenance, original order sounds easy to implement. In practice, however, it is not so clear-cut. What was the office of origin for the records found in the North Fork University basement after 20 years of hibernation? Should the archivist maintain an original order that looks like it came from Mount Saint Helens rather than a file cabinet? If my predecessor as archivist completely destroyed provenance and original order, should I maintain this system or try to return to the archival ideal? Archivists face these decisions more often than they like to admit.[2]

FIVE LEVELS OF ARRANGEMENT

As archivists move from arrangement theory to practice, they have developed some helpful concepts and approaches. Perhaps the most useful is the concept of levels of arrangement articulated by Oliver Wendell Holmes of the U.S. National Archives.[3] No, this is not the Supreme Court justice—as versatile as Justice Holmes may have been, he was not also an archival theorist.

Holmes the archivist found it "elementary" that records have different levels of arrangement. Each level has an arrangement that can be coordinated with—but still different from—the other four. This concept has been accepted by both archivists and manuscript curators. It is effective with collections of historical materials of every size. The five levels are:

- repository
- record group (collection) and subgroup
- series
- file unit
- item

From a practical standpoint, Holmes's major contribution was in detailing the different activities archivists must perform at the five levels of arrangement. The following sections explain the levels and their associated archival activities.

REPOSITORY

A repository's total holdings usually are divided into a few major and distinct categories. Repository level decisions are not the kind that an archivist makes every day. This usually is done at the highest administrative levels and, once determined, tends to remain in effect for a long period of time. For example, a university might divide its holdings into "institutional archives" generated by the university itself and "special collections" created by other organizations and individuals. The U.S. National Archives uses such repository level divisions as "civil archives" and "military archives," as well as special format divisions for electronic records and other special media.

RECORD GROUP AND SUBGROUP

Record group is a term unique to archivists and, therefore, confusing to almost everyone else. A record group is a body of organizationally related records established on the basis of provenance, with particular regard for the complexity and volume of the records and the administrative history of the record-creating institution or organization. An example is the records of the president's office. A subgroup is a subordinate administrative unit or a major division within the record group. To continue with the example, a subgroup might be the assistant to the president.

In establishing record groups, an archivist is concerned with both the *complexity* and *quantity* of the body of records. One must be able to manage the record group system physically. Archivists have tended to use one of the following strategies in establishing a record group system:

- Establish record groups *strictly according to provenance.* Records of each creating agency are kept together as a record group and assigned a unique number. The National Archives, for example, assigns each major federal agency or institution its own record group number. Manuscript repositories tend to use this approach since they assign each collection a unique number.
- Establish *general groups for records relating to an organization as a whole,* not merely one unit of it. An example would be one record group for the officers of an organization (each officer, in turn, would be considered a subgroup).
- Establish *collective groups* to bring together *like bodies of material.* This usually is done when an institution has a large number of small entities. University archives, for example, might establish one record group for student organizations rather than have 75 separate record groups.[4]

The key to any record group system is that it be clear, unambiguous, and understandable. It is preferable, too, especially in a small archives setting, to have a system that is easy to remember without frequent references to a lengthy list of numbers.

Establishing a record group structure is a very personal decision—it reflects the personality of the archivist as well as his or her analysis of what is significant in the history of the institution. Whatever the system, there should only be one logical place to assign any collection or group of records; otherwise the system will appear to reflect a dysfunctional archival personality.

SERIES

A series is a group of files or documents maintained together *as a unit* because of some relationship arising out of their creation, receipt, or use. The records may relate to a particular subject or function, result from the same activity, or have a common form. Series usually are identified by common filing order, subject matter, or physical type. Some examples are: general correspondence, invoices, minutes, and patient case files. Subseries occur when the series is partitioned. For example, the originating department may have divided "general correspondence" into "incoming correspondence" and "outgoing correspondence," thereby making two subseries.

Record series is perhaps the most crucial archival arrangement level for a number of reasons:

- Here the archivist expresses the character of the collection by the divisions identified in it.
- Work on subordinate levels merely refines the order within each individual series.
- Description also focuses heavily on the series.
- Archivists usually direct researchers to series they believe may provide answers to their queries.

Series level arrangement actually involves two considerations: the order *within* a series (which file folder comes first in a series) and the order *among* series (which series comes before another series in the final collection arrangement). The creator of the records usually cares about order within a series, but not order among series. He or she established an original order based on intended use of the information. The creator seldom dictates which series should come first—the archivist decides this. In fact, when records are still active, the decision about which series comes before another is often based more on which drawer of a filing cabinet is free rather than any intellectual effort. The archivist's job, therefore, is to restore the order *within* series and to create an order *among* the series (see Figure 5.1).

Figure 5.1 Order at the Series Level		
	Within Series	**Among Series**
Who determines the order?	The creator/originator of the series	The archivist
When is this order determined?	When the records are active in the originating department	When the inactive records are processed in the archives
What is the archivist's role?	Restore	Create

FILE UNIT

Records creators place individual items into units for ease of filing. These units may be file folders, bound volumes, magnetic disk packs, and countless other items. File folders are the most common unit that archivists face at this level. File folders tend to be arranged in one of several common schemes:

- alphabetical
- chronological
- geographical
- subject
- numerical

An archivist respecting original order would determine the filing sequence (alphabetical, let's say), and put the folders in proper order. Obvious misfiles would be corrected—they would not be preserved as a monument to someone's inability to alphabetize.

ITEM

The fifth level of arrangement is item level. An *item* is a letter or other document, regardless of length. Items are the letters, memoranda, and reports found within file folders. Usually items in folders are arranged chronologically or alphabetically. Once again, the archivist would retain the original order of items within file folders if at all possible.

THE FIVE LEVELS AT NORTH FORK UNIVERSITY

Figure 5.2 shows how Holmes's five levels apply to the North Fork University Department of Archives and Special Collections.

At the repository level, the holdings are divided into two major categories: university archives and special collections. This separation made sense to the university because of the differences in ownership and copyright that might apply. Official university records are placed in the Archives while all other records or papers become part of Special Collections.

The record group/collection level differs somewhat between Archives and Special Collections. Archives uses the term "record group" for its major holdings. Among the record groups are Board of Trustees, Vice President for Academic Affairs, Office of Financial Aid, and Student Organizations. Special Collections uses the term "collection" for its major holdings, the equivalent of record groups. Among the collections are the Long Island Winegrowers Association, the Dr. Andrew Seligman Papers, and the James Anderson Papers.

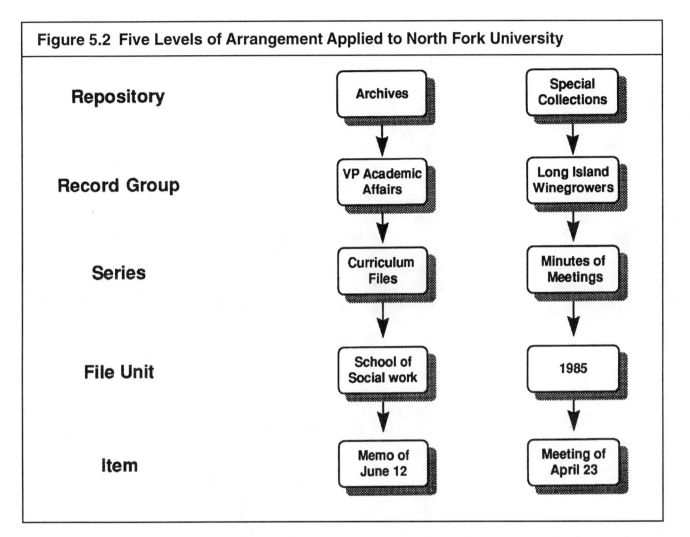

Figure 5.2 Five Levels of Arrangement Applied to North Fork University

Repository	Archives	Special Collections
Record Group	VP Academic Affairs	Long Island Winegrowers
Series	Curriculum Files	Minutes of Meetings
File Unit	School of Social work	1985
Item	Memo of June 12	Meeting of April 23

The remaining three levels will be less confusing if I work through the levels first for Archives and then for Special Collections. For the Archives, there are several series within the records of the Vice President for Academic Affairs: Curriculum Files; Correspondence with the President and Board of Trustees; University Departments; and Faculty Files. Within the Curriculum Files Series, there are individual file units (file folders) for each academic area. The School of Social Work, for example, has its own folder. Inside this folder are many items, including a memorandum dated June 12 of last year dealing with changes to the curriculum.

In Special Collections, the Long Island Winegrowers Association Collection contains such series as Minutes of Meetings; Correspondence; Financial Data; Membership Applications; and General Reference. Within the Minutes series, there are file folders for each year. Finally, inside the 1985 folder one will find the minutes of the meeting of April 23, 1985.

RELATING THE FIVE LEVELS TO ARCHIVAL PROCESSING

Levels of arrangement is another modular concept. It is as valuable for establishing work priorities as it is for processing individual collections. Most nitty-gritty archival work involves arrangement at levels three, four, and five. Even here, however, archivists must make choices. If there is a large backlog of unprocessed collections, an archivist may opt not to work down to the item level. Taking this approach, an archivist first would process all collections down to the file unit level. Once caught up (if ever), the archivist would return to the collections and worry about the order of individual items within file folders.

Certainly there are trade-offs in this approach. Some archivists would cringe at the thought of having items within file folders not in perfect chronological or alphabetical order. Wouldn't researchers think that I was not a very careful archivist? While some researchers might think so, others would be pleased that archival processing time led to the availability of more collections rather than the precise micro-arrangement of just one collection. The bulk of modern collections forces archivists to balance time against resources at every step of the archival enterprise.

ARRANGING A COLLECTION

How, then, do archivists arrange a collection? How do they make sense of a mass of boxes and folders? How do they approach this task without losing heart? To paraphrase the Marx Brothers, do archival job descriptions have a "sanity clause" or is this just a Christmas legend?

While there are different approaches to arranging a collection, the following nine steps have proven successful in a number of settings:

1. *Prepare to process the collection.* Make certain that there is sufficient work space to spread records out during sorting. Place supplies (acid-free file folders, staple removers, erasers, and dry cleaning pads) in the same locations each day. This will relieve you of searching for supplies each time you need them.

"Robert M. Gates, the Director of Central Intelligence, has ordered a sweeping overhaul of how the C.I.A. maintains its vast store of files, government officials said today.

"Mr. Gates's order is a result of the embarrassment suffered by the Central Intelligence Agency over its role in the criminal investigation of an Atlanta branch of an Italian Bank. The Justice Department complained in the summer that the nation's prime intelligence and espionage agency failed to pass on crucial information in the files about the bank Banca Nazionale del Lavoro....

"Computer-security experts said that the C.I.A.'s system of filing its secrets is so compartmentalized for security's sake that it is often difficult or impossible to track down all relevant information on a subject. At the same time, they said, the complicated system also provides a ready excuse for the agency when its officers want to withhold information."—*New York Times,* January 1, 1993.

2. *Review the accession register and other acquisitions documents.* Remember, the accession register serves as the interim finding aid until processing is completed. If prepared in sufficient detail, these documents should outline series and other major sections of the collection.

3. *Go through the entire collection without rearranging anything.* This initial pass is to confirm the information in the accession register, give you a feel for the collection, and allow you to come to some conclusions about series. It is best to take extensive notes during this stage. Some archivists use a pad; others prefer to use index cards so they can reshuffle the entries to try out possible arrangements.

4. *Develop the processing plan.* Sketch out the order the final collection will have. Review this order with coworkers or superiors, especially if you are new to archival processing. Determine the appropriate level of detail for processing, including any preservation work that must happen at this stage.

5. *Sort the collection into series.* In this second pass through the collection, separate records into the series identified in the processing plan. Place the series in the order in which they will appear in the processed collection.

6. *Process each series to the filing unit level.* Take the series in order, "re-folder" them using acid-free materials, and place them in uniform boxes. The acid-free folders should be labeled but not numbered at this stage—there still may be some changes to filing sequence as the collection is processed. Placing the folders in uniform acid-free boxes not only helps one plan for the ultimate size of the collection

Figure 5.3 Steps in Arranging a Collection

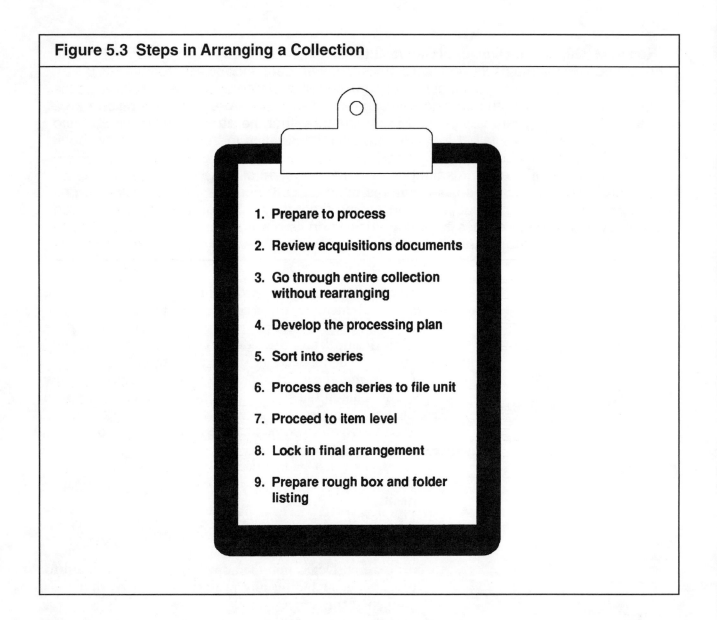

1. **Prepare to process**

2. **Review acquisitions documents**

3. **Go through entire collection without rearranging**

4. **Develop the processing plan**

5. **Sort into series**

6. **Process each series to file unit**

7. **Proceed to item level**

8. **Lock in final arrangement**

9. **Prepare rough box and folder listing**

(which usually is reduced during processing), but it gives a feeling of accomplishment as we see the collection move from unprocessed to processed. (Remember the sanity clause!)

7. *Proceed to the item level.* If resources permit, there are different types of item processing one can undertake. The simplest is just removing paper clips, rubber bands, and other fasteners that will cause the collection to deteriorate. (Most archivists will remove these fasteners even if they can do nothing else at the item level.) More effort is

"University of Illinois physicist Albert Wattenberg didn't go to the Chicago branch of the National Archives last year looking for trouble. But when he could barely lift an 8-inch metal rod from a box containing artifacts used by nuclear physicist Enrico Fermi and his colleagues to build a nuclear pile under the University of Chicago football stadium, he knew something was wrong. 'There's only one metal that heavy,' says Wattenberg, who was part of Fermi's team in the 1940s. 'It was obviously uranium.'

"Wattenberg had literally put his fingers on a half-century of carelessness in preserving the beginnings of the nation's nuclear history. Thousands of artifacts contaminated by radionuclides during the testing and production of nuclear materials—laboratory notebooks, classified documents, components from experiments, and the like—were being stored along with nonradioactive material in files open to public inspection. Although the health hazards associated with these materials are small . . . the contamination is presenting the Department of Energy and the National Archives with a major cleanup problem."—*Science,* January 14, 1994.

required to place items in correct date order or other sequence. Many archives remove certain items (such as photographs or publications) from a collection for special handling. If such items are removed for storage elsewhere, it is customary to leave a "separation sheet" in the originating collection so that researchers will know where to look for the item. On the other side of the transaction, the removed item should contain enough information so that one can locate the collection from which it came.

8. *Lock in the final arrangement.* Place folders in final order. Do not overpack them into boxes. (Leave enough room to remove and return folders easily, but not so much room that items fall over and curl.) Place box and folder numbers on each folder.

9. *Prepare a rough box and folder listing.* List all folders in box and folder order. Write down dates and any other information you will need to describe the collection (see Chapter 6).

As one can see, archival arrangement is a labor-intensive process. It requires multiple passes through a collection. It also requires a great deal of discipline. Most archivists are interested in history to some degree, whether or not they majored in it in college, and they are tempted to read every word of every item, just because the story is so interesting and the contact with primary sources is so rewarding. Archivists must avoid the temptation if collections are ever to get processed. An archivist must read *just enough* to understand the nature and significance of the collection in order to make this known to researchers through finding aids. Any more than this is a waste of scarce archival resources.

TEN ARRANGEMENT "HINTS"

Even following the steps outlined above may not answer all of the questions that arise during arrangement. The following ten "Hunter's Hints" provide some additional insights:

1. *Box the records yourself prior to transfer.* As noted in Chapter 4, this is the best way to understand and preserve the original order of the collection. The boxing procedure also offers the opportunity to identify series and processing priorities even before the collection reaches the repository door.

2. *When in doubt, chicken out.* If you have any doubt about the original order, or if there is an original order that does not make sense, be cautious before changing it. Order always can be changed and divisions made later; rarely can order be reconstituted, and divisions undone. (Even if they can be undone, this takes time and energy away from other activities.) Particularly troublesome are "Dewey-Decimal-type" filing systems where someone, long dead, grouped files under a classification scheme now forgotten and probably further hidden behind an array of file numbers. Archivists have been known to spend a great deal of time undoing an indecipherable system only to find the "cipher," or list of codes, in a subsequent file. Ouch!

3. *Remember the "test of creation."* You can distinguish one record group from another by asking "who created these records?" Similarly, if you are unclear if a body of records is a record group or series, try to focus on who created it. Multiple series can be part of a record group.

4. *Records follow function.* Functions usually remain constant in organizations though department names and locations may change. The records of a predecessor department are maintained with the successor department, if that is the way the archives received them. Arrange the files under the name of the unit making the transfer. Consider, for example, an organization that once had a separate research department. It subsequently was closed and the research responsibility was transferred to public relations, along with all the extant records. Ten years later, the public relations department transferred

its records to the archives. Intermingled throughout the public relations materials are files from the now-defunct research department. The archivist should not try to re-assemble the records of the research department, because their integration into the public relations files tells a great deal about how the department functioned. The finding aid should explain the shift in responsibility and steer researchers to the public relations records for answers to their questions.

5. *What do you do if there is no original order,* or if there is an original order but it is an unserviceable one? Frank Boles argues that archivists should not be slaves to original order. He offers "simple usability" as a higher law than original order (like Hebrew National's "higher authority" for making hot dogs). Boles makes a great deal of sense; there is no point maintaining an unusable original order. The key is to do the least rearranging possible to make the collection serviceable. If there is no order at all, the archivist should use the simplest order possible.[5]

6. *What about manuscript collections?* Original order sometimes does not make as much sense with personal papers—the collection often arrives in a state of disarray. Imagine if someone took the contents of your desk top, shoveled them into a box, and shipped them to a manuscript repository. What was the original order of your desk? Perhaps it was an embodiment of the Big Bang Theory? Faced with such situations, manuscript curators often have to be more creative than their archival colleagues. Curators tend to divide personal papers in one of four ways:

   - *Chronology.* Regardless of type of document, everything is placed in straight date order, since people (except perhaps Shirley MacLaine) only live once and do so in a chronological sequence. A chronological arrangement can be easy to implement but likely will require extensive cross-referencing for subject access.
   - *Topics.* The potential problem is who defines the topics. Will researchers be looking for the same topics as the curator who arranged the collection?
   - *Types of materials.* The curator would establish separate series for such materials as correspondence, diaries, and minutes. Researchers find this arrangement very helpful since some types of materials tend to be more valuable for research than other types.

- *Functions of the creator.* The papers of a college professor active in professional and community affairs could have the following series: personal life, teaching and research, professional service, and community service.

7. *Avoid establishing more than one system within any one collection.* Such combinations create more than one proper place for some documents. This can lead to confusion and frustration for the staff as well as for researchers. For example, if you begin dividing the collection by type of material, do not also have part of the collection divided by topic, or there will now be two logical places to file a particular item.

8. *Arrange series in order of the value of the information they contain.* This hint deals with the order among series in a collection. The series that provide the greatest insight and the fullest overview come first. If the series are ordered by types, then minutes, diaries, and correspondence usually come first. Indexes come before the records they illuminate. (There is nothing more frustrating for a researcher than to wade through a collection, only to find an index after the fact.) Archivists usually arrange records according to the administrative hierarchy: the president comes before the vice president, the main office comes before the field offices, records covering more than one function precede those documenting a single activity. Curators usually arrange manuscript collections from the most personal types of items (diaries and correspondence) to the least personal (newspaper clippings).

9. *Order within file folders.* Curators place the earliest items first, so the researcher may follow events as they developed. Archivists, following standard business practice, tend to put the most recent document on top. Naturally, if one does not get down to the individual item level, this point is moot.

10. *Create folder titles that are complete but terse.* Description will be based on information gathered during the arrangement stage. Folder titles are particularly important, since the archivist preparing a finding aid wants to avoid having to look inside folders once again. A concise list of folder titles is as much the end product of the arrangement phase as a neat array of acid-free boxes.

CONCLUSION

Archival arrangement, once mastered, can be a very satisfying activity. Where once there was disorder and an inherently valuable collection inaccessible to researchers, there now is a body of records whose arrangement helps illuminate the significance of the collection. But arrangement is not the end of the story. The best-arranged collection, without description just as carefully prepared, will remain a historical resource in potential only. The next chapter deals with description as a bridge to the use of archival collections.

NOTES

1. The best sources of further information are Fredric M. Miller, *Arranging and Describing Archives and Manuscripts* (Chicago: Society of American Archivists, 1990); David B. Gracy II, *Archives and Manuscripts: Arrangement and Description* (Chicago: Society of American Archivists, 1977); David W. Carmicheal, *Organizing Archival Records: A Practical Method of Arrangement and Description for Small Archives* (Harrisburg, Penn.: Pennsylvania Historical and Museum Commission, 1993); *Guidelines for Arrangement and Description of Archives and Manuscripts: A Manual for Historical Records Programs in New York State* New York State Archives and Records Administration (Albany, N.Y.: University of the State of New York, 1991).

2. For more on provenance and original order, see Miller, *Arranging and Describing Archives and Manuscripts*, 25–27.

3. Oliver W. Holmes, "Archival Arrangement: Five Different Operations at Five Different Levels," *American Archivist* 27 (January 1964): 21–41.

4. For more information on different types of record groups, see Lewis J. Bellardo and Lynn Lady Bellardo, *A Glossary for Archivists, Manuscript Curators, and Records Managers* (Chicago, Ill.: Society of American Archivists, 1992).

5. Frank Boles, "Disrespecting Original Order," *American Archivist* 45 (winter 1982): 26–32.

6 DESCRIPTION

Description is the process of establishing administrative and intellectual control over archival holdings through the preparation of finding aids. The archivist takes what he or she has learned about a collection during the arrangement stage and translates it into a collection road map for the archival staff and researchers. Without adequate description, even the most historically valuable and best-arranged collection will remain unused and, hence, worthless from a research perspective.

Finding aids are the descriptive media, published and unpublished, created by an originating office, an archival agency, or a manuscript repository, to establish administrative and intellectual control over holdings. As noted in Chapter 4, the accession register is the first finding aid created by archives or manuscript repository; it is the beginning of a unified descriptive system.

OBJECTIVES OF A DESCRIPTION PROGRAM

As noted above, a description program has two objectives: to provide administrative control for the repository and to establish intellectual control for staff and researchers.

ADMINISTRATIVE CONTROL

Finding aids provide administrative control for the repository in a number of ways:

- Finding aids *give the location* of collections on the repository's shelves.
- Finding aids *identify the source,* or provenance, of the collections. This feature provides an important link in the "chain of custody" should it ever be necessary to document for legal reasons the administrative history of a collection.
- Finding aids *outline the general contents* of collections so that archivists can provide reference services from the moment the collection reaches the repository.

INTELLECTUAL CONTROL

Finding aids also establish intellectual control for staff and researchers in the following ways:

- Finding aids sketch the *general nature of a repository's holdings.* Is this the archives of an art museum or a special collection focusing on urban affairs?
- Finding aids identify the *general contents of individual collections.* What are the titles of all the collections and what do they contain?
- As the descriptive system develops, finding aids offer researchers *detailed information about individual collections.* What is in each box of the collection?
- Finding aids *summarize information on a specific topic* available in several collections. For example, what does the repository contain that would be useful for genealogical research?

THREE CATEGORIES OF FINDING AIDS

To meet the above objectives, most archives use three categories of finding aids: internal control tools, in-house reference aids, and external reference aids.[1] A well-rounded archival program will prepare at least one finding aid in each category, usually in the order outlined below.

INTERNAL CONTROL TOOLS

As soon as a collection reaches a repository, an archivist or manuscript curator creates one or more finding aids. Accession worksheets, location registers, and checklists of various kinds are intended solely for the repository staff. While researchers never see these finding aids, they benefit from them nonetheless. Until other finding aids are created, these internal control documents provide the major access points for the collection.

IN-HOUSE REFERENCE AIDS

As arrangement and description proceed, and as the archival staff becomes familiar with the collections by answering reference requests, they create more detailed finding aids. These still are "in-house," in the sense that the finding aids are not intended to be

Figure 6.1 Categories of Finding Aids

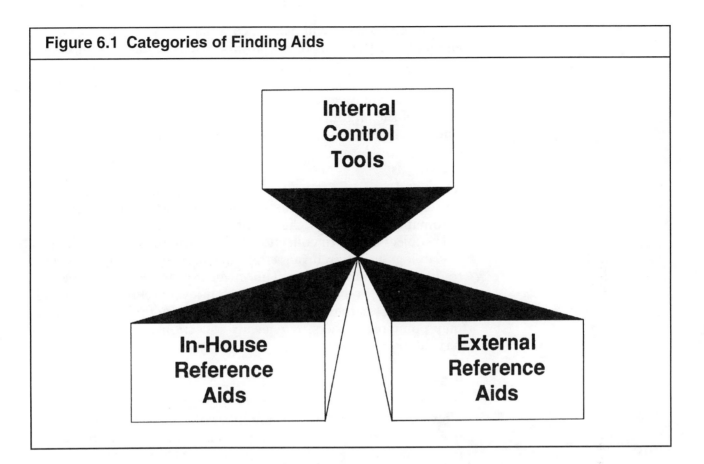

published and distributed to the research community. Unlike the previous category of finding aids, however, researchers are permitted to use these reference aids during visits to the repository. The three most common in-house reference aids are container lists, catalogs, and indexes.

Container Lists

Container lists are called different things in different repositories: shelf lists, box lists, and folder lists, to name a few. Whatever the name, the finding aid usually takes the form of a columnar listing of box numbers, folder numbers, and folder titles.

During the arrangement stage, the processing archivist takes detailed notes on the final order of the collection. These notes, once typed in columns, become the container lists used by staff and researchers alike. Many repositories use three-ring binders to hold container lists. Some also make electronic versions of container lists available for searching, even if the list is nothing more than a word-processing document.

Since researchers will use the container lists, it is important to eliminate jargon and abbreviations. Some of the jargon comes from the subject matter of the collection; other jargon comes from the abbreviations archivists use to save themselves time (for example, the abbreviation "mss" for manuscripts). Whatever the source of the jargon, the usefulness of the container list is diminished if a researcher must have an archivist present to translate.

Catalogs

Many archives use catalogs as in-house reference aids. This is true especially for archives located in library settings. Before wide-scale automation of archives, there probably was no better way to provide subject access to collections than through a card catalog.

Catalogs in an archival setting are used differently from in a traditional library setting. The inventory or register, to be discussed below, is the primary collection-level archival finding aid. Catalog entries, therefore, are not the primary finding aid; rather, they point researchers to relevant collections that are fully described in an inventory.

Indexes

The catalog also can serve as an index to archival collections. However, an index can take a number of other forms. In the electronic environment, it increasingly is a database or even a word-processing document that can be searched by keywords. There will be more later in this chapter on the impact of computers on archival finding aids.

EXTERNAL REFERENCE AIDS

The last step in the description process is the creation of external reference aids. In a modular approach to description, external reference aids build upon internal control tools and in-house reference aids; there is no wasted effort in a well-planned descriptive system. Researchers are likely to encounter the following four external reference aids: calendars, inventories, guides, and networked information systems.

Calendars

Today, calendars exist as archival artifacts. Earlier in the century, archivists created detailed, item-level descriptions of collections. These item level descriptions were called calendars. It was common to create calendars for collections of the "Great White Fathers" (such as Washington and Madison).

One can imagine the time and effort involved in creating calendars for even a small collection. In some cases, the text in the description of an item may have been longer than the text in the item itself.

Although researchers probably would be pleased if archivists continued to produce calendars, it does not happen very often. Collections are too large to describe at the item level. Furthermore, if an archivist is describing one collection down to the item level, some other archival task is not being accomplished; another collection remains undescribed, fragile originals are not preserved, or the response to a reference request is delayed even longer. What is the best use of archival resources?

Inventories

An inventory (also called a register) is the basic archival finding aid. The National Archives developed the inventory after World War II. (The National Archives also has "preliminary inventories," some of which have not been completed in decades and probably never will be.) The Library of Congress has a similar finding aid which it calls a register.

Inventories or registers provide detailed information about one collection or record group/subgroup. Inventories go beyond *content*, however, to provide *context*. Where did these records come from? What were the circumstances of their creation? How do these records relate to other records? Why are they significant for research now and in the future?

There are seven sections to a typical inventory:

- preface
- introduction
- biographical sketch or agency history
- scope and content note
- series description
- container listing
- index or item listing[2]

Preface. A published inventory usually begins with a preface. A repository will use the same preface for all of its inventories, thereby providing continuity to its finding aids. A preface explains the institution's policies on access and restrictions. It also can provide information about photocopies and microfilm of collections. A well-written preface can be a welcoming experience to a potential researcher.

Introduction. The introduction provides an overview of the contents, provenance, and research strengths of the collection. It re-

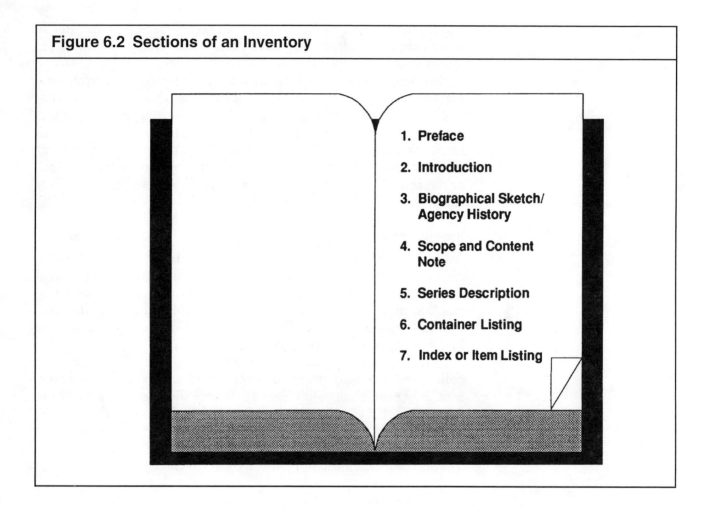

Figure 6.2 Sections of an Inventory

1. Preface

2. Introduction

3. Biographical Sketch/
   Agency History

4. Scope and Content
   Note

5. Series Description

6. Container Listing

7. Index or Item Listing

lates the contents of the collection to the history of the creating institution or the biography of the creator. It also includes information on restrictions that apply to this specific collection.

The sections of the inventory discussed below are specific to the collection in question. They are also modular; a researcher should be able to learn a little more about the collection in each section. An inventory should make it easier for the researcher to avoid reading a lengthy description of an irrelevant collection.

Biographical Sketch or Agency History. The next section of the inventory expands on the context of the collection. There is a brief overview, in either outline or narrative form, of the principal events in the history of the person or agency during the period encompassed by the collection. This is not a daily record included for its own sake. Rather, it is relevant detail included to illuminate events documented in the collection.

Focus is the key. A biographical sketch in a collection of personal papers might go on at great length about the person's Civil War exploits. In beautiful prose, it could wax eloquent about battle after battle. Is this the proper focus for a collection that does not begin until 1880? It would be better for the biographical sketch to focus on the time period covered by the collection of papers.

Scope and Content Note. The scope and content note discusses in narrative form the extent and depth of the collection—its strengths, weaknesses, and gaps. This and the series description are a dialog between the archivist and the researcher. At a minimum, the scope and content note mentions

- types of materials
- dates (both "outside dates" that indicate the beginning and end of the collection, and "bulk dates" that let the researcher know where most of the material is concentrated)
- important divisions (usually series)
- significant correspondents and subjects

The best scope and content notes bring out what is hidden—what researchers would otherwise miss because they did not process the collection. In order to identify these hidden treasures, the archivist must understand researchers and what they need.

Series Description. The series description builds upon the scope and content note. It lists each series in order and reviews the elements within each; each series description is an abbreviated scope and content note. After the series title, it includes five elements:

- inclusive dates
- quantity
- main types of material
- arrangement
- major subjects

The series description draws heavily upon the notes that the archivist takes while arranging the collection.

Container Listing. At this point in an inventory, the container list prepared as an in-house reference aid usually reappears. If not done previously, the list should be carefully edited for style and format. The container listing serves as a detailed table of contents providing specific information on the filing order and the contents of the collection, usually at the subseries or file unit level. The container list should be consistent and enumerate equivalent filing units.

Index or Item Listing. All published inventories, and larger unpublished ones, should include an index. As with card catalog entries, it is common for indexes to point the researcher to a particular series. If financing permits, the index may identify the relevant file folder. An item listing is rare, usually only for small and important manuscript collections. Literary collections, for example, may be listed at the item level because of the monetary value of individual documents.

"In 1980, Texas Pacific Land Trust Certificate Number 390 surfaced in Wells Fargo's five-year-old archives in San Francisco. The most famous missing trust certificate in U.S. history was spotted by an alert archivist in a box of documents recovered from a Manhattan subbasement.

"Worth only a few hundred dollars when lost at the turn of the century, the certificate was worth $5 million when found. Wells Fargo's archivists also helped document transactions relating to it. Three medical schools and an elderly woman were the successful claimants to the money, and the company got good publicity for its frontier slogan, 'Wells Fargo never forgets!' "—*Wall Street Journal,* January 16, 1989.

Having outlined the order in which sections of an inventory appear, I must point out that it is very difficult to write the sections in that order. In fact, I usually write the sections of an inventory almost in reverse order. I always find it easier to start with the detail (the container listing) and to summarize and shorten the information for other sections. I write series descriptions and then condense them for the scope and content note. The biographical sketch or agency history also embodies what is fresh in my mind from the container listing. The scope and content note is further condensed for the introduction. I find it easier to edit and condense rather than to wait for a clear and concise introduction to pop into my head.

Figure 6.3 provides examples of sections of an inventory. These sections are considerably shorter than they would be in a typical inventory.

Guides

The third type of external finding aid is the guide. The reference section of almost any university library probably contains guides to several archival collections. Guides tend to fall into two categories: repository guides and subject guides.

Repository Guides. A repository guide briefly describes and indicates the relationships among holdings, with the record group

---

Figure 6.3   Inventory to a Collection at NFU
Peconic Bay Yachting Association Records, 1899–1960, 30 Cubic Feet

---

PREFACE

The North Fork University Department of Archives and Special Collections exists to identify, preserve, and make available records and papers of enduring value. Its mission is twofold:

- *University Archives.* To collect and maintain records of enduring value created or received by the university and its employees.
- *Special Collections.* To collect and maintain nonuniversity records and papers that support the academic mission of the university. Areas of collecting interest are specified in a separate Collection Development Policy.

The department serves members of the NFU community and outside researchers. The department provides access to its collections under a separate policy that is available from the Director of the Department of Archives and Special Collections. It is recommended that researchers make an appointment before visiting the department.

INTRODUCTION

The Records of the Peconic Bay Yachting Association were received in the NFU Department of Archives and Special Collections in October 1995. The collection totals 30 cubic feet.

The collection documents the activities of a voluntary organization that was very prominent on the East End of Long Island. The organization's membership changed over time, reflecting the larger changes taking place in society. The collection, therefore, offers research possibilities outside the world of yachting.

The records are open for research without restrictions, under conditions of the Department's Access Policy. The suggested citation to the collection is: "Peconic Bay Yachting Association Records, North Fork University Department of Archives and Special Collections."

ORGANIZATIONAL HISTORY

The Peconic Bay Yachting Association was incorporated in 1899. Its original membership was wealthy individuals who spent their summer on the East End of Long Island. During the Depression years, the nature of the yachting association changed as fewer people could afford to maintain sailboats. After World War II, the Yachting Association became an organization of middle-class individuals who shared a love of sailing. Its focus became families and the recreational use of the waters around Long Island. The organization disbanded in 1960, when many of its members moved west on Long Island to take jobs in the expanding defense industry.

SCOPE AND CONTENT NOTE

The collection is composed of six series: organizational documents, minutes, membership information, correspondence, racing programs, and photographs.

Figure 6.3   (cont.)

The collection is particularly strong in the membership area. Most of the correspondence is with individual members and reflects the full range of their interests. The Yachting Association prided itself in its involvement with the wider community; this involvement is reflected in the correspondence.

The photographs are another unique source. Photographs of the East End of Long Island, especially during the 1940s and 1950s, are difficult to locate. The photographs in this collection would be useful in any number of historical projects.

SERIES DESCRIPTION

Organizational Documents

This series contains the Certificate of Incorporation as well as a list of charter members and notices of meetings that were published in the newspaper.

Minutes

There is a complete set of minutes of meetings of the association. The minutes for the early part of the century are especially rich in social commentary and include detail on the policy debates that took place at the meetings.

Membership Information

There are complete rosters of members as well as application forms completed by all members. Of particular interest are the essays that prospective members had to write as part of the application process. Applicants were asked to tell why the waters of Long Island were important to them. The essays, therefore, offer a grassroots look at the development of environmental consciousness.

Correspondence

The correspondence series is one of the strengths of the collection. As the largest series, it provides a detailed glimpse into the life of the members of the association. The correspondence documents the changing nature of communication as the membership shifted from wealthy to middle-class individuals. Because of the involvement of the association and its membership in many community activities, this series is an important source for anyone researching the history of the North Fork.

Racing Programs

The racing programs document the ebb and flow of interest in sailing. During the early years of the association, the Vanderbilts and the Morgans were regular contestants in association races. Their yachts required large crews in order to race. By the end of the association's life, races were composed of "yachts" with crews of one or two.

Figure 6.3 (cont.)

Photographs

The members of the association kept very good photographic documentation. There is one subseries of member photos and a second subseries of event photos. The event photos, in particular, are a rich historical resource and offer beautiful views of Long Island and its environs.

CONTAINER LISTING

[Note: This example does not include the full 30 cubic feet.]

Box	Folder	Contents
1	1	Certificate of incorporation, 1899
1	2	Minutes, 1899–1925
1	3	Minutes, 1926–1960
10	1	Membership rosters, 1899–1960
18	1	Correspondence, 1899–1910
18	2	Correspondence, 1911–1920
25	1	Racing programs, 1945–60
29	1	Photographs of members, 1950–1960
29	2	Photographs of events, 1954–60

or collection as the unit of entry. The guide used to be the epitome of archival description. A repository would spend years developing its guide. After lengthy editorial, typesetting, and printing steps the guide would be issued—already out of date. Modern word processing has dramatically cut the time and effort involved in producing a guide.

Entries in a repository guide should be similar in style and content, with an equivalent amount of text for each entry. The researcher rightfully expects all collections to be treated equally.

Entries are usually listed in alphabetical order and frequently are numbered. Indexing is keyed to the entry number of the collection or record group. This simplifies the indexing and shortens the final product.

Subject Guides. Subject guides describe the holdings of one or more repositories relating to particular subjects, time periods, or geographical areas. They offer researchers a different perspective on the holdings of the repository.

Many archives found that, beginning in the 1960s, they attracted new types of researchers or familiar researchers asking new questions. Interest in minority studies, women's studies, and gay and lesbian studies has led archivists to review their collections and describe them in new ways. Special subject guides often are the result.

Government archives find that genealogists are now their largest category of researchers. A subject guide can make accessible collections likely to contain genealogical information. Chapter 9 discusses in greater depth how to identify and meet the needs of archival researchers.

Networked Information Systems

The spread of local and wide area networks has given archivists new opportunities to reach researchers. The Research Libraries Information Network (RLIN) offers archivists the opportunity to distribute collection-level information via a library bibliographic system. The Internet makes it possible for researchers to review finding aids as well as digitized historical documents. Effective use of these and other networked information systems requires a clear statement of goals and a plan to meet these goals.

ARCHIVAL INFORMATION EXCHANGE, THE USMARC FORMAT, AND THE INTERNET

Archives exist within a larger context of information resources (for example, libraries, museums, and historic sites). Researchers seeking answers to questions often need to consult multiple sources within this information environment. In the last two decades, archivists have come to realize how important it is that archival records be part of larger information systems.

THE USMARC FORMAT

Beginning in the 1960s, archivists attempted to develop their own information system for sharing collection information. The U.S. National Archives created one such system, called Spindex. Despite its promise, Spindex never found widespread use.

During this same time, the library community took great strides in information exchange. In 1968 the Library of Congress began developing a family of MARC formats (Machine Readable Cataloging). Drawing upon a century of cataloging experience, each MARC format defined specific fields for use with particular media formats.

The MARC format—now called USMARC—had an important difference from archival automation efforts. MARC was a *format* for the exchange of information rather than being an information *system*. The MARC format simply provides a standard structure for arranging pieces of information—it does not require particular hardware or software.

By the mid-1980s, archivists saw the wisdom of including their records in the large library bibliographic systems built upon the MARC format. To do otherwise would relegate archival sources to an information backwater.

Through the leadership of the Society of American Archivists and the Research Libraries Group, archivists began to enter collection information in MARC format into the Research Libraries Information Network (RLIN). What began as an experiment has become a common part of archival practice.

In order to use the MARC format, archivists have had to become familiar with various elements of library cataloging: standardized rules, subject classifications, and authority files. The most important of these are the *Anglo-American Cataloging Rules, 2d edition* (commonly called AACR2) and the *Library of*

Figure 6.4 Selected USMARC Fields for Archival Description

Field Name	Field Number
Personal name	100
Corporate name	110
Title statement	245a,b
Inclusive dates	245f
Bulk dates	245g
Physical description (volume)	300
Arrangement/organization	351
Biographical/historical note	545
Scope and content note	520
Restrictions on access	506
Terms governing use	540
Provenance	561
Subject added entry – topical term	650
Subject added entry – geographical	651
Personal name as added entry	700
Corporate name as added entry	710
Personal name as subject	600
Corporate name as subject	610

Congress Subject Headings (referred to as LCSH). An SAA publication, *Archives, Personal Papers and Manuscripts* (called APPM), adapted and extended AACR2 to provide descriptive rules for archives and manuscripts.[3] Generations of archivists had maintained that archival collections were so specialized that descriptive standards could not possibly apply. This generation of archivists has proven their predecessors wrong.

The original MARC format for archives was called MARC AMC, with the last three letters standing for "Archives and Manuscripts Control." This was one of a number of MARC formats for specialized materials; the library community now is moving toward an integrated format rather than a number of separate formats.

Archival repositories can use the USMARC format whether or not they have a computer, since it provides a standard set of information elements to be gathered on each collection. The format makes the most sense, however, if an archives collection plans to exchange information via national databases.

The USMARC format contains numbered "fields" that one uses in describing a collection. These fields are similar to the elements of archival finding aids previously discussed in this chapter. Figure 6.4 lists some of the most important fields for archival description. Learning to use these fields takes time and practice. Archival professional organizations regularly offer workshops in the USMARC format.

THE INTERNET AND THE WORLD WIDE WEB

At the same time that archivists are becoming part of the standardized information environment known as the library bibliographic utility, they also are becoming part of the still chaotic information environment known as the Internet.

The Internet had its roots in the U.S. Department of Defense. The military wanted to develop a computer network that was sufficiently distributed to survive an attack, either foreign or domestic. The original network was called ARPANET, after the Advanced Research Projects Agency, the research and development arm of the Department of Defense. The first two ARPANET sites were linked in late 1969.[4]

The World Wide Web was created at CERN, the European particle Physics laboratory in Switzerland. As explained by Eric Gagnon:

Figure 6.5 Archival Sites on the World Wide Web		
Site Name	**Site Address**	**Contents**
U.S. National Archives and Records Administration	http://www.nara.gov	Information for archivists, online exhibits
New York State Archives and Records Administration	http://www.sara.nysed.gov	Information about holdings; searchable online catalog and databases
Australian Archives	http://www.aa.gov.au	Information about national, state, and territory archives; exhibits
British Columbia Archives and Records Service	http://www.bcars.gs.gov.bc.ca	Collection summaries, including audiovisual records
University of Notre Dame	http://archives1.archives.nd.edu	University archives; special collections; calendars of documents; indexes to student publications' on-line, searchable inventories
Duke University Special Collections	http://odyssey.lib.duke.edu	Exhibits; searchable finding aids
Immigration History Research Center, University of Minnesota	http://www.umn.edu/ihrc	Collection information; publications; colloquia and lectures
University of Arizona	http://dizzy.library.arizona.edu	Images of the U.S.S. Arizona and other exhibits; clearinghouse of image databases

Originally designed as a standardized method to help physicists organize and access their research data for international distribution online, the World Wide Web standards are essentially a text coding, or "markup" method, where selected elements in a text file, such as article headlines, subheads, images, and important words highlighted in the body of a text file can, by the insertion of special, bracketed codes (called HTML, or Hyper Text Markup Language codes), be turned into hotlinks that are easily and instantly accessible by anyone with a Web browser.[5]

Children and other computer experts have discovered the World Wide Web, using it to "surf the net" on a regular basis. Archives are rushing to create Web pages and link them to other Internet sites. We wouldn't want to be left out of the surf!

Archivists are beginning to use the World Wide Web as part of their descriptive programs. They are providing information about their general holdings as well as their specific collections. The problem of out-of-date guides may be a thing of the past when finding aids can be revised and made available to millions at the blink of an eye.

An approach that holds great promise is the application of publishing standards to electronic finding aids. Beginning in 1993, the library at the University of California at Berkeley has investigated the feasibility of developing "encoding standards" for electronic versions of finding aids. The goal was to find a way to go beyond just creating a USMARC record for each collection by offering more extensive electronic access points for researchers.

After much investigation, the Berkeley team decided to use SGML (Standard Generalized Markup Language), an international publication standard, to encode archival findings aids. SGML is a set of rules defining and expressing the logical structure of documents. This makes it possible for software products to control the searching, retrieval, and display of documents—independent of the hardware platform. The rules are applied in the form of codes (or tags) that can be embedded in an electronic document to identify and establish relationships among component parts.

During the summer of 1995, a team of archivists assembled at the Bentley Historical Library of the University of Michigan to review current work and help refine the encoding standard. The team's work was shared with the archival profession in early 1996.

Called the "Encoded Archival Description (EAD) document structure," it now will be subjected to widespread professional review and critique before being finalized as an additional descriptive tool for archivists.[6]

The Web archivist, however, is going beyond just making finding aids available. Many archivists are scanning parts of their collections, converting them to digital form. These digital representations of archival documents—including photographs, film, and sound—are available for viewing with a Web browser like Netscape Navigator or Microsoft Internet Explorer. Figure 6.5 is an unscientific sampling of archival sites on the World Wide Web. Because of the explosive growth of the Web, the list is neither inclusive nor representative. It does, however, hint at the range of information currently available.[7]

FIVE CHARACTERISTICS OF A GOOD FINDING AID

Whatever form they take, good finding aids tend to have certain things in common. A good finding aid is

1. *Intended for the researcher,* not for the edification of the archivist (who often is a frustrated researcher). The focus should be on *use* by others, rather than on showcasing the literary abilities of the archivist. First and foremost, a finding aid must help the researcher to *find* materials.
2. *Objective about the collection.* Finding aids should have a professional tone. Whether one is describing a collection from the NAACP or the Ku Klux Klan, an archivist's personal sentiments should not cloud the description.
3. *Aware of the needs of a wide variety of researchers.* An archivist who knows the interests of current and potential researchers can prepare finding aids useful to many people. A good finding aid anticipates how various researchers will approach the collection.
4. *Clear, concise, and consistent.* It avoids jargon and terms that make the finding aid inaccessible to researchers. There is a uniform level of description for each entry, thereby establishing consistency.
5. *Efficient.* It presents the maximum usable information in a minimum of space. It is easy for the researcher to scan:

it uses headings, indentations, skipped lines, and an appropriate mix of fonts, to move the researcher through the finding aid. The researcher should be able to grasp the essence of the collection at a glance, and know where else to turn for more information.

FORGING A DESCRIPTIVE SYSTEM: FINAL CONSIDERATIONS

As with any system, a descriptive system takes planning. The archivist must define needs, analyze resources, and determine priorities in order to develop a realistic plan. Staff size and budget will affect the description program one can design.

Description follows (and proceeds along) the five levels of arrangement identified by Holmes and discussed in Chapter 5. A descriptive system should provide basic bibliographic control. It is better to describe all collections *to the same level* than to focus all effort on one collection. The latter approach will result in a skewed descriptive program. One approach is first to describe everything at the collection/record group level. After this, one can establish priorities for further description. The staff can then proceed through the series level and the file unit level, if resources permit.

Efficient archivists take a "building block" approach to their descriptive system. There is no wasted effort; work on one finding aid is carried over to another one. For example, in-house reference aids are the basis for published finding aids. Also, each section of an inventory builds upon the previous section. This can only happen if the system is planned from the very beginning rather than growing up like Topsy.[8]

A good descriptive program is also flexible. It allows the archivist to expand and emphasize different information as required. But the inventory remains the *key*; everything else builds upon it.

A final note concerning computers: As countless organizations have learned, computers are not magic boxes that solve all problems. I still remember the telephone call I received from a newly appointed archivist. He wanted to know which computer hardware and software to buy, as though this would solve everything. I talked at length about a descriptive program and the role of computers in it. We discussed staff and other resources that would be available for description. Only in this context could I begin to offer advice about automation. As a researcher, I would prefer a well-thought-out manual system to a poorly designed automated one. The proof of the finding aid is in the finding.

NOTES

1. This distinction comes from David B. Gracy II, *Archives and Manuscripts: Arrangement and Description* (Chicago: Society of American Archivists, 1977).

2. The best source on inventories remains Gracy, *Archives and Manuscripts.* See also Fredric M. Miller, *Arranging and Describing Archives and Manuscripts* (Chicago: Society of American Archivists, 1990).

3. See Steven L. Hensen, *Archives, Personal Papers, and Manuscripts: A Cataloging Manual for Archival Repositories, Historical Societies, and Manuscript Libraries,* 2d ed. (Chicago: Society of American Archivists, 1989); *Anglo-American Cataloging Rules,* 2d ed. (Chicago: American Library Association, 1988); Library of Congress, Subject Cataloging Division, *Library of Congress Subject Headings,* 10th ed. (Washington, D.C.: Library of Congress, 1986).

4. Peter H. Salus, *Casting the Net: From ARPANET to Internet and Beyond* (New York: Addison-Wesley, 1995).

5. Eric Gagnon, ed., *What's on the Web* (Fairfax, Va.: Internet Media Corp., 1995), 6. Although many archival finding aids still exist in text form on Gopher servers, they can be accessed with Web browsers.

6. "Encoding Standards for Electronic Aids: A Report by the Bentley Team for Encoded Archival Description Development," *Archival Outlook, Newsletter of SAA,* January 1996: 10–13.

7. For general information about the contents of the World Wide Web, see Gagnon, *What's on the Web;* Paul J. Perry, *World Wide Web Secrets* (Chicago: IDG Books, 1995); and Harley Hahn and Rick Stout, *The Internet Yellow Pages,* 2d ed. (New York: Osborne McGraw-Hill, 1995).

8. See Lydia Lucas, "Efficient Finding Aids: Developing a System for Control of Archives and Manuscripts," *American Archivist* 41 (winter 1981): 21–26.

7 PRESERVATION

Preservation encompasses a wide variety of interrelated activities designed to prolong the usable life of archives and manuscripts. It is a broad term that covers protection, stabilization, and treatment of documents.[1] Preservation is one of the three core functions of the archivist, the other two being identification and use.

Most preservation programs in small archives take a phased approach that emphasizes broad stabilizing actions to protect a repository's entire holdings, rather than concentrating resources solely on item-level treatment. Such an approach includes

- understanding the nature of the preservation problem
- conducting preservation surveys to establish priorities
- controlling the storage environment
- planning for disasters
- performing holdings maintenance
- treating selected materials[2]

Except for disaster planning, which is covered in chapter 8, each of these activities is discussed below.

THE PRESERVATION PROBLEM

Before trying to address preservation problems, it is necessary to understand the nature of the materials in question and the causes of deterioration. This section deals with paper and photographic media. Chapter 10 discusses the specific challenges posed by electronic records.

PAPER

Because most archival collections, by volume, are on paper, the fragile nature of this medium is a major problem for archivists as well as librarians. Modern papers exacerbate this problem. The title of a popular article summarized the all-too-common sequence of events: pulp to paper, paper to dust.[3]

Modern paper, it turns out, contains the seeds of its own destruction; the very production of paper introduces elements, particularly sources of acid, which lead to deterioration. While raised consciousness bodes well for future paper production, archivists are left with almost 100 years of paper that is rapidly deteriorating.[4]

First of all, just what is paper? It is a thin, flat sheet composed of fibers that have been reduced to pulp, suspended in water, and then matted. Paper is usually made of cellulose fibers, the light-weight material that forms the cell walls of plants. Cellulose fibers dissolve—breaking into shorter and shorter strands—when they come into contact with acid. Hence the problem with modern papers.

Paper was introduced into Europe from China in the twelfth century. It still is made the same basic way:

- Plant matter is beaten with water to produce a pulp.
- The pulp is shaped in a mold with a wire screen at the bottom. It is this wire screen that produces a watermark.
- Water is drained off the mold and squeezed out of the paper.
- The paper is sized (coated) to prevent the absorption of water. Unsized paper acts like blotting paper or a paper towel—ink is absorbed into and spread throughout the fibers.[5]

If paper is still produced the same basic way, why are we having problems now? Until the nineteenth century, paper was made from cotton and flax plants, obtained from rags. These plants had long, strong fibers. The paper also was sized by hand—dipping it sheet by sheet in a gelatin or animal glue.

After 1840, trees replaced rags as the principal raw material for paper. Wood pulp was cheaper than rags and more widely available. Wood's cellulose fibers, however, are relatively short and contain impurities. In particular, lignin, which holds the cellulose fibers together, comprises 25 percent of most wood. When exposed to air, lignin's chemical structure changes: it turns brown and gives off acid.

To complicate matters further, sizing changed after 1836. Mass producers of paper began to add rosin from pine trees while the

"As if keeping track of 3 billion pieces of paper weren't enough trouble, the National Archives has discovered that most of its historic government documents dating from World War II and the cold-war period are rapidly disintegrating. Cheap, high-acid paper—a wartime austerity measure—is the major culprit. The acid eats the cellulose fibers of the paper, causing it to fall apart. Hundreds of millions of one-of-a-kind documents may be unreadable in 10 years."—*U.S. News & World Report,* September 22, 1986.

The archives of Radio Free Europe are to move to Budapest's Central European University. "The archives' extensive collection of *samizdat* writings—the typed or hand-copied manuscripts of banned authors and dissidents that were circulated underground—needs the immediate attention of preservationists. Many of the documents are brittle or fading. 'A lot of the stuff only had 10 or 15 years left before it would have been un-photographable. People were writing with poor ink on poor-quality, high-acid paper, which was then circulated hand-to-hand, so the materials are very fragile. Part of our goal in this project is to save this world treasure and make it available to the citizens who produced it.' "—*Chronicle of Higher Education,* November 2, 1994.

paper was being beaten. It no longer was necessary to dip one sheet at a time. But in order to make the rosin adhere to the pulp, manufacturers added alum (potassium aluminum sulphate). When alum comes into contact with moisture, it forms sulfuric acid, which attacks the cellulose fiber in pulp paper. Most paper even today has alum-rosin sizing. Such paper will only last 10-50 years, as opposed to the hundreds of years for handmade paper.

Preservation problems are compounded by the increasing volume of paper. Every four months, the federal government produces a stack of records equal to all those produced in the 124 years between George Washington and Woodrow Wilson. Paper still makes up most of this volume.[6] The impermanence of the physical medium of paper, combined with the huge volume of records stored on it, has led some archivists to question whether or not preservation really is still possible.[7]

PHOTOGRAPHIC MEDIA

Photographic images are formed by the action of light on chemical compounds. Photographs are composed of a number of layers, each of which responds differently to environmental conditions. Figure 7.1 is a generic model of layers in photographic images.

A major problem with photographic preservation is that the failure of any of these layers can lead to the loss of the image. Accordingly, the long-term preservation of photographic materials involves a number of interrelated factors:

- the inherent stability of the component materials
- the quality of original processing, including proper or improper fixing and washing
- exposure to an uncontrolled environment, including high temperature and relative humidity, light, and pollutants
- physical and chemical suitability of enclosure materials
- handling and use procedures

Figure 7.1 Layers in Photographic Images[8]

Layer	Comments
Final image material	The most common image material, especially in archival photographs, is finely divided metallic silver. Other final image materials have included platinum, pigments, and dyes.
Binder	The most common binder has been gelatin, though albumen and collodion were common nineteenth-century binders.
Support	Supports have included paper, metal, glass, and plastic film (cellulose nitrate, cellulose acetate esters, and polyester).
Surface treatments, adhesives, and other layers	There can be anticurl and antiabrasion layers; coatings such as wax or varnish; adhesives; and applied colors.

Balancing all these factors can be a very complex task.[9]

Figure 7.2 summarizes the slow and subtle forms of deterioration to which paper, photographs, and all media are subject.

PRESERVATION SURVEYS

Planning even a modest preservation program begins with information about the situation as it now exists. Without this information, how can an archivist possibly determine the best use of its limited preservation resources? For this planning to be effective, surveys or other data collection must happen at both the repository and collection levels.

REPOSITORY LEVEL

Information gathered at the repository level is used to plan an integrated preservation program. It leads to policies and procedures that influence preservation of all the collections. This information also focuses attention on environmental shortcomings in storage and other areas.

The archivist should gather information about

Figure 7.2 Forms of Deterioration[10]

Form of Deterioration	Description	How Controlled
Inherent chemical	The material itself undergoes the reactions of decay. It does not need external pollutants or light. Examples are brittleness, discoloration, and fading.	Control rate of deterioration by controlling temperature and relative humidity in the storage environment.
Pollutant-induced	Since pollutants are external, they are not always present. Pollutants can affect both organic and inorganic materials.	Use air purification systems and protective enclosures.
Light-induced	Light is a form of energy that breaks chemical bonds, thus causing decay. Damage depends on a number of factors: nature of the object, relative humidity, kind of light, intensity, and duration.	Keep illumination intensities down and store objects in dark places.
Biological	Primarily affect organic materials. Divided into three categories: bacterial, fungal, and insect-related. Involve a complex set of factors: temperature, relative humidity, light, ventilation, and housekeeping practices.	Tailor control measures to the particular circumstances of each collection.
Physical	Mechanical forms of deterioration such as warping, cracking, or separation of layers. Changes in moisture content cause different materials to swell or shrink at different rates.	Keep relative humidity stable.

- fire detection, alert, and suppression systems (for example, sprinklers, halon gas)
- water detection and alert systems
- environmental conditions in storage, processing, and reference areas
- recurring problems such as leaks or floods
- problems with insects or other infestations
- housing and storage equipment for records
- exhibition practices
- level of staff familiarity with preservation practices[11]

Once the information is gathered, it may be necessary to secure outside assistance with such technical areas as environmental monitoring and fire protection. Any expert advice, however, should be used in the context of the overall archival program. As noted throughout this book, balancing competing demands for resources is one of the toughest tasks facing an archivist.

COLLECTION LEVEL

Preservation planning cannot remain solely at the repository level. The archivist must look at individual collections, assess their preservation needs, and plan for the meeting of those needs within the overall context of the institution's budget.

An institution new to preservation planning will have a backlog of collections that have never been addressed from this perspective. Even conducting the collection-level survey may be a daunting task in such a situation.

The best way to make the task less daunting is by using a form designed for the purpose. The form systematizes the collection of *necessary* information—and nothing more. There is always a temptation to collect every conceivable bit of information archives may ever need. This presupposes that the archivist can define at this stage of program development all the preservation program possibilities for the future. Even if this were possible, such detail still might not be desirable because of the time and expense it adds to the collection-level survey.

The advice, then, is: gather only information necessary for program planning at the present time. In addition, using closed-ended questions (where the responses are predefined and one need only check or circle the answer) is faster than using open-ended questions (where response choices are not provided). The goal is to gather the information as quickly as possible and move on to planning and program development.

Figure 7.3 presents some of the fields typically found on a collection-level survey form.

Figure 7.3 Fields on a Collection Level Survey Form[12]	
Field	**Common Responses**
Primary housing	File drawer, records center carton, archives box
Secondary housing	File folders, envelopes, ring binders
Types of records	Loose papers, bound volumes, index cards, photographs, sound recordings, videotapes, electronic media
Condition of records	Folded, rolled, brittle, torn, molded, water damaged, taped, dirty
Special concerns	Impermanent media, faint text or images, colored media, use of fasteners, artifact value (seals, etc.)
Recommendations	Rehousing, duplication, treatment
Preservation priority	High, medium, low, none

If preservation is to become an integral part of an archival program, each collection should have a preservation assessment at the time of accessioning. This can be done by adding one or more fields to the accession form to gather some of the same information obtained in the collection-level survey described above. Preservation planning, as with all types of planning, is best done as an ongoing activity rather than according to the "locust model"—planning only once every seven years.

THE STORAGE ENVIRONMENT

In the film *The Graduate,* the character played by Dustin Hoffman is pulled aside by a relative and told the one word that is the key to the future: "plastics." If the relative had been an archivist, however, he would have whispered: "environment." The proper environment will prolong the life of the collections and reduce the repair and restoration activities the archives must undertake. In fact, without a proper environment, restoration activities are a

"The sealed glass cases protecting the Declaration of Independence, the Constitution and the Bill of Rights are undergoing unexpected deterioration that could affect the condition of the nation's three most prized documents, experts told the National Archives today....

"More than 1.2 million people a year visit the Archives to see the documents, which are written on several parchment pages. Each of those pages, which are raised for viewing each day from a 55-ton bombproof vault, has been enclosed since 1952 in a bronze-framed glass case filled with helium (to prevent oxidation) and water vapor (to keep the parchment from drying out). At the time they were enclosed, scientists estimated that the documents would be protected by the cases for at least 100 years."—*New York Times,* April 1, 1995.

waste of money; why place a restored item back in an environment where it will deteriorate again?

First it is necessary to know precisely what the environment is like. I recall a visit to a new colleague in the profession who gave me a tour of the archives he recently inherited. Although it was July, his facility was comfortably air-conditioned. I asked him if it was like this all the time. He responded that this was the temperature when he arrived in the morning, so he assumed the answer was "yes." At my suggestion he purchased a hygrothermograph, a device used to measure and record both relative humidity and temperature. The archivist was surprised to learn that the air-conditioning was turned off every evening at six o'clock and not reactivated until seven o'clock the next morning. On weekends, the air-conditioning was off from Friday night until Monday morning. In the interim, the hygrothermograph documented that the records were nice and toasty. Once the nature of the problem was understood (rather than assumed) it became possible to design improvements.[13]

An archivist should look at the following specific aspects of the storage environment:

- temperature
- relative humidity
- air quality
- light
- biological agents
- holdings maintenance practices

TEMPERATURE

Temperature is important for preservation because higher temperatures speed up chemical reactions. It has been estimated that the useful life of paper is cut approximately in half with every ten degree Fahrenheit increase in temperature above 68 degrees. Conversely, for every ten degree decrease, the expected life of paper is effectively doubled.[14]

Archival collections are complex, containing a variety of media. The proper temperature and humidity, therefore, will be a compromise. Each medium will have its own ideal conditions—but for an archives program to function, there must be a happy medium acceptable to the records as well as to the archives staff.

Many preservation administrators, therefore, recommend a temperature of 68 degrees Fahrenheit, plus or minus two degrees.[15] While a colder environment might be better for preservation, it can be difficult to maintain relative humidity within an acceptable range. Furthermore, before items can be used, they must be gradually reconditioned to room temperature to avoid condensation.

The range in which the temperature is permitted to vary is a very important consideration. Archivists try to avoid rapid cycling—dramatic shifts in temperature and humidity on a daily or weekly basis. It would be better to have a slightly higher constant temperature than one that varies greatly over a short period of time.

RELATIVE HUMIDITY

We talk about humidity as being relative—it relates to temperature. The warmer the air, the more water vapor it is capable of holding. The amount of moisture in the air contributes to chemical activity; high humidity accelerates some chemical reactions, including the formation of acids.

Humidity also affects organic materials. High humidity encourages the growth of mold and mildew; it also creates a resort environment preferred by some varieties of insects. Low humidity, on the other hand, causes materials to become dry and brittle.

Paper, vellum, and parchment all are hygroscopic; their moisture content changes as the environment around them changes. Rapid cycling of humidity causes these materials to shrink and expand—a workout that will not promote the physical fitness of the collection.

Over the course of a year, the relative humidity in a building may range from nearly 100 percent in summer (if no dehumidification is provided) to as low as 10 percent in winter (if heating is provided without humidification).[16]

As noted with temperature, each archival medium has an ideal humidity range. The target recommended for a collection of mixed media materials is 45 percent relative humidity, plus or minus 2 percent.[17]

Recent work at the Image Permanence Institute of the Rochester Institute of Technology provides archivists and librarians with a framework for evaluating the effect of particular combinations of temperature and relative humidity on the rate of chemical deterioration in collections over time.[18] This new methodology promises to become a powerful management tool, especially for determining cost-benefit ratios. Archivists will be able to calculate how much longer a collection will last at improved temperature and humidity conditions. They then will be able to determine if this extra life is worth the cost of construction and annual operation—or if another option, such as microfilming, makes better economic sense.[19]

AIR QUALITY

Atmospheric pollutants also cause deterioration of archival materials. Some lead to the formation of acids that damage the records. Others break down the cellulose in paper fibers. Still others lead to abrasion, which damages materials over time. The main atmospheric challenges to archival materials are listed in Figure 7.4.[20]

An ideal archival environment includes systems for air circulation and filtration. Some of the elements to look for are

- a dedicated system, rather than one shared with such sources of indoor pollution as kitchens, laboratories, and staff lounges
- sealed windows and gaskets on doors
- positive air pressure within the controlled area, to eliminate the introduction of contaminated air
- even circulation of a constant volume of air in and around stack ranges, including compact shelving
- filters in the air handling system to eliminate external pollutants
- air intakes situated away from loading docks, exhaust fans, or street traffic
- regular monitoring and replacement of filters

Achieving these system requirements will involve consultation with engineers and architects—and with the keepers of the institutional budget. Problems are particularly acute in urban areas, although virtually no part of the country is immune from some of the conditions noted above.[21]

Figure 7.4 Atmospheric Pollutants[20]

Pollutant	Source	Effect
Sulfur dioxide	When sulfur-containing fuel (coal, natural gas, petroleum, or oil) is burned, the sulfur combines with water to form sulfur dioxide.	Sulfur dioxide combines with water in the air to form sulfuric acid, a strong corrosive.
Nitrogen dioxide	By-product of combustion and other chemical reactions.	Combines with water in the air to form nitric acids, also strong corrosives.
Ozone	By-product of the combination of sunlight and nitrogen dioxide, especially from automobile exhaust. Also a by-product of some air-conditioners and photocopy machines.	A strong oxidizing agent that causes severe damage to organic materials.
Acetic acid	Generated by out-gassing of wood, particularly oak, birch, and beech.	Especially damaging to photographs.
Sulfides	Vulcanized rubber.	Especially damaging to photographs.
Other gaseous pollutants	Smoking, cooking, cellulose nitrate film, paint finishes.	Can cause chemical reactions and abrasion.
Solid particles (dirt, dust, carbon, soot, tar)	Deposited on materials through the air.	Cause abrasion. Absorb moisture and other pollutants from the air, which they deposit on the records (not the kind of deposit arrangement archivists like to encourage). May contain traces of metal, such as iron, which can become a focus for deterioration.

LIGHT

When God said, "Let there be light," a footnote might have been added: except in archives. Light speeds up the oxidation of paper and thus its chemical breakdown, resulting in a loss of strength. This oxidation of cellulose is accelerated by sulfur dioxide, nitrogen dioxide, and water. Light becomes the final ingredient in the bouillabaisse of deterioration.

Light also has a bleaching effect, causing some papers to whiten and some inks to fade. Lignin-containing papers can darken very quickly—just leave a newspaper in your car during a summer trip to the beach to try your own accelerated aging test.

Archival records must be protected from ultraviolet (UV) radiation, visible light, and infrared radiation. Ultraviolet radiation is a particularly damaging component because of the way it accelerates photochemical decay.

Some of the ways archives can minimize the damaging effects of light are to

- box or otherwise protect records from direct exposure
- have no windows in stack areas (if windows are present, cover or block them in some way)
- treat windows in work or reference areas with UV-filtering glazes or films
- cover fluorescent lights with UV filters (tubes or sheets)
- keep light levels low by turning off unneeded lights and removing some bulbs
- design exhibit cases and rooms to minimize the amount of light exposure the records receive[22]

BIOLOGICAL AGENTS

Last but not least, archival records require a storage environment free of biological agents. In general, a warm and humid environment is more likely to attract these unwanted visitors. Figure 7.5 lists the major biological agents and the challenges they present.

Many of the above problems can be controlled by stabilizing the temperature and humidity. Good housekeeping practices are an important second step. Among the practices archives should adopt are to

- prohibit smoking, eating, or drinking in or near archival storage, processing, or reference areas
- remove garbage from the building on a daily basis
- keep stack and storage areas free of debris
- prohibit plants in areas where records are stored and used

Figure 7.5 Biological Agents[23]		
Biological Agent	**Preferred Conditions**	**Potential Damage**
Fungi (mold and mildew)	Warm (above 75 degrees), humid (above 65 percent relative humidity), dark, and little air circulation	Feed on cellulose, starch adhesive, sizing, and gelatin. Can weaken, stain and obliterate material.
Insects (especially cockroaches, silverfish, termites, and beetles)	Dark, warm, and damp	Eat away image-bearing materials (like gelatin emulsions); damage structures by boring through them.
Rodents (rats, mice, and squirrels)	Need food or garbage	Nibble away at items; use shredded paper as nesting material; droppings are corrosive and can leave permanent stains.

- damp-mop or vacuum floors at least once per week
- dust shelves, boxes, and the exteriors of bound volumes on a regular basis

Most archives arrange to have cleaning services present during normal working hours. This is important for security reasons. It also is a way for the archivist to be certain that the cleaning staff neither inadvertently damages materials nor uses chemicals harmful to their long-term preservation. The archival heavy artillery of fumigation and extermination should be done by a trained professional aware of the particular preservation concerns in an archives.[24]

HOLDINGS MAINTENANCE PRACTICES

Holdings maintenance practices include unfolding or unrolling documents, removing or replacing harmful fasteners, reproducing unstable documents, placing materials in acid-free folders and boxes, and shelving them in environmentally controlled and secure storage.

In addition, staff and researchers must understand proper handling of various media. Some hints are found in Figure 7.6.

Figure 7.6 Tips on Proper Handling[25]	
Medium or Type of Item	**Proper Handling**
Paper records	Support and protect records being moved. Remove entire folder from box before looking for an individual item. Do not lean on or write on top of records. Do not use pressure-sensitive tape. Avoid paper clips and staples.
Bound volumes	Do not pull volumes from the top. Support volumes from the bottom when removing them from shelves. Be careful when turning pages, especially brittle ones. Use book cradles and supports in reference areas.
Photographic media	Avoid bending or creasing. Use two hands rather than picking up items by one edge. Wear white, lint-free gloves when handling.
Audio and video magnetic tapes	Handle only by the housing supports (reels, cartridges, and cassettes). Never touch tape surfaces. Assure proper threading and mounting on playback equipment. Rewind with even tension.

TREATMENT OF MATERIALS

All archives reach a point where environment and holdings maintenance have done all they can do. Some materials may need conservation treatment, either by the archives staff or a professional conservator.

"Conservation" has replaced an earlier term, "restoration."[26] Conservation treatments attempt to stabilize materials in their original format by chemical and physical means. Among the main objectives are to

- return deteriorated or damaged items to stable and usable condition
- render archival materials capable of being safely duplicated
- reverse previous treatments that have proven unsuitable or have placed a document in jeopardy[27]

Conservators practice the rule of reversibility which can be stated as follows: to the degree possible, no procedure or treatment should be undertaken that cannot later, if necessary, be undone without harm to the document. Materials and procedures used during the course of treatment must be stable and incapable of interacting with the item being treated in ways that alter its physical, chemical, aesthetic, or historical integrity.

Managing a practical archives program involves knowing which treatments can be done in-house and which should be sent to a conservator (either one who works for the same institution as the archivist or an independent professional). Naturally, the exact placement of the dividing line will depend on the size and resources of the archival facility. For a small repository just beginning an archival program, I recommend the division of tasks outlined in Figure 7.7.

Figure 7.7 Recommended Specific Treatment of Archival Materials	
Place of Treatment	**Specific Treatments**
The archives itself	Surface cleaning, humidification and flattening, polyester film encapsulation, repairing simple tears
Outside conservator	Fumigation, deacidification, repairing extensive tears, and other paper strengthening

Reformatting—onto paper or another medium such as microfilm—is also a preservation option. If a large collection needs item-level treatment, it probably would be cost-effective to microfilm the collection instead. This becomes an even more attractive option if the documents lack intrinsic value as defined in Chapter 3. In this case, the original documents can be destroyed after microfilming. The microfilming could be done by the repository's own staff or a service bureau.

TREATMENTS HANDLED BY THE ARCHIVES

The following treatments should be simple and inexpensive enough that any archival program can perform them as needed:

- surface cleaning
- humidification and flattening
- polyester film encapsulation
- repairing simple tears

Remember, however, that even simple conservation treatments will take staff time away from the myriad other archival activities discussed in this book. Conservation treatment quickly can consume all available time and energy. This may currently be an appropriate focus in the life of the archives—or it may not. The only way to determine the appropriate amount of time to spend on conservation is to analyze needs and develop plans in the systematic way discussed above.

The following sections present an overview of each technique. A more complete discussion, including diagrams of the steps for each technique, is found in Mary Lynn Ritzenthaler's book *Preserving Archives and Manuscripts*.

Surface Cleaning

Loose surface dirt, dust, and debris can be gently removed from paper strong enough to withstand moderate handling. Photographic materials and documents composed of more than one medium (a letter attached to a cardboard exhibit mount, for example) are much more complex and should be approached with healthy caution.

The following techniques for cleaning paper are listed in increasing order of potential damage:

- *Gently dust with a soft brush.* The brushing should proceed from the center to the edge.
- *Work eraser particles across nontext and nonimage areas.* Work the eraser particles in a circular motion. As they become dirty, dust them away with a soft brush.
- *Clean with an eraser.* This must be done lightly—not with a scrubbing motion. The abrasive action can damage paper fibers.

Humidification and Flattening

Humidification and flattening techniques are designed to introduce moisture into the paper so that it can be unrolled or flattened without tearing. It is important to understand the nature and structure of the paper in question. Coated papers and moisture-sensitive inks could be damaged by the introduction of moisture. It also takes an experienced eye to know just how much moisture is enough without being too much.

Archivists can use a passive humidification process to introduce moisture gently into the environment; the paper, in turn, will absorb the moisture. This process is done by using a humidification chamber constructed of an airtight, noncorrosive, rustproof enclosure. Some archives use a pair of plastic trash containers; others use an unplugged refrigerator devoid of rusting internal components.

The humidity in the closed chamber increases the moisture content of the paper, which should relax the fibers. The time required to accomplish this will vary according to the type and weight of the paper—anywhere from 30 minutes to several hours.

The humidified papers must be handled carefully to avoid tearing. They also must be dried between clean, dry blotters under moderate weight to complete the flattening. It may be necessary to change the blotter paper one or more times during the drying process.

Polyester Film Encapsulation

Polyester film encapsulation offers a way to support and protect fragile single sheets of paper. It involves sandwiching the paper between two layers of polyester. The sandwich is sealed on all sides, which offers increased security as well.

A simpler option is just placing the item in a polyester sleeve. This is particularly appropriate if the item has not yet been deacidified (see below). Some items, however, would slip out of a sleeve; full encapsulation would thus be preferable, whether or not the items are deacidified.

There are different approaches to sealing the four edges of the polyester film capsule:

- stable, double-coated, pressure-sensitive adhesive
- ultrasonic welding
- electromagnetic radiation sealing
- sewing machine using a thread with nonbleeding dyes

The choice of sealing method depends on such factors as staff time and capital budget levels. While encapsulating machines are expensive, they are cost-effective for institutions that require a large number of encapsulations.

Repairing Simple Tears

It is possible to mend documents using long-fiber Japanese paper and a starch adhesive. This is a tried-and-true approach to paper repairs. Though a time-consuming process, the end result is a strong, safe, long-lasting repair.

There are a number of pressure-sensitive mending tapes advertised as "archival quality," acid-free, non-yellowing, and reversible. Archivists are advised to use these products cautiously, if at all, until independent testing can either confirm or refute manufacturers' claims.[28]

TREATMENTS BEST REFERRED TO AN OUTSIDE CONSERVATOR

Practical archivists know when they are in over their heads. Though some archivists are comfortable with the following conservation treatments, many others are more than happy to refer the following treatments to outside experts:

- fumigation
- deacidification
- repairing extensive tears and other paper strengthening

Fumigation

Fumigation and other chemical aspects of pest management certainly could be done by the archivist. However many archives, especially smaller ones, contract for these services, particularly in light of environmental and employee health and safety concerns.

The long-term effects of fumigants on archival materials still are unknown. Therefore fumigation should be seen as a last resort—only used when there are signs of an active infestation. It is better to improve the environment to make it less hospitable for our crawling friends.

Reading the literature about specific fumigation agents also leads to a "do not try this at home" mindset. Ethylene oxide, a commonly used fumigant, is flammable, toxic, and explosive. Carbon dioxide can be used as a fumigant if its concentration is high enough. Thymol, which was once used to treat mold-infested books and documents, is known to pose serious health hazards and is no longer recommended. Low-level gamma radiation (Cobalt-60) shows promise, although it appears to weaken the structure of cellulose. Freezing is an alternative to fumigation, but it must be done quickly and at a low enough temperature; otherwise some pests will continue to pester after their winter vacations.

Most local exterminators do not understand the particular needs of archival materials: to them, bugs are bugs. It may take a few telephone calls to neighboring archives, museums, or libraries to locate an exterminator for whom not all boxes are just boxes. There is no way around this exercise of archival concern.[29]

Deacidification

As noted previously, acid attacks the cellulose in paper, breaking down the strands and weakening the paper. Deacidification processes are intended to neutralize the paper's acidity and deposit an alkaline buffer to prevent the return to an acidic state—the cellulose equivalent of a long-lasting Tums.

Deacidification in archives is a labor-intensive process still done most often at the individual item level. Candidates for deacidification must be tested for solubility and color change prior to treatment. The two options are

- *Aqueous deacidification.* Water-based treatments can only be done with loose papers—any bound volumes must be disassembled before immersion. Items usually are washed before treatment and then immersed in one or more baths. Documents often emerge with stains and discoloration removed, a bonus for a visit to the deacidification spa.
- *Nonaqueous deacidification.* This option is appropriate for the nonswimmers in the archival collection, usually because water would damage the paper or its inks. Organic solvents are used as a carrier for the chemicals. Using such solvents, however, requires a fume hood, protective clothing, and a breathing apparatus.

Archives and libraries have been trying to reach the promised land of low-cost mass deacidification. This appears to be the only way to treat the huge volume of deteriorating archival holdings effectively. Several processes have been used with books and other bound volumes. Conservators, however, remain skeptical of manufacturers' claims until they can be independently verified. The promised land still is beyond several hills.

A final point about deacidification: it will not *strengthen* the paper. While it will stabilize the paper and sometimes improve its appearance, there is no Lazarus effect restoring life. Following deacidification, weak papers must be strengthened or protected in polyester film.[30]

Repairing Extensive Tears and Other Paper Strengthening

While archives may do simple repairs, extensive repairs or paper strengthening are best left to professional conservators. Even simple repairs may be appropriate for referral if they involve records of high intrinsic value—the original charter of North Fork University, for example.

Experiments are under way to strengthen entire sheets of paper. At the present time, there are no standards in this area and little independent verification of manufacturers' claims. Reformatting onto microfilm is probably the preferred option for small archives with collections of embrittled documents.

CONCLUSION

A phased approach to preservation is the most appropriate approach for the small archives. Once the problems are identified, committing resources to stabilizing the environment will have the greatest preservation return for the dollar. Other aspects of preservation can be integrated into the archival program as funding and staff permit. In this way, a small archives program can achieve the proper balance between preservation and use.

NOTES

1. According to Paul Conway, "At one time, advocates for the protection of cultural artifacts, including books, primary source documents, and museum objects, used the terms 'conservation' and 'preservation' interchangeably. Today preservation is an umbrella term for the many policies and options for action, including conservation treatments. Preservation is the acquisition, organization, and distribution of resources to prevent further deterioration or renew the usability of selected groups of materials." Paul Conway, *Preservation in the Digital World* (Washington, D.C.: Commission on Preservation and Access, 1996), 5.

2. This framework is taken from Lewis J. Bellardo and Lynn Lady Bellardo, *A Glossary for Archivists, Manuscript Curators, and Records Managers* (Chicago: Society of American Archivists, 1992). The best one-volume discussion of preservation for archivists is Mary Lynn Ritzenthaler, *Preserving Archives and Manuscripts* (Chicago: Society of American Archivists, 1993). See also Norvell M. M. Jones and Mary Lynn Ritzenthaler, "Implementing an Archival Preservation Program," in James Gregory Bradsher, ed., *Managing Archives and Archival Institutions* (Chicago: University of Chicago Press, 1989), 185–206.

3. Flora Skelly Johnson, "Pulp to Paper, Paper to Dust" *Newsday,* April 2, 1985.

4. Librarians have a similar problem with many of the "brittle books" on their shelves. For more information, see *Preserving the Intellectual Heritage: A Report of the Bellagio Conference, June 7–10, 1993* (Washington, D.C.: Commission on Preservation and Access, 1993).

5. For a more detailed description, see Mary Lynn Ritzenthaler, *Preserving Archives and Manuscripts,* 19–37. For an overview of

reproduction technologies on paper and other media, see Gregory S. Hunter, "Reprography," *World Encyclopedia of Library and Information Services*, 3d ed. (Chicago: American Library Association, 1993), 711–715.

6. Page Putnam Miller, *Developing a Premier National Institution: A Report from the User Community to the National Archives* (Washington, D.C.: National Coordinating Committee for the Promotion of History, 1989).

7. See James O'Toole, "On the Idea of Permanence," *American Archivist* 52 (winter 1989): 11–25. For recommendations on dealing with these limitations, see *The Preservation of Archival Materials: A Report of the Task Forces on Archival Selection to the Commission on Preservation and Access* (Washington, D.C.: Commission on Preservation and Access, 1993).

8. James M. Reilly, *Care and Identification of Nineteenth-Century Photographic Prints* (Rochester, N.Y.: Eastman Kodak Company, 1986).

9. For more information, see Barbara Applebaum, *Guide to Environmental Protection of Collections* (Madison, Conn.: Sound View Press, 1991), 198–200.

10. Adapted from James M. Reilly, Douglas W. Nishimura, and Edward Zinn, *New Tools for Preservation: Assessing Long-Term Environmental Effects on Library and Archives Collections* (Washington, D.C.: Commission on Preservation and Access, 1995), 2, 19–20.

11. Ritzenthaler, *Preserving Archives and Manuscripts*, 8–11.

12. For another approach to a survey form, see Bruce W. Dearstyne, *The Archival Enterprise: Modern Archival Principles, Practices, and Management Techniques* (Chicago: American Library Association, 1993), 157–158.

13. For photographs and descriptions of hygrothermographs and other measuring devices, see Gregor Trinkaus-Randall, *Protecting Your Collections: A Manual of Archival Security* (Chicago: Society of American Archivists, 1995), 29–33.

14. Ritzenthaler, *Preserving Archives and Manuscripts*, 46.

15. "Other things being equal, most objects would last longer at low temperatures. Higher temperatures of 60 or 70 degrees Fahrenheit are usually needed for human comfort, but not for the benefit of the collection. In almost all collections, the lower the temperature the better, with 65 to 68 degrees Fahrenheit a good compromise with human needs and other practical concerns. Due to their particular sensitivity to temperature, every attempt should be made to segregate any important photographic and film collections, particularly color, and keep them at temperatures below 55 degrees Fahrenheit." William P. Lull, with the assistance

of Paul N. Banks, *Conservation Environment Guidelines for Libraries and Archives* (Albany, N.Y.: New York State Library, 1990), 4.

16. Lull, *Conservation Environment Guidelines,* 4.

17. Ritzenthaler, *Preserving Archives and Manuscripts,* 53.

18. Reilly, Nishimura, and Zinn, *New Tools for Preservation.* This work built upon an earlier effort; see Donald K. Sebera, *Isoperms: An Environmental Management Tool* (Washington, D.C.: Commission on Preservation and Access, 1994).

19. For more information on temperature and humidity, see Appelbaum, *Guide to Environmental Protection of Collections,* 25–64. For excellent advice on the design and implementation of improved preservation environments, see Lull, *Conservation Environment Guidelines,* 19–73.

20. Adapted from Ritzenthaler, *Preserving Archives and Manuscripts,* 47.

21. For more information, see Appelbaum, *Guide to Environmental Protection of Collections,* 97–116.

22. Appelbaum, *Guide to Environmental Protection of Collections,* 65–96.

23. Adapted from Ritzenthaler, *Preserving Archives and Manuscripts,* 48–49.

24. For more information, see Appelbaum, *Guide to Environmental Protection of Collections,* 117–144.

25. Adapted from Ritzenthaler, *Preserving Archives and Manuscripts,* 67–75. See also Appelbaum, *Guide to Environmental Protection of Collections,* 145–158.

26. As one might expect, terminology has changed over time. "Conservation" used to be the broadest term even a few years ago, the equivalent of the way we now use "preservation." Restoration was used to indicate one specific aspect of the conservation program.

27. Ritzenthaler, *Preserving Archives and Manuscripts,* 2.

28. Ritzenthaler, *Preserving Archives and Manuscripts,* 149.

29. Ritzenthaler, *Preserving Archives and Manuscripts,* 140–143; and Appelbaum, *Guide to Environmental Protection of Collections,* 119–141.

30. Ritzenthaler, *Preserving Archives and Manuscripts,* 144–147.

8 SECURITY AND DISASTER PLANNING

Security and disaster planning are not the stuff of pleasant archival dreams. Naturally, archivists prefer to think about the good times—a collection finally processed or a happy researcher leaving the reference room. Part of being responsible for an archival collection, however, is also trying to minimize or plan for the bad times through a security and disaster program.

The Society of American Archivists (SAA) defines security broadly enough to include disaster planning. According to SAA, security is "an archival and records management function concerned with the protection of documents from unauthorized access and/or damage or loss from fire, water, theft, mutilation, or unauthorized alteration or destruction."[1]

Although it is difficult to separate the two subjects, I will try to do so as follows:

- *Security* deals with potential human problems.
- *Disaster planning* deals with problems caused by natural elements.

Integrating both elements into a unified program for the protection of records is part of the archivist's mission.

SECURITY

Security presents archivists with a dilemma: how do we balance our desire to provide access with the responsibility for protecting records? (This dilemma is discussed in greater depth in Chapter 9). Archivists must balance present-day use of the records against long-term preservation. Part of that preservation is protection from human and natural catastrophes.

An archivist trying to address security issues needs to consider two aspects:

- physical security
- collection security

PHYSICAL SECURITY

Physical security deals with the repository and the building. Although most thefts take place during normal working hours, it is also prudent to examine the building's after-hours security.

The following six "Hunter's Hints" address the physical security of the repository. An archives program that is part of a larger institution may not have direct responsibility for all of these considerations. A smaller archives program, however, will need to review all of these considerations.

- *Doors* should be strong and well made, including the frame. In most burglaries the door is broken down.
- *Locks* should not be the key-in-the-knob type which can be pried open using a credit card—for this reason, most thieves "do not leave home" without one. Archivists should insist on a deadbolt lock which has a bolt separate from the knob. Also, the bolt should extend well into the frame to provide extra protection against the breaking down of the door.
- *Windows* on the lower floor should be locked and secured. Depending on the local environment, gates and grills may be in order.
- *Alarms* to detect after-hour entry are highly recommended. If the archives does not have alarms, try to have at least regular patrols by building guards.
- *Keys* should be carefully issued and monitored. Archives often remove themselves from the building master. When cleaning or maintenance staff need to be in the archives, they must do so during normal working hours or after hours in the presence of a security guard.
- *Box labels* can be a security measure. I recommend that archives place only the minimum information on the box label: collection name and box number. Anything more than this is available from the finding aids—why make it easier for an unauthorized person to find items of interest?[2]

COLLECTION SECURITY

Collection security involves making sure that documents do not disappear either during use or at other times. Anyone in the proximity of documents may be the source of a security problem.

Staff certainly have the opportunity to steal documents. A potential archival employer should carefully check the references of all applicants. It is important to contact previous employers, whether or not they are listed as references. It is not just that the archivist is looking for potential thieves; it is also necessary to know if the applicant will respect privacy and other aspects of administering archival collections.

There are certain patterns that emerge when employee thefts are involved. In particular, archivists should be alert to the following:

- materials consistently not in their usual locations
- the same person reporting items missing or always being the one to find missing items
- a staff member unconcerned about pursuing missing items
- regular inconsistencies or discrepancies in the repository's documentation and records
- a staff member's disregard for established rules and procedures
- a staff member's lifestyle that does not match salary and known assets[3]

"The first clue that anything was amiss in the rare books collection of Columbia University came on a hot day last July. A librarian preparing a catalogue entry went to the shelves on the sixth floor, where medieval manuscripts are stored in boxes. But one of the boxes was empty. The head librarian ordered an inventory of the medieval manuscripts. By the time it was complete, it was clear that 22 were gone, including a papal bull written in 1202 and a French copy of the Book of Hours from the 14th century."—*New York Times,* October 8, 1994.

Patrons are another cause of worry; there have been numerous cases of thefts by researchers. There are a number of things archives can do to reduce the danger, some of which are discussed in greater detail in Chapter 9.

- Require the researcher to present valid identification (driver's license or other photo ID). Note the identification on the form the researcher completes during the entrance interview. Some archives photocopy the identification and add it to the researcher's file.
- Establish and enforce some basic research room rules— require that all personal belongings be left at a check point; limit the number of items used at any one time; recheck items when the researcher is done; inspect researchers' personal belongings before they leave.

- Close the stacks to researchers.
- Control access to the research room: have only one exit, past the reference desk.
- Supervise researchers' use of materials: always have one staff member in the research room; make sure you have a clear field of vision, so you can see all researchers all the time (don't let them build a "Berlin Wall" with manuscript boxes); make sure the researchers know you are watching them.
- Know what's in your collection, so you can tell if something is missing. Keep all call slips: they provide evidence of what a researcher requested, and they also document that a particular item was previously used by other researchers.
- Consider ways to protect valuable items from your collections
  - remove originals and replace them with photocopies (keep the originals in a safe).
  - microfilm the entire collection if all of it is particularly valuable, and require researchers to use the microfilm.
  - mark valuable items with a property stamp and acid-free ink.[4]

Despite all the precautions, there may come a time when archives suspects a researcher of theft. Before getting to this point, it is imperative that all staff know what to do: remember that a false arrest or an improper detention might lead to a lawsuit. The archives should have policies and procedures in which all staff members are trained. Role playing often works well in this kind of training.

The following guidelines will help archives facing the difficult task of confronting a patron over a potential theft:

- Before detaining someone, make sure you have "probable cause" (such as seeing the person take an item). Do not rely on third-party witnesses.
- Notify security or the police, as dictated by the repository's written security plan.
- Make sure there is a credible witness for your upcoming discussion with the patron (to avoid "my word against your word.")
- Interrupt the researcher's activity—engage him or her in conversation.
- Take a quiet but firm approach.

- Try to avoid a scene, especially shouting and other displays of anger.
- Do not touch the patron, except in self-defense.
- Inform the patron that there appears to be a problem and ask the patron to go into an office to discuss it. The patron must go into the office voluntarily.
- Wait for security or the police, who will take over the investigation.
- If the patron denies there is a problem and leaves the building, one person should carefully follow the patron to get a license plate number and a description of the patron's car.[5]

Confronting a patron is not something archives should take lightly. It is a serious matter with serious legal implications for the patron as well as for archives, which is why most archives try to establish a research environment that minimizes the opportunity for theft and makes it easy to identify stolen materials. The former is done by having researchers check personal belongings and work under staff observation. Consider using colored paper for photocopies and providing the paper for researchers to use in taking notes.

One major repository, for example, distributes note paper with a hole in it. When researchers are ready to leave, they must stop at a security desk. The guard places a pencil or similar object into the stack of note paper and shakes vigorously. Anything that falls out is examined very carefully—especially if it is signed by George Washington.

Will the precautions detailed above prevent all thefts? Of course not—even the best car alarm will not prevent all auto thefts. The prudent archivist attempts to raise the stakes for a potential thief so that the repository will not be viewed as an "easy mark." This, perhaps, is the best we can hope to accomplish.

DISASTER PLANNING

As if human challenges were not enough, archives also face risks from natural events such as fires, floods, hurricanes, and earthquakes. An archivist can be consoled, however, that this is not a "personal" thing—hurricanes usually do not have a vendetta against archives. On the other hand, a natural disaster will not avoid a repository just because it contains historically valuable records. The archivist must be prepared without being panicked.

Disaster planning in an archival context can have either a narrow or a broad focus.

- The *narrow focus* plans only for the protection and restoration of records already in the archives. Other departments within the organization have to plan for themselves and be responsible for their own records.
- The *broad focus* involves planning for *all* the "vital records" of the organization, no matter who holds custody.

I recommend that an archivist take the broad focus, especially in an organization where there is no other records professional. Such a void can have a negative impact on the organization in the case of disaster. If the archivist does not fill the void, nobody will. While information systems professionals will deal with computer records, especially those on centralized systems, no one is likely to consider paper records.

DEFINING TERMS

First of all, what are vital records? These are records necessary for the maintenance of the function, reason, and objective of the organization. Some archival records may be vital; others may not. Similarly, some records of short-term value will be vital but not archival.

According to the federal government, vital records fall into one or both of the categories presented in Figure 8.1.[6]

The National Archives and Records Administration (NARA) makes a distinction between a disaster and an emergency[7] and defines them as follows:

- A *disaster* is an unexpected occurrence inflicting widespread destruction and distress and having long-term adverse effects on organization operations.
- An *emergency* is a situation or occurrence of a serious nature, developing suddenly and unexpectedly, and demanding immediate action. This is generally of short duration, like a power failure or minor flooding caused by broken pipes.

Using NARA terminology, an archivist in a small repository needs to plan for emergencies as well as disasters. In fact, the average archives is more likely to face a localized emergency than an extensive disaster. Certainly a disaster will receive more pub-

Figure 8.1 Categories of Vital Records		
Category	**Description**	**Examples of Records**
Emergency operating records	Essential to the continued functioning or reconstitution of an organization during and after an emergency	Emergency plans and directives, orders of succession, delegations of authority, staffing assignments, selected program records needed to continue the most critical organizational operations
Legal and financial rights records	Essential to protect the legal and financial rights of the organization and of the individuals directly affected by its activities	Accounts receivable, social security, payroll, retirement, insurance

licity and can completely devastate a repository, but the day-to-day survival of most archival records will depend on the way a repository plans for and responds to smaller emergencies.

Developing a vital records program involves four steps:

- identifying records that should be protected
- anticipating potential disasters and emergencies
- devising methods of protection
- planning responses

IDENTIFYING RECORDS

An archivist taking the broad approach to disaster planning needs to look at all the records of the organization to determine

- the ability of the organization to continue in business without the record
- the cost of replacing or reconstructing the record

The entire process is similar to deciding whether or not to purchase an insurance policy. What are the risks? Do these risks justify protection that will cost a certain amount? Records exhibiting both high cost of replacement and high need for continuing operations are the prime candidates for the insurance policy of a vital records program.

It is best to identify vital records as part of a larger process: conducting a records inventory and developing a retention schedule for all of an organization's records. This process encourages an integrated approach to recordkeeping practices.

If such an integrated approach is not possible, however, one can identify vital records by asking the following questions:

- Do the records assure the collection of income due?
- Do the records protect against fraud or overpayment?
- Do the records provide information about real property of other assets?
- Do the records protect the rights or interests of employees, shareholders, customers, or other stakeholders?

Figure 8.2 lists some categories of records often identified as vital.

Even within these broad categories of vital records, an archivist needs to establish priorities for protection and recovery. Are

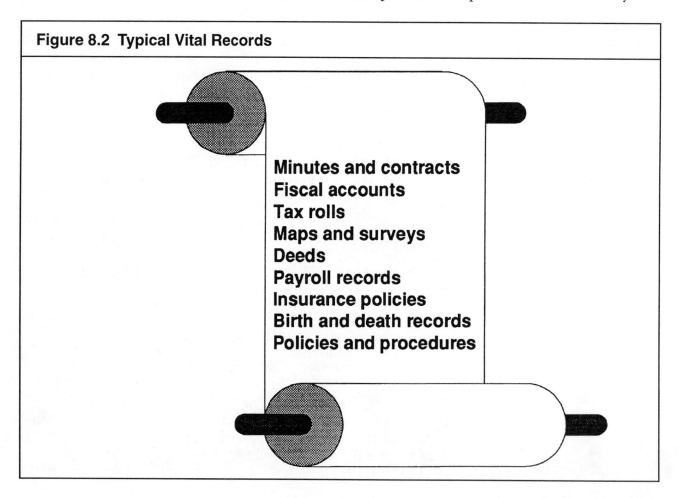

Figure 8.2 Typical Vital Records

Minutes and contracts
Fiscal accounts
Tax rolls
Maps and surveys
Deeds
Payroll records
Insurance policies
Birth and death records
Policies and procedures

the payroll records "more vital" than the tax rolls? Does the fact that payroll records are duplicated in the payroll service bureau make them a lower priority for protection? How does the archivist make these choices?

Judith Fortson has developed a framework for determining vital records priorities. This framework is summarized in Figure 8.3[8]

Figure 8.3 Priorities for Protection	
Priority	**Types of Materials**
Top priority	Difficult or impossible to replace or replicate and are either essential for the ongoing operations of the institution or some larger body, such as a state agency Have prime research value Have significant monetary value
Second priority	Difficult to replace or replicate and provide significant operational or research resources
Lowest priority	Can be replaced, either in original or reprographic form. Can be considered expendable, if necessary, to the institution and its constituents

In an archival setting, the finding aids should be a top priority, especially if only one copy of them exists. Without the finding aids, it would be difficult if not impossible even to determine what had been damaged in a disaster or emergency. The lowest-cost option is to duplicate the finding aids and store a copy off-site.

ANTICIPATING DISASTERS AND EMERGENCIES

Articles on disaster planning from the 1960s usually begin with a map, quite often of New York City, on which are superimposed a number of concentric circles. Those of us who grew up in major cities—and who were within the first or second ring—can remember school drills in which we hid under our desks to protect us from a nuclear blast. In retrospect, organizational records certainly were better protected in their mines and vaults than we were under our desks and bookbags. Perhaps it is reassuring to know that our utility bill would have been delivered on the first of the month following the blast to the giant crater where our mailbox once stood.

While the nuclear threat has diminished, there are other disasters for which we still must plan. Some of these are acts of nature: hurricanes, tornadoes, and major fires and floods. The vivid images of the Mississippi River flooding a couple of years ago come quickly to mind. Other disasters are human in origin and relatively recent to our shores. Among the first people permitted in the World Trade Center after it was bombed were employees retrieving records necessary to restart business. The bombing of the Oklahoma City federal building destroyed records as well as shattered families.

Often an archivist can guard against potential damage by understanding the nature of the likely types of disasters, examining the facility with an eye toward potential emergencies, implementing simple solutions, and advocating more extensive precautions. Two disasters for which all archivists need to plan are fire and water damage.

Figure 8.4 North Fork University: Assessment of Potential Major Disasters

TO: University President
FROM: Director, Department of Archives and Special Collections
RE: Potential Major Disasters

In addition to the localized disasters and emergencies like fires and floods, the university should prepare for major disasters that may affect the region as well as the campus.

Located as we are on Long Island, NFU's vital records program must take into account the potential damage caused by a major hurricane. While high winds are a concern, all but the oldest buildings on campus have been constructed to withstand their force. At the present time, there are no vital records in these oldest buildings.

Massive flooding, however, is not so easy to address—especially with our location near Long Island Sound. Regional disaster impact studies have projected that a major hurricane hitting at high tide would submerge the campus under several feet of water. It could take days before the water recedes to normal levels.

For this reason, I recommend that a copy of all university vital records be stored off Long Island. Storing these records in another building on campus, or even in a location a few miles away, would not prevent their destruction in a major disaster such as a hurricane.

I will explore options for off-island storage as part of the disaster planning program in which the university is engaged.

Fire

In a fire, both flames and smoke are a cause for concern. Smoke, in fact, can be almost as damaging as flames, especially to sensitive items like records on magnetic media.

In planning for fires, it is essential to consult local building codes as well as the publications of the National Fire Protection Association dealing with libraries, archives and records centers. This is not an area where the archivist should learn by doing (especially by doing incorrectly).

Archivists can adopt certain practices, however, to reduce the risk of fire. Figure 8.5 presents a fire prevention checklist.[9]

The main way to avoid extensive fire damage is to have a fire suppression system in the archives. While some archives rely exclusively on fire extinguishers, such an approach is dangerous; fire extinguishers are only appropriate for small fires and they offer no protection at all unless someone is there to operate them.

The best protection is a sprinkler system installed in the archives. In the past, some archives installed a suppression system using Halon 1301 gas, a practice common in computer environments. Halon gas no longer is produced, however, because it proved damaging to the environment. Sprinklers, therefore, are the only alternative.

But isn't the threat of water damage from malfunctioning sprinklers a concern? While archivists would prefer not to introduce a source of water into the storage environment, the benefits outweigh the risks. As a subsequent section of this chapter shows, water-damaged records can be restored at a reasonable cost; the same is not true of badly burned records. Furthermore, modern sprinkler systems are quite reliable—false discharges or leaks happen infrequently. The sprinkler systems are designed, moreover, to discharge water only in the immediate area of a fire. Unlike depictions in Hollywood films, the sprinkler heads do not all discharge and soak the entire facility.[10]

Water Damage

Water damage often happens as a result of a storm that brings wind and other damage. An engineer should examine the building's structure to be certain that the roof, foundation, and other components are able to withstand windstorm damage. Archives in areas subject to earthquakes face additional requirements for the building structure and such internal components as shelving.[11]

Water damage can also result from efforts to control fire. For this reason, an archivist should be prepared to cope with water-damaged materials after almost any kind of disaster.

Figure 8.5 Fire Prevention Checklist

✔ Prohibit smoking in records storage areas.

✔ Keep food and trash away from records.

✔ Do not store flammable and combustible materials with records or in adjacent storage areas.

✔ Keep all chemical and solvent containers closed, even when in use.

✔ Ensure that air circulation is adequate throughout the building.

✔ Ensure that electrical appliances are operated at a safe distance from flammable materials and that they are turned off when not in use.

✔ Check electrical outlets, fixtures, equipment, and appliances regularly.

✔ Check fire suppression system/fire extinguishers regularly.

✔ Check security alarms regularly.

✔ Keep all fire doors closed.

✔ Keep aisles clear of impediments to firefighters.

✔ Store as many loose items as possible in boxes or other enclosures.

✔ Use fire-retardant furnishings whenever possible.

✔ Make certain that repair people, contractors, and other temporary workers are aware of and follow the above practices.

"NASA has recovered the data and voice recorders that investigators hope will provide valuable information about Challenger's 73-second flight that may not have been picked up by ground computers....The devices had been recovered in about 650 feet of water about 32 miles off shore, along with tons of other debris from the crew cabin....In a statement written before the recorders were recovered, NASA said they would be submerged in cool water until they can be cleaned and dried under controlled temperature and humidity conditions at a NASA facility."—*Newsday,* March 14, 1986.

Quick action is especially important with water-damaged records. Mold will develop within 48 to 72 hours when the temperature exceeds 75 degrees and the relative humidity exceeds 60 percent. Under these circumstances, the archivist must act quickly to prevent permanent damage to the records.

As with fire, certain practices will lessen potential water damage. Figure 8.6 presents these practices in a checklist.[12]

Figure 8.6 Water Prevention Checklist

✔ Avoid basement storage as much as possible.

✔ Do not store records below pipes or restrooms.

✔ Do not store records near windows, skylights, or heating/cooling units.

✔ Do not store records on the floor. Records should be stored at least 4 inches off the floor (higher if flooding is more common).

✔ Locate all drains and check them regularly.

✔ Inspect the roof regularly for leaks.

✔ Do not install carpet in storage areas.

✔ Store records at least 12 inches from outside walls to prevent condensation.

✔ Keep plastic sheeting nearby to cover records quickly in case of water.

✔ Place drip pans under exposed pipes. Protect pipes vulnerable to freezing.

✔ Do not store particularly valuable records on the bottom or top shelves.

✔ Consider installing a sump pump with an alternate source of power.

DEVISING PROTECTION

A broad approach to disaster protection includes weighing three options for the protection of records:

- duplication and dispersal
- on-site protection
- off-site storage

Duplication and Dispersal

An effective way to protect records against disasters is to store a second copy at another location. Some records have a natural dispersal: additional copies are distributed elsewhere as part of the normal course of business. In these cases, it usually is possible to re-create the records in case of disaster, though the re-creation may involve some time and expense.

For other records, there is no natural dispersal. In certain instances, it may be desirable to create one or more additional copies specifically for remote storage. If copies must be made of a large volume of records, microfilm usually is the most cost-effective option.

An archives that has copied records onto preservation microfilm also has disaster protection, provided the original records or original microfilm are not stored in the same facility as the duplicate microfilm.

When choosing duplication and dispersal as a protection method, the copy of the vital record stored off-site is normally a duplicate of the original record. This facilitates the destruction of obsolete duplicates when replaced by an updated copy.

Computer backup tapes created in the normal course of systems maintenance, or other electronic copies routinely created in the normal course of business may be used as a vital records copy. This natural dispersal is the simplest way to protect electronic vital records.

Archivists need to consider several factors when deciding where to store copies of vital records.

- Copies of emergency operating vital records, to use the federal term, must be accessible in a very short time for use in the event of a disaster or emergency.
- Copies of legal and financial rights records may not be needed as quickly. They can be stored far away from the institution.[13]

On-Site Protection

For some records, duplication and dispersal is not an option. For example, current accounting records may have to be kept on-site so they are available for immediate reference. There also are times when the most current version of a document is the vital record—when the document is updated tomorrow, today's document no longer is vital. The crucial time, in this case, is overnight.

On-site protection usually involves fireproof storage, either in cabinets or vaults. Such storage must be used on a daily basis if the organization's interests are to be protected adequately. As discussed above, however, fire is not the only disaster from which records must be protected. Records should be stored as far away from potential sources of water damage as possible.

One important caveat with fireproof cabinets is in order: not all cabinets offer an equal level of protection. Before purchasing any cabinet, it is important to review the "fire rating" to determine the following:

- Will the cabinet protect the records as long as it will take to extinguish the fire? The fire rating gives the protection in hours.
- Is the cabinet rated for the proper medium? Cabinets designed to protect paper records should *not* be used for magnetic or photographic media; in the event of fire, their interior temperature and humidity will get too high for these fragile media.

Off-Site Storage

In some cases, the only copy of a record will be stored off-site. For example, archives may opt to store the original corporate charter off the premises. This option is only appropriate for records not needed for reference on a regular basis. If the record is needed for reference, it must be duplicated before being sent off-site.

Archives storing vital records off-site will need to evaluate the potential storage location carefully. Most archivists insist on a personal visit rather than just reviewing promotional materials. In conducting the visit, the archivist should try to answer the following questions:

- Is the facility secure? What does one need to do to gain access?
- Do they keep logs of visitors?
- Are there alarms, video monitors, and other security devices?

- Are temperature and humidity readings recorded? If so, what were their recent readings?
- Is the facility located beyond the area likely to be affected by a disaster that befalls your archives?
- How does the facility control records once entered into its system?
- How easy is it to retrieve records? What is the turn-around time?
- Are you willing to stake your reputation within your own organization on the adequacy of this off-site facility?

The last question is probably the most important one. If there is a problem with the off-site facility, others within the organization are likely to emphasize that the "archivist approved the off-site facility." The archivist must have a very high comfort level with any off-site facility before entrusting it with records.

PLANNING RESPONSES

Archives and libraries use disaster plans to summarize the above thinking, state it clearly, and provide a blueprint for use during an actual disaster or emergency. All the debating should happen at the planning stage—not at the time of a disaster, when minutes count.

Figure 8.7 presents the sections of a typical disaster plan.[14]

Figure 8.7 Sections of a Disaster Plan	
Section	**Contents**
Introduction	Purpose or rationale, scope of the plan, references to related institutional documents or policies
Establishment of authority and assignment of responsibilities	List of names and recovery duties (especially the recovery manager), work and home phone numbers of key people
Recovery procedures	Step-by-step instructions for disaster response activities, sections dealing with each type of medium (paper, photographic, etc.), lists of necessary supplies for each procedure, names and phone numbers for consultants or vendors (vacuum freeze-drying, for example).
Appendixes	Phone tree, additional contacts, supplies, floor plans, checklists.

Upon completion, the disaster plan should be submitted for approval by administrators at various levels, including the board of trustees in a small institution. Discussing and revising the plan becomes a way of educating administrators about the risks, how to minimize them, and how to deal with the disaster if it occurs.

Disaster plans should be tested regularly. I know of one business that tested its disaster plan by assuming that the entire facility had been destroyed. The recovery team was given a list of questions that they had to answer based upon information that was supposed to be duplicated off-site. Among the questions were

- Who were the employees assigned to the facility at the time of the disaster?
- What was the current status of a major product then under development?
- What were the locations of the gas mains serving the facility?
- What was the current cash position of the facility?

Such rigorous tests are the only way to make certain that the plan will work when needed.

While it may seem obvious, the disaster plan itself is a vital record. Copies must be accessible outside the area in which the disaster occurs. Copies must also be accessible any time of the day or night—especially for the first people to respond to a disaster after hours (often the maintenance or security staff). After all the planning, it would be a shame to have the plan unused because no one could find it.[15]

DISASTER RESPONSE AND RECOVERY

General

Once the archivist either discovers a disaster or is informed about one, it is time to implement the disaster plan. The following steps offer a general framework for disaster response:

1. *Assess the disaster situation.* It may be helpful to use an initial damage assessment form to record responses. In the chaos following a disaster, it would be easy to miss something important.
2. *Contact the insurer.* Insurance companies should be contacted immediately. It is helpful to begin taking photographs as soon as the disaster is discovered, for insurance and other purposes. A Polaroid or other instant camera should be part of the disaster response kit.

3. *Convene required staff and experts.* Once there is an initial assessment, it is time to call in staff members and relevant experts. All members of the team are working members—there are no honorary members. Furthermore, normal reporting relationships are suspended during the disaster: even a senior executive helping with recovery takes direction from a lower-ranking person identified in the plan as the disaster response coordinator.

4. *Set up a command post.* There must be a safe place that can be used to coordinate activities. Communication with the command post is important and may require the temporary use of cellular telephones.

5. *Activate plans for supplies, additional staff, and volunteers.* Depending on the severity of the disaster, other parts of the plan may be activated. If volunteers are needed, "on the job training" is necessary to ensure that well-meaning volunteers do not injure themselves or damage records.

6. *Make sure the building is safe.* Firefighters or other emergency personnel must certify that the building is safe before archivists can enter. Not only must the structure be sound, but the area must be free of contamination from asbestos, PCBs, or other hazardous substances. There is a risk of electrical shock in any wet environment. An archivist needs to avoid the temptation of being a hero—rushing into an unsafe area can result in personal injury.

7. *Stop the source of the problem.* If there is a fire, it must be extinguished before recovery can begin. Similarly, if there is a flood, the flow of water must first be stopped. It is important to note that heat can cause delayed ignition of paper in file cabinets and vaults for up to three days.

8. *Stabilize the environment.* The archivist should try to keep the temperature in the room below 60 degrees and to reduce humidity by using dehumidifiers. It is important to keep air moving to prevent mold growth. Records should not be returned to an unstable environment.

9. *Protect or remove records.* Records can be covered with plastic sheeting for a short period of time to protect them from imminent water damage. Also consider moving records to a higher location to protect them from rising water.

10. *Recover damaged records.* If records are damaged, they will need to be dealt with in a systematic way, from highest to lowest priority. The next two sections provide de-

tail on recovery of fire- and water-damaged records.

11. *Conclude the initial response phase.* The initial response phase should end with a debriefing about what worked and what did not. This feedback should lead to revisions of the institution's disaster plan. Also, restored records remain more vulnerable than other records. They should be checked periodically for mold, fungus, or other deterioration.[16]

Recovering Fire-Damaged Records

In many instances, fire-damaged records are beyond recovery. The information they contain, however, might be found in other records stored elsewhere.

Charred paper can be trimmed and gently cleaned. It may be possible to return these records to the files. If the records are too fragile, extensively damaged, or contaminated, it is best to photocopy or microfilm the records and substitute the copies for the originals.

Photographic and magnetic media are likely to melt in a fire, making recovery even more difficult.

Recovering Water-Damaged Records

Water damage is common in most archival disasters. Every archivist, therefore, should be prepared to deal with water damage on a small or large scale. I can remember sacrificing more than one business suit to the recovery of records damaged by leaking pipes.

The following are some hints for the archivist facing water damage to collections and storage areas:

- Wear sturdy shoes when reentering the area, because of the possibility of broken glass.
- Resist the temptation to try to restore items on-site. First get them out of the wet area, then worry about restoring them.
- Do not try to press water out of items. Also, do not stack wet items. Both practices are likely to damage the materials.
- It is possible to air dry items, especially if they are merely damp or wet around the edges. In a well-ventilated area, stand books upright and fan them open slightly; at regular intervals they should be re-fanned and inverted. One can also interleave items with absorbent blotter paper or unprinted newsprint.

- Separate groups of soaked records with freezer or waxed paper.
- Use cubic-foot boxes or plastic milk crates for packing records.
- If items are severely soaked, or if large numbers are involved, freeze them. Freezing buys time by stopping mold growth and other deterioration.
- Frozen records can be dried in a self-defrosting freezer. Expect this to take several weeks to several months.
- Vacuum freeze-drying is another option. This process vaporizes ice crystals without permitting them to melt. Another benefit is that mud, dirt, and soot are lifted to the surface, facilitating later cleaning.
- Microfilm and other photographic media are more susceptible to water damage than is paper, and, as already noted, they are very sensitive to temperature and humidity. Because of the time and expense required for the recovery of these media (and the frequent need to consult outside experts) it is imperative that the archivist identify priorities for restoration, and procedures to follow, *before* a disaster occurs. In general, improper or sudden drying of these media may cause more damage than keeping them wet until an expert can restore them.[17]

Electronic Records Disasters

With electronic records, the best choice is to have backup files of records, so recovery can be done at a keyboard rather than in a flooded basement. If damaged magnetic records must be recovered, the archivist is well advised to seek professional assistance.

Many electronic records disasters, however, are of much smaller scale, involving everything from power surges to lost documentation. Some hints for minimizing electronic records disasters are

- Use an uninterruptable power supply (UPS) for crucial systems.
- Use virus detection software.
- Implement a system of password-protected access to electronic files.
- Store copies of software and documentation off-site.
- Develop and implement a regular, off-site, backup schedule.
- Assess recoverability of information from other sources (such as paper or microfilm)
- Set up a cooperative recovery agreement with another institution possessing a similar computing infrastructure.[18]

CONCLUSION

This chapter began by equating security and disasters with archival nightmares. However, unlike nightmares that scare us in the dark, archivists can take some control during the day—by anticipating problems and planning against them. Moreover, archivists *must* anticipate and plan in order to fulfill the part of their mission that deals with preserving records of enduring value. Those records, once preserved and protected, are ready for use by researchers.

NOTES

1. Lewis J. Bellardo and Lynn Lady Bellardo, *A Glossary for Archivists, Manuscript Curators, and Records Managers* (Chicago: Society of American Archivists, 1992). Two helpful volumes on security are: Gregor Trinkaus-Randall, *Protecting Your Collection: A Manual of Archival Security* (Chicago: Society of American Archivists, 1995); and Timothy Walch, *Archives and Manuscripts: Security* (Chicago: Society of American Archivists, 1977). For an excellent one-volume treatment of disaster planning, see Judith Fortson, *Disaster Planning and Recovery: A How-To-Do-It Manual for Librarians and Archivists* (New York: Neal-Schuman, 1992).

2. For more on physical security systems, see Trinkaus-Randall, *Protecting Your Collections*, 43–59. This book contains photographs of locks, alarms, and detection devices.

3. Trinkaus-Randall, *Protecting Your Collections*, 63–64.

4. "The Office of Preservation of the Library of Congress advises repositories to use an ink that is nonfading, ineradicable with solvents or bleaches, neutral or slightly alkaline in pH, essentially nonbleeding and nonmigratory, stable at heat up to 300 degrees Fahrenheit, resistant to light for at least one hundred years, and slow drying on the stamp pad but fast drying on the document. At the present time, inks with these requirements are not commercially available, but the Office of Preservation of the Library of Congress, in conjunction with the Government Printing Office, has formulated and tested such an ink that is available from the Library free of charge to all who request it. A single two-ounce bottle will last at least ten years if properly used. The

Library will not divulge the ink's formula, since such knowledge might make it possible to develop an effective means of eradication." Trinkaus-Randall, *Protecting Your Collections,* 13.

5. For more on dealing with a suspected theft, see Trinkaus-Randall, *Protecting Your Collections,* 62–63.

6. "Management of Vital Records," final rule issued by the National Archives and Records Administration, *Federal Register* 60:109 (June 7, 1995), 29989–29992.

7. For the latest NARA thinking on the topic see *Vital Records and Records Disaster Mitigation and Recovery: An Instructional Guide,* available from the NARA World Wide Web site at http://www.nara.gov.

8. Adapted from Fortson, *Disaster Planning and Recovery,* 82.

9. This checklist was drawn from two sources: the New York State Archives and Records Administration (SARA) and Fortson's *Disaster Planning and Recovery.* The SARA information was prepared by its Local Government Records Advisory Services and is accessible at the SARA Internet site: http://nyslgti.gen.ny.us:80/empireweb/SARA/home.html.

10. Trinkaus-Randall, *Protecting Your Collections,* 32–33.

11. For more on earthquakes, see Fortson, *Disaster Planning and Recovery,* 33–43.

12. This checklist comes from the New York State Archives and Fortson, *Disaster Planning and Recovery.*

13. "Management of Vital Records," NARA.

14. Fortson, *Disaster Planning and Recovery,* 88–95. See also "How to Design a Disaster Recovery Plan," *News Digest,* International Institute of Municipal Clerks (October 1992): 1–9; and Trinkaus-Randall, *Protecting Your Collections,* 33–36.

15. For more on disaster plans, see Mildred O'Connell, "Disaster Planning: Writing and Implementing Plans for Collections-Holding Institutions," *Technology and Conservation* (summer 1983), 18–25; Sally Buchanan, "Disaster: Prevention, Preparedness and Action," *Library Trends* (fall 1981), 241–252; *Hell and High Water: A Disaster Information Sourcebook* (New York: New York Metropolitan Reference and Research Library Agency [METRO], 1988); and Trinkaus-Randall, *Protecting Your Collections,* 33–36.

16. These steps were drawn from Sally A. Buchanan, *Resource Materials for Disaster Planning in New York Institutions* (Albany: New York State Library, 1988) and other documents found on the New York State Archives' Web site.

17. Adapted from Fortson, *Disaster Planning and Recovery,* 31–32, 45–75. See also *Western Association for Art Conservation Newsletter,* May 1988 and Peter Waters, *Procedures for Sal-*

vage of Water-Damaged Library Materials (Washington, D.C.: Library of Congress, 1975).

18. Adapted from *Electronic Records Management: Checklist for Disaster Planning and Preparedness* (Albany, N.Y.: New York State Archives and Records Administration, 1995).

9 ACCESS, REFERENCE, AND OUTREACH

Archival records exist to be used. Identifying and preserving records, though laudable goals, are not enough for an archival program. This is not to say that all archives exist primarily to serve the general public. In many institutions (for example, businesses), the archives exists to serve the organization itself. In these cases, very few nonemployees may ever gain access to archival records.

Whatever the organizational setting, the dual archival responsibility—preservation and use—leads to a tension. Archivists try to make materials available to the fullest extent possible, consistent with a reasonable regard for their preservation. The use of records can lead to deterioration, damage, and theft. If records were locked away in a "perfect" environment, they certainly would last longer. Every time someone uses a record, the lifetime of that record is shortened. Archivists must weigh the demands of present day researchers against the potential demands of posterity—use versus preservation.

Archives are not unique in this tension—it also applies to library materials. The tension is compounded, however, by the one-of-a-kind materials found in an archives. An archival program must constantly work to achieve the proper balance.[1]

ACCESS

Access is defined as the "right, opportunity, or means of finding, using, or approaching documents and/or information."[2] Access is the authority to obtain information from or perform research using archival materials. As will be noted below, granting *access* is not the same as granting permission to *duplicate* the materials in an archives collection. The latter involves archivists in the area of copyright.

ACCESS TRADITIONS

In the United States, there are two traditions in administering access: the historical manuscripts tradition and the public archives tradition. Elements of each tradition continue to influence contemporary archival practice.

Historical Manuscripts Tradition

The historical manuscripts tradition is exemplified by the Library of Congress. In this tradition, access is based on an agreement between the repository and donor that exchanges possession of the papers for restrictions on their use. In negotiating the deed of gift agreement, the donor is able to define access parameters, usually along one of the following lines:

- The donor or designee approves each application for access.
- The donor imposes an absolute restriction on access, usually for a fixed period of time.

In this tradition, ultimate preservation is viewed as more important than quick access. This viewpoint leads to a major disadvantage: the entire "forest" of a collection may be closed to protect a few sensitive "trees."

Public Archives Tradition

As exemplified by the National Archives, access policy in the public archives tradition is based on the assumption that records with a high public policy content should be open. Since these records belong "to the people," the people should have access to them as quickly and as fully as possible.

In the public archives tradition, restrictions are regarded as a necessary evil. They usually are administered as follows:

- General restriction categories are established (such as national security).
- Archivists conduct a page-by-page review of the records against these categories, restricting records that fit each category.

This categorization leads to fast access to *most* of a collection, rather than restricting the entire collection. The forest is open quickly because the sensitive trees can be identified and segregated. There are disadvantages, however, to the page-by-page review:

- It is time-consuming, labor-intensive, and expensive.
- It relies on the judgment of the archivist; there is an element of subjectivity.

These traditions sometimes overlap. High-ranking public and private officials, for example, often consider their files to be personal papers rather than organizational records. If these are personal papers, then the high-ranking official would be able to negotiate access policies through a deed of gift agreement. If these are archival records, then access would be governed by organizational policies rather than the wishes of the official. In this case, the two traditions would have dramatically different impacts on access to the materials.

ADMINISTERING ACCESS

With these traditions as a foundation, the archivist faces the task of administering access on a daily basis. Four related concepts help the archivist meet the challenge:

- equal access
- full access
- competing rights
- restrictions

Equal Access

Archivists try to make materials available to researchers on equal terms. Archivists should neither permit access by only one researcher nor discriminate against particular types of researchers. These are basic tenets of the *Code of Ethics for Archivists* reprinted in Appendix B. Even such basic tenets, however, can be difficult to implement.

For example, the Director of the Department of Archives and Special Collections at North Fork University faced the following two situations:

- A faculty member in the political science department was instrumental in securing the donation of the papers of a local politician. The professor asked that, as a way of saying thank you, the archivist give her six months of exclusive access before the collection is opened to other researchers.
- An astrologer, considering sending his son to North Fork, visited the archives to examine the founding documents of the university. He wanted to know if the stars were favorable for his son's academic career at NFU.

How should the archivist handle these situations? Should the professor be given special treatment? The obvious answer may be "no," but how will the archivist then deal with a potential enemy within NFU, someone who may talk negatively about the archives within university circles?

What about the astrologer? Is this the kind of researcher that the university wishes to encourage? If the records are open, should they be open to everyone willing to abide by the rules and regulations? Is it the archivist's responsibility to determine the worthiness of a research request?

As these examples illustrate, the ethical challenges of granting equal access often involve shades of gray.

Full Access

Archivists try to grant access to *all* materials that may help a researcher, except those materials closed by law or other restrictions (either donor- or repository-imposed). Full access is not always easy to provide, however.

Some researchers are very secretive about their projects. The North Fork archives, for example, was visited by a doctoral candidate embarking on dissertation research. The archivist attempted to learn more about the dissertation topic in order to help the researcher. The researcher, however, would only discuss the topic in general terms; he was afraid that someone would "steal" the topic before he could finish the dissertation, thereby invalidating all his work.

On the other hand, assisting even a forthright researcher can be hindered by the nature of modern archives and manuscript collections. As collections get larger, it becomes more difficult to know their contents in detail. Archivists who do not know their collections will have a difficult time guiding researchers. The only solution is to rely on finding aids. Full access implies that an archives collection has basic bibliographic control over *all* collections—both processed *and* unprocessed.

Competing Rights

Administering access places an archivist at the intersection of often-competing rights: the right to know and the right to privacy. Both are part of the American legal and cultural tradition. Archivists try to respect both rights, realizing that such respect may place the archivist in a difficult position.

Right to Know. Americans pride themselves in having an open society, especially as it relates to government actions. The Freedom of Information Act outlines specific procedures whereby citizens can request access to government records and information. Declassification procedures recently have been changed to allow more records to be open sooner. Some states have "sunshine laws" and "open meeting laws" meant to prevent secret decision making. Taken together, Americans expect to be able to get access to

> "The heart of writer Alex Haley thumped. He was examining microfilmed census records in the National Archives Building in Washington, D.C.
>
> "'Suddenly in utter astonishment I found myself looking down there on "Tom Murray, black, blacksmith . . . " "Irene Murray, black, housewife . . . " followed by the names of Grandma's older sisters—most of whom I'd listened to countless times on Grandma's front porch. "Elizabeth, age 6"—nobody in the world but my Great Aunt Liz! At the time of that census, Grandma wasn't even born yet!' he has written.
>
> "Haley had just discovered the first documentary evidence that led him to his past and to his best seller *Roots*."—*Newsday,* March 31, 1985.

information, even information that once involved the nation's deepest secrets.

The right-to-know tradition also appears in the private sector. Genealogists and family researchers expect churches to provide information about their ancestors from sacramental records. Potential investors expect corporations to disclose information from their records that may affect share price. Patients expect to have access to their medical records to confirm a diagnosis or to monitor treatment. Therefore all archivists, regardless of institutional setting, want information available and usable to the fullest extent possible while respecting the right to privacy.[3]

Right to Privacy. Americans also cherish an individual's right to be left alone—to live free of unwanted publicity or interference. This is enshrined in legislation such as the Privacy Act and the Family Educational Rights and Privacy Act (FERPA). The latter act, dealing with student records, has changed the way educational institutions handle recommendations, transcripts, and other records.

> "A Nassau [County, N.Y.] judge yesterday refused to give the state permission to review confidential court records of divorce cases to gather statistical information on child support. . . .
>
> "[The judge] turned down the request from the state Department of Social Services after matrimonial lawyers argued that access to the records would be an unnecessary invasion of privacy. Before ruling, [the judge] said she was concerned about researchers reading files they might find 'titillating' and misinterpreting the financial information."—*Newsday,* April 23, 1986.

Archivists respect the right to privacy partially out of a desire to prevent embarrassment. In these litigious times, however, archivists also are aware of the possibility of lawsuits and other legal actions. Whatever the motivation, understanding and respecting privacy is part of the archival consciousness.

At the time of donation or transfer, an archivist tries to determine privacy issues in the records and how to address these concerns. It is important to note that there is no privacy right for the dead. Heirs and other living relatives, however, *do* have a right to privacy that the archivist should consider when administering access.

Case files are the most difficult records to administer from a privacy standpoint. Case information usually is given as part of a confidential relationship with a doctor, social worker, clergyperson, or other professional. The information in the file is personal in the truest sense: it relates to a person at his or her deepest levels. Revealing the information could certainly be embarrassing for the subject.

A couple of years ago, the world witnessed a dramatic example of the conflict between these competing rights. After the fall of East Germany and other Communist regimes, once-secret police files were opened for research. On more than one occasion, people learned for the first time that the informant whose testimony condemned them to years in prison was none other than their spouse. In these situations, the move to an open society was accompanied by much personal pain.

Restrictions

Restrictions are the way an archivist attempts to balance the competing rights. Restrictions usually flow from a desire to protect privacy, either of the donor or a third party. Restrictions should be noted on all finding aids, especially those distributed to researchers before they arrive at the archives. Imagine how frustrating it would be for a researcher to travel across the country to visit an archives collection, only to learn that all or most of the collection is restricted—an "unhappy camper" would be an understatement.

There are three broad categories of restrictions:

- completely closed or sealed
- partially closed or restricted due to contents
- restricted for preservation or security reasons

Completely Closed or Sealed. If a collection is completely closed or sealed, no one—sometimes not even the archival staff—may see the contents. This drastic step is difficult to justify in light of the archivist's mission to make records available.

If complete closure *is* imposed, however, it is best to do so for a set period of time rather to leave the issue open-ended. This guarantees that everyone, including the donor, knows that the collection will eventually be open for research.

It is common to close unprocessed collections completely—except, of course, to the archivists who must process them in order to lift the closure. How can an archivist administer privacy, copyright, or other concerns if relevant items remain unidentified in an unprocessed collection? Most archivists take the safer course of not granting access until the collection is processed.

Closed or Partially Restricted. In many cases, a collection is open, but researchers are permitted to use only some of the material. As with the previous category, it is best if restrictions are for a specific length of time rather than remaining in effect indefinitely. It is also best to avoid situations where the archivist must approach the donor (or other designee) for permission each time a researcher wants to consult a collection. Not only is this a time-consuming process, but it can pose questions about whether or not access is equal for all researchers.

Figure 9.1 lists the most common reasons for restricting access due to content. If only part of a collection exhibits these categories, the sensitive part would be removed from the collection prior to researcher use. It is customary to insert a separation sheet at the point of removal so researchers know that part of the collection was removed and why. Naturally, if an entire collection consists of sensitive material as defined in Figure 9.1, the entire collection would be closed to researchers.

In some cases, access is *conditional*: researchers may use the collection if they agree in advance to certain conditions. Usually this agreement with the researcher is made in writing to prevent future misunderstandings. Some typical conditions are

- review of notes by the archives staff before the researcher leaves
- prior review of any potential publication
- limitation on or prohibition against quotation or publication

Some of these conditions may seem strange, especially to librarians accustomed to dealing with previously published materials. The unpublished nature of archival materials, however, means that an individual or organization—other than the archi-

Figure 9.1 Reasons for Restricting Access Due to Content	
Reason	**Description**
Privacy	Information that would violate the right to privacy.
Business information	Trade secrets and other proprietary business information.
Personnel data	Salaries, performance reviews, and other employee data.
Investigative information	Kept closed to protect both the individuals involved and the institutional investigative process.
Statutory and other directed restrictions	National security restrictions, for example.

val repository—may hold the copyright, including the right to first publication. As noted in Chapter 4, copyright *may* be transferred to the archives along with the transfer of the physical property—or the copyright holder may retain this right. The deed of gift agreement should be specific on this point.

Conditions on researcher access usually originate with the donor of the materials. They are also common in archives that have had a negative experience with a researcher—either unauthorized publication of information or inaccurate citation of sources. The most important point is this: if conditions are imposed, they should be imposed equally on all researchers.

Restricted for Preservation/Security Reasons. Access may be restricted for reasons other than the *content* of the collection. The *physical condition* of the items, or their market value, may also lead to restrictions. Fragile or deteriorated originals may suffer further damage if handled by researchers. Items with a monetary value may disappear in the course of research use.

In such cases, it is common for the archivist to replace the original with a duplicate on paper or another medium. If only a few items are of concern, replacing the original with a photocopy is the usual practice. (The original is then stored in a secure environment.) If a larger number of items are of preservation or security concerns, microfilm becomes the duplicating medium of choice.

Access and the Archival Repository

Administering access in an individual archival repository usually involves three steps:

1. *Prepare a general access policy for the repository.* This document should outline access and reference policies, indicate fees (if any), and detail searching and reference services. Some institutional archives also establish a default closure period for organizational records. The access policy should be approved by the governing body of the institution.[4]

2. *Determine specific restrictions for individual collections or parts of collections.* Some collections or parts of collections will be closed for longer or shorter periods than the default period. Corporate minutes, for example, may be closed longer while press releases may be open immediately.

3. *Consistently apply the restrictions by developing a procedure manual and training staff in its use.* The larger the staff that administers access, the more important this third point becomes.

Once the access policies are established, the manuals are written, and the staff is trained, it is time for the archives to admit researchers.

REFERENCE

Reference service includes a range of activities to assist researchers in using archival materials. These activities make the past accessible to present and future generations. Effective reference service can make the difference in an archives fulfilling its mission. Such effective service does not happen by accident.

When providing reference services, archivists tend to deal with two broad categories of individuals: researchers of the interpretation and researchers of the fact.[5]

Researchers of the interpretation are the traditional archival users. These researchers—the stereotypical scholars on sabbatical—have weeks or months to spend wading through the collections in archives. They are "panning for gold" rather than "expecting a quick strike." Researchers of the interpretation want archives to produce any bit of evidence that may relate; they are willing to make the links and connections, even if it takes a great deal of time. Contrary to popular opinion, this type of researcher no longer is the predominant user of archives.

Researchers of the fact now predominate. These researchers want a quick strike. They are looking for specific information and want to find it as soon as possible. Rather than developing a theory of immigration, they want to know if their great-grandfather was on a particular ship. Genealogists, journalists, and many in-house users fit this category.

Why does this distinction matter? Because each type of researcher will have different expectations about and preferences toward the range of research services archives provides. Researchers of the interpretation may not mind the finding aids that offer only a general overview of a collection—in fact, they may not use the finding aids at all, preferring to locate their own nuggets of gold. Researchers of the fact, by contrast, may not be so tolerant of a finding aid system they believe fails to meet their needs.

It may seem obvious to say that archivists need to understand their researchers. Sometimes, however, the obvious does not happen. Studies have shown that much of archival administration has been *material-centered* rather than *client-centered*. Many archivists believe that they are oriented to users, yet they do not even know who their users are. In one user survey conducted by a major archives program, 30 percent of the users checked "other" as the best description of them—implying that the archives program did not even know how to define the categories of its users, an important first step to meeting their specific needs.[6]

Among the range of reference services archives use to meet the needs of both types of users are

- providing information about and from holdings
- assisting with research visits
- providing or making duplicates

PROVIDING INFORMATION

Archivists provide two types of information: information *about* their holdings and information *from* their holdings. As with all aspects of archival work, the trick is to achieve the proper balance.

Providing information *about* holdings is recognized universally as part of the archivist's mission. Potential researchers need to know what is contained in a particular archival repository. Archivists provide this information through the range of finding aids discussed in Chapter 6: guides, inventories, entries in online catalogs, and Internet sites for example. As noted above, information about holdings should include statements about restrictions, both general restrictions applicable to all collections and specific restrictions relating to individual collections.

Providing information *from* holdings is more controversial. It is common for archives to receive mail or telephone requests from researchers unable to visit the repository but who still want information from the collections. This places the archivist, especially in a small institution, in a difficult position. Should we do the research requested? If so, how much time should we spend on it?[7]

The main problem is with providing equal access, one of the goals outlined above. An archives program will need to be consistent in the way it handles such requests in order to provide equal access to its collections. As in so many other areas, it is necessary to develop policies and implement them consistently.

Many archives set a time limit for how long they will spend researching a particular request. Typical time periods are anywhere from ten minutes to an hour. A distant researcher who needs more time than this will often be referred to professional researchers near the archives who are willing to work on a contract basis. In order to avoid any appearance of a conflict of interest, the archivist should never recommend only one person.

Service to internal users often is treated separately. Archivists in businesses and similar institutional settings find that they spend a great deal of time doing research for others in the institution. This is a fact of institutional life. The archivist provides a service, as other staff members do with legal research or library services. Employees of the institution do not expect to perform these services themselves—that is why the institution established a library or an archives in the first place. When a vice president calls looking for information from the archives, the best response probably is not "We have dozens of boxes that may relate. Come down between 9:00 a.m. and 5:00 p.m. and we'll bring them out for you to examine." Others in the organization would consider this the equivalent of a lawyer saying, "If you'd like to know if we can be sued, I have shelves full of law books you're welcome to consult."

Some archives waive the time limit on research in the case of senior administrators. This waiver is a different kind of archival survival than that associated with preservation efforts. Once again, it all comes down to understanding one's patrons in general and the specific person we are trying to assist at the moment.

Archivists publicize their holdings through external and internal means. Externally, archivists use various outreach efforts:

speeches before professional and community organizations, finding aids, exhibits, and sites on the Internet. Internally, contacts with researchers who visit the repository offer archivists opportunities to publicize holdings—through interviews with researchers, explanation of in-house finding aids, and other approaches. The next section discusses these approaches in more detail.

ASSISTING WITH RESEARCH VISITS

An effective research visit to archives involves three steps:

- entrance interview
- reference room activities
- exit interview

At each of these steps, both the archivist and the researcher have specific things they wish to accomplish as shown in Figure 9.2. The trick is to achieve these differing purposes in a collegial rather than an adversarial way.

Figure 9.2 Research Visit Goals: Archivist and Researcher Perspectives

Step	What the Archivist Wishes to Accomplish	What the Researcher Wishes to Accomplish
Entrance interview	• Confirm the identity of the researcher • Determine researcher interests • Explain rules and regulations • Explain the use of finding aids	• Find out about relevant collections • Learn how the research room operates
Reference room activities	• Protect the records from damage or theft • Retrieve and refile records efficiently	• Find the desired information as quickly as possible • Have someone available to answer questions
Exit interviews	• Get feedback on the collections, finding aids, and procedures	• Be certain that follow-up work by the archives (photocopies, etc.) will take place

Unless there is clear communication between the archivist and the researcher, there is likely to be misunderstanding about these three steps. In such cases, a chart of inaccurate perceptions and expectations might look like Figure 9.3.

Figure 9.3 Research Visit Goals: Inaccurate Perceptions and Expectations		
Step	**What the Researcher Thinks the Archivist Wishes to Accomplish**	**What the Archivist Thinks the Researcher Wishes to Accomplish**
Entrance interview	• Tell the researcher how wonderful the archives is	• Get out of the room quickly as possible
Reference room activities	• Put as many obstacles as possible in the way of the research visit • Make the researcher's life as miserable as possible	• Receive undivided attention • Have the rules changed if they are inconvenient for the researcher
Exit interviews	• Find one more way to delay the process	• Get out of the room as quickly as possible.

Entrance Interview

An entrance interview is a key part of archival reference service. It gives both parties in the reference process (the researcher and the archivist) a chance to communicate their expectations, needs, and limitations. An entrance interview can save time and frustration for both parties.

The entrance interview has the following specific objectives:

- *Confirm the identity of the researcher.* Most archives have researchers complete a registration form that gives such information as name, address, institutional affiliation, and research topic. Many archives require the researcher to furnish identification. Sometimes a photocopy of the ID is made; in case of theft or another security problem, this identification can be very important. If identification is required, it should be consistently required of *all* researchers.
- *Determine the researcher's needs.* The archivist tries to clarify the researcher's topic and available time. The ar-

chivist also will suggest secondary sources the researcher should consult as well as other archives holding related primary sources.

- *Discuss the exchange of researcher information.* Researchers have a right to the privacy of their research. The archives should not identify researchers or their topics to other researchers without permission. Some researchers are willing to have archives share this information, provided they also learn of related research. Such permission should be given in writing.

- *Explain the institution's rules and regulations.* The archivist will explain rules covering the use of materials, citation and quotation, and photocopying. Many archives have the researcher sign a copy of the rules as an acknowledgment that the rules have been discussed and understood.

- *Explain the use of finding aids.* In particular, the archivist describes in-house finding aids and suggests collections where the researcher may want to begin research.

- *Explain fees.* If the archives charges any fees, these should be clearly explained in the entrance interview. Charging for *use* of the archives is controversial (it is done by some historical societies); however, almost all archives charge for photocopies and other duplicates (such as photographs, videotape, and audio tape).

Reference Room Activities

With preliminaries out of the way, the researcher moves to the reference room to see the archival records. Since the physical aspects of the reference room are discussed in Chapter 8, "Security," this chapter only covers policies and procedures.

The following is a summary of reference room activities:

1. *Researchers check all personal belongings.* Hats, coats, briefcases and other belongings are placed in a secure area. Notepaper and writing instruments (including personal computers) are the only items permitted in the reference room.

2. *Researchers sign a logbook each day they are in the reference room.* While this may seem an unnecessary step, the log could be important in case of theft. It would demonstrate that a researcher *was* in the reference room on a particular day, with the notations made in the researcher's own handwriting.

3. *Researchers complete a call slip for each collection or part of a collection.* Staff members use these call slips to pull collections off the shelves. The slips are also important in case of theft—they document that a person used a particular collection.
4. *A staff member retrieves the requested materials.* Since there are no open stacks, the researcher remains in the reference room while the records are retrieved.
5. *One staff member is always in the reference room to watch researchers.* The unique nature of archival materials means that researchers should always be observed in the reference room. While this need not be *obtrusive*, it should be *apparent* to researchers.
6. *Researchers return the records to the archives staff.* A staff member checks the records for completeness and refiles the material when time permits.
7. *Researchers leave the reference room.* In some archives, researchers and their belongings are subject to search. This should be spelled out in the rules and regulations as well as posted on signs.[8]

Exit Interview

An exit interview is an important—but often overlooked—part of archival reference service. All too often, a researcher just leaves without any further contact with the archives staff. When this happens, some real opportunities are lost.

The exit interview takes the form of a conversation with a colleague. Among the questions an archivist asks are:

- How valuable were the collections to you? Did they contain what you thought they would contain?
- How helpful were the finding aids? What can the archives do to make them more helpful?
- Did you encounter any problems with the records? Were items out of order or missing?
- How helpful were archival staff members?
- Do you know of other repositories with related collections?

MAKING DUPLICATES

Many researchers request copies of archival materials in the course of their visit. Archives usually try to be as accommodating as time and staff will allow. The reproduction of archival materials, however, enmeshes the archivist in questions of copyright; can the archives duplicate or permit the duplication of the requested items?

General Considerations

Copyright is the right vested by law in the author of a document and his or her heirs or assignees to publish or reproduce a document, or to authorize publication or reproduction of a document. Copyright is a property right that pertains to original works of authorship. It is one part of what is known as intellectual property, which also includes patents and trademarks.[9]

The first question for the archivist is who is the copyright holder? It is not always the author, since a document may have been produced as a "work for hire" or as part of one's employment responsibilities. The determination of the copyright holder can be a complex matter best discussed with legal counsel. As noted in Chapter 4, the resolution of copyright questions should be addressed in a deed of gift agreement.

Organizations or persons can only grant permission to duplicate an item for which they possess the copyright. In general terms, institutions hold the copyright to their *outgoing* correspondence, but not their *incoming* correspondence. The same is true of individuals acting in a personal capacity. As one can see, a large collection of materials would contain items from numerous copyright holders.

The Copyright Law of 1976, which took effect in 1978, eliminated a previous distinction between published and unpublished items. In the past, published items were governed by statutory law while unpublished items were governed by common law copyright. The intention of the new law is that eventually *all* published and unpublished materials, including those in archival institutions, will be in the public domain where they can be reproduced without infringing copyright.

"The Supreme Court yesterday refused to allow publication of an unauthorized biography of J. D. Salinger that includes quotations from [unpublished] letters the novelist wrote. The justices, without comment, let stand a federal appeals court ruling that publication of *J. D. Salinger: A Writing Life* would violate federal copyright law. . . .

"Ian Hamilton, a literary critic for *The London Sunday Times* . . . completed work on the Salinger biography in 1986.

"Hamilton located, and quoted from, letters sent to and from Salinger that had been placed in university libraries across the country."—*Newsday,* October 6, 1987.

There are some additional provisions for unpublished, noncopyrighted works created before January 1, 1978—precisely the kinds of documents that fill archives:

- Protection extends for the life of the author plus 50 years.
- No matter how long ago the author died, all unpublished works are protected for 25 years from the time the new copyright law took effect. Thus on January 1, 2003, a large amount of unpublished material will enter the public domain.[10]

Until items reach the public domain, the archives must protect the rights of the copyright holder. Two sections of the Copyright Act most directly affect the way archives and libraries protect copyright holders and themselves.

Section 107 deals with "fair use" of materials. According to the law, if the use is fair, then it is permissible without authorization or payment of royalties. Fairness is determined by meeting four criteria:

- the purpose of the use
- the nature of the work used
- the substantiality of the use
- the effect of the use on the actual and potential market for the work used

The definition of fair use is an evolving one, especially in the electronic environment. A key determinant, however, is the purpose of the use. According to the Copyright Act, fair use of a copyrighted work "for purposes such as criticism, comment, news reporting, teaching (including multiple copies for classroom use), scholarship, or research, is not an infringement of copyright."

Section 108, titled "Limitations on Exclusive Rights: Reproduction by Libraries and Archives," is a special section dealing with the duplication of materials by archives and libraries. It goes beyond Section 107, which applies to everyone copying a work.

According to Section 108, for an institution to copy a work without infringement, the institution

- must be open to the public or open to researchers in a specialized field
- must not be copying for a commercial purpose
- must include a notice of copyright in the copies produced

Having met these tests, an institution can copy certain works as outlined in Figure 9.4.[11]

Figure 9.4 Works for Which Copying Is Permissible

Nature of Work	Copies for	Considerations
Unpublished work	The institution itself	Copying permitted for preservation or security purposes.
Unpublished work	Another institution	Copying permitted for deposit for research use in another institution that is either open to the public or open to researchers in a specialized field.
Published work	The institution itself or another research institution	Copying permitted to replace a damaged, deteriorating, lost, or stolen work if an unused replacement cannot be found at a fair price.
Musical works, pictorial works, graphic works, sculptural works, motion pictures	The institution itself	Copying permitted only for preservation, security, or replacement of the work.
Published or unpublished work	Researcher or other user	Before proceeding, the institution should have a reasonable belief that the copy will be used for private study, scholarship, or research. The notice (discussed below) must be posted at the place where the institution accepts copy orders and on any order forms.

Procedures for Duplication for Researchers

Archives use two approaches to comply with researcher requests for copies. Some archives make the copies for the researchers. Other archives researchers make their own copies. In either case, the archives must make certain that they are protected from damages due to infringement of copyright.

If the archives makes copies for researchers, it is advisable to have the researcher complete a request form. This form should contain the warning printed in Figure 9.5. The warning also should be posted in the area where the archives accepts copying orders. By signing the request form, the researcher acknowledges that he or she is aware of copyright issues and has assumed responsibility for complying with them.

If an institution has an unsupervised photocopying machine that is made available to researchers, the institution may escape liability if the equipment displays a notice that copying may be subject to the copyright law. A basic step, therefore, is to make certain that all photocopy machines display the notice in Figure 9.5.

While these precautions may seem extreme, they are essential if an archives is to protect itself from liability resulting from a researcher's infringement of copyright.[12]

Figure 9.5 Warning from the Copyright Act of 1976

NOTICE
WARNING CONCERNING COPYRIGHT RESTRICTIONS

The copyright law of the United States (Title 17, United States Code) governs the making of photocopies and other reproductions of copyrighted material.

Under certain conditions specified in the law, libraries and archives are authorized to furnish a photocopy or other reproduction. One of these specified conditions is that the photocopy or reproduction is not to be "used for any purpose other than private study, scholarship or research." If a user makes a request for, or later uses, a photocopy or reproduction for purposes in excess of "fair use," that user may be liable for copyright infringement.

The institution reserves the right to refuse to accept a copying order if, in its judgment, fulfillment of the order would involve violation of copyright law.

OUTREACH AND PROMOTION

One of the most frustrating things for an archivist is to know that the collections have great research value, but that very few people are using them. Over the past decade, archivists have come to realize that outreach and promotion must be an integral part of archival work—not something done occasionally, as with an anniversary celebration.[13]

In an era of downsizing, rightsizing, reengineering, and plain-old-fashioned staff reductions, an unknown or underappreciated archives is likely to be closed. Outreach has moved from being an optional activity to one essential for survival.

Any outreach activity begins by defining the "publics" that the archives serves and the needs of those publics that the archives can meet. Defining publics depends on the nature of the organization of which the archives is a part. For example, North Fork University's Department of Archives and Special Collections defined the publics it served as follows:

- *NFU students.* The archive serves both undergraduate and graduate students, including all areas of the university.
- *NFU faculty.* While this includes all faculty, there will be a special emphasis on the needs of faculty in the university's areas of scholarly distinction: environmental studies and social work.
- *Alumni.* The NFU archives will try to use history as a way of keeping alumni connected with (and, the university hopes, contributing to) the university.
- *Local community.* NFU prides itself on its involvement with, and commitment to, the local community. NFU will try to make the resources of its archives available to all community members, not just to scholars.
- *News media.* NFU has defined new media, especially regional print and broadcast outlets, as an important group to serve.

An archives program in a different type of organization would have different publics to serve. State archives would define the citizens (and taxpayers) of the state as a key public. Archives in a religious congregation would serve the needs of members of the congregation. A small historical society might try to add services for genealogists and other family historians.

Once publics are defined, the archivist can design an outreach program that includes activities designed to meet their needs.

Among the activities typically used by archives are

- exhibits
- public performances
- newsletters
- presentations at meetings and conferences
- tours
- newspaper articles
- appearances on radio and television
- in-house receptions
- electronic publication on the World Wide Web

Many archives find that a volunteer friends group can help with outreach and promotion. Individuals interested enough in the archives to accept the title of "friend" are a special resource not to be underestimated. Friends can spread the word about the archives and its services, often to circles that the archives otherwise never would reach. The friends group also provides a sounding board and a feedback mechanism for assessing the effectiveness of public programs. Finally, friends can become "angels" (either through their own fundraising or by the pressure they bring to bear on institutional administrators) if funding of the archives becomes a source of contention.

The North Fork University Department of Archives and Special Collections realized it needed to improve outreach. In consultation with administrators, users, and other stakeholders (to use a term popular in the management literature), the archives developed the plan for outreach and promotion printed in Figure 9.6.

Any archivist involved with outreach and promotion activities usually asks: Are these activities effective? Are they worth the time and money I spend on them? Would my time be better spent elsewhere? At NFU, the archives is gathering information on a regular basis to help answer these questions. Everyone who calls or visits the archives, for example, is asked how they heard about the archives. Over time, the archives will be able to devote more resources to effective strategies and to design other strategies to replace those found to be less effective.

Figure 9.6 North Fork University Outreach and Promotion Audiences and Activities	
Target Audience	**Activity**
NFU students	Write a regular column in the student newspaper: "This Week in NFU History."
NFU faculty	Prepare packets of historical materials dealing with NFU during World War II for the U.S. History survey course.
Alumni	Prepare a historical calendar for next year that includes photographs from the NFU archives and key dates in NFU history.
Local community	Prepare a traveling exhibit on the environment of the North Fork. Try to get the local wineries to take turns displaying the exhibit.
News media	Prepare press releases each time a new collection is received or a closed collection is opened for research.

CONCLUSION

This chapter began with a discussion of the tension that arises in archives due to the sometimes-competing goals of preservation and use. Detailed policies and procedures, like those outlined above, are a means for archives to keep this tension from leading to anxiety and paralysis. Policies and procedures also provide a sound foundation for the more extensive outreach and promotion efforts that are so necessary for archival survival. As the next chapter discusses, reference and access—and, indeed, all archival activities—must face the challenge posed by electronic records.

NOTES

1. The best one-volume treatment of the subject is Mary Jo Pugh, *Providing Reference Services for Archives and Manuscripts* (Chicago: Society of American Archivists, 1992). See also Sue Holbert, *Archives and Manuscripts: Reference and Access* (Chicago: Society of American Archivists, 1977); and David R. Kepley, "Reference Service and Access," in James Gregory Bradsher, ed., *Managing Archives and Archival Institutions* (Chicago: University of Chicago Press, 1988), 161–173.

2. Lewis J. Bellardo and Lynn Lady Bellardo, compilers, *A Glossary for Archivists, Manuscript Curators, and Records Managers* (Chicago: Society of American Archivists, 1992).

3. Luciana Duranti believes that archivists in the United States overemphasize potential use of records. This overemphasis leads archivists to assign "value" to records based largely on anticipated use. According to Duranti, the search for value in appraisal has taken U.S. archivists away from their traditional role—one still practiced in the rest of the world—of impartial selector of archival documents. Luciana Duranti, "The Concept of Appraisal and Archival Theory," *American Archivist* 57 (spring 1994): 328–344.

4. Pugh, *Providing Reference Services,* 55–64.

5. This distinction comes from Trudy Huskamp Peterson, "Archival Principles and Records of the New Technology," *American Archivist* 47 (fall 1984): 383–393.

6. Elsie T. Freeman, "In the Eye of the Beholder: Archives Administration from the User's Point of View," *American Archivist* 47 (spring 1984): 111–123. See also Pugh, *Providing Reference Services,* 11–24.

7. For more information, see Pugh, *Providing Reference Services,* 25–39.

8. Pugh, *Providing Reference Services,* 68–77.

9. William Z. Nasri, "Copyright," *World Encyclopedia of Library and Information Services,* 3d ed., (Chicago: American Library Association, 1993), 228.

10. Pugh, *Providing Reference Services,* 82. For more information on copyright, see the Library of Congress' Web Site at http://www.loc.gov. See also a very helpful site at Stanford University—http://fairuse.standard.edu.

11. Adapted from Gary M. Peterson and Trudy Huskamp Peterson, *Archives and Manuscripts: Law* (Chicago: Society of American Archivists, 1985), 81–89. For a review of recent court decisions that indicate a move toward narrowing the provisions

of the Copyright Act, see Pugh, *Providing Reference Services,* 82–84.

12. For more information, see Pugh, *Providing Reference Services,* 79–91.

13. The best one-volume treatment is Elsie Freeman Finch, ed., *Advocating Archives: An Introduction to Public Relations for Archivists* (Metuchen, N.J.: Society of American Archivists and Scarecrow Press, 1994). Still useful is Ann E. Pederson and Gail Farr Casterline, *Archives and Manuscripts: Public Programs* (Chicago: Society of American Archivists, 1992). See also two articles in Bradsher, ed., *Managing Archives:* Kathleen Roe, "Public Programs," 218–227; and James Gregory Bradsher and Mary Lynn Ritzenthaler, "Archival Exhibits," 218–240.

10 ELECTRONIC RECORDS

Electronic information systems are much in the news these days. On the positive side are stories about the explosion of the Internet and the World Wide Web, the increasing power of personal computer hardware and software, and the ability of organizations to network their information sources effectively. On the negative side are stories about errors caused by defective computer chips, fear of the dehumanization of work, and the effects of such rapid changes on organizations and people.

"Buried in bulging files and stored in computers in doctors' offices, drug stores, insurance companies and hospitals is information on nearly everything that the health care profession has done to or prescribed for Americans in recent years. To some, the records are a gold mine. To others, they are a minefield.

"But one thing is certain: the material is being unearthed. Insurers, drug companies and large health maintenance organizations are mounting an extensive effort to use medical data to decide which treatments are best, which doctors are best and which health plans keep people healthiest."—*New York Times,* August 8, 1994.

Hollywood plays upon our greatest hopes and our deepest fears—as it has always done. In the 1950s we had giant crabs and other mutations caused by nuclear fallout. By contrast, in the summer of 1995 we had *The Net*, the tale of a computer expert systematically removed from all databases—effectively no longer existing.[1]

Moving from Hollywood to the real world, Peter G. Neumann published a book in 1995 called *Computer Related Risks*. The book chronicles hundreds of incidents involving computers and the risks of relying upon them.[2] Among the incidents Neumann reports are

- An $18.5 million Atlas-Agena rocket, launching what was intended to be the first satellite to fly by Venus, had to be destroyed when it went off course. Subsequent analysis showed that the computer flight plan was missing a hyphen that was a symbol for a particular formula (p. 26).
- The Voyager 1 mission lost data over a weekend because not all five printers were operational: four were configured improperly (including being off-line) and one had a paper jam (p. 29).

- A woman on trial in Dusseldorf, Germany, used as her defense that she had been the victim of a computer error. She had been erroneously informed that medical test results showed that she had incurable syphilis and had passed it on to her daughter and son. As a result, she strangled her 15-year-old daughter and attempted to kill her son and herself. The woman was acquitted (p. 71).
- A physician reported that a 99-year-old man in the emergency room had a highly abnormal white-blood-cell count that the computer reported as being within normal limits. The computer, it turns out, was reporting results for an infant, assuming that the birth year of "89" was 1989 rather than 1889 (p. 72).
- The Air Force sold as surplus more than 1,200 used digital tapes and almost 2,000 used analog tapes, many with sensitive data that had not been erased (p. 145).
- The confidential files of a federal prosecutor in Lexington, Kentucky, remained on disks of a broken computer sold to a used equipment dealer for $45. The data included sealed federal indictments and confidential employee data. (p. 145).
- An alleged cocaine dealer was released from Los Angeles County Jail in 1987 on the basis of a phony e-mail message ordering his release (p. 174).
- A Washington newspaper published computer records of video rentals by Supreme Court nominee Robert Bork (p. 186).
- Payroll printouts from a San Diego school accidentally wound up as Christmas giftwrap in a local store (p. 188).
- The names of 14 Americans were mistakenly carved on the Vietnam Memorial in Washington (p. 190).
- On July 18, 1989, actress Rebecca Schaeffer was murdered by an obsessed fan who traced her home address through computer records at the California Department of Motor Vehicles (p. 184).

As an archivist reading these and other examples, I was struck by one major "risk" that does not appear in Neumann's book: the risk of not being able to use information over time. The above instances deal with access to current information. What about the person who in 30 years cannot collect a pension because no system exists to read today's computerized payroll records? What about the municipality that cannot renovate a deteriorating bridge in the future because all the Computer Assisted Design (CAD) drawings were created on a proprietary system by a vendor long defunct? What about an ill person whose digital X-rays deteriorated in an improper storage environment and are now unreadable for comparison with current images?

These and similar questions worry archivists who are already dealing with electronic records. Fulfilling the archival mission—identifying, preserving, and making records available—may have to change in this new environment. In the next few years, more and more archives will have to determine how they will face the challenge of electronic records. To offer some guidance, this chapter will have two sections:

- the nature of the problem
- the outline of a solution

Archival thinking, especially on the second point, is evolving. Research studies now under way may change the future approach of archivists.[3] But for now, the following sections summarize the way leading archivists are defining the problem and trying to solve it.

THE NATURE OF THE PROBLEM

Electronic records are more than information on a new medium—they are not the same old product in a "new and improved" package. Rather, there are dramatic shifts in the nature of the records themselves. Figure 10.1 summarizes these shifts.

At the heart of these changes is the following: paper records are tangible things, while electronic records are often evolving processes. Different versions of electronic records appear and disappear. Managers now make decisions based on snapshots of information combining text, data, and image. At a very basic level, it is even unclear when, if ever, a "record" appears.

We can begin to see the shape of an electronic records spiral—some would call it a tornado. This spiral is gaining speed as a number of factors swirl around one another:

- cheaper information technology
- decentralized information systems
- downsized, leaner organizations
- process redesign and workflow improvements, especially among office workers

Figure 10.1 Shifts Caused by Electronic Records[4]		
From	**To**	**Explanation**
Physical entities	Logical entities	We can no longer identify records from their physical characteristics.
Linear documents	Nonlinear documents (hypermedia)	Documents are composed of images (still and moving), sound, and data—as well as text. These elements are combined in different ways by individual users.
Centralized information	Decentralized information	Not only are central paper files disappearing, but the control offered by mainframe computing environments is diminishing.
Time and space dependent	Time and space independent	To use a record, a person previously had to go to the office when it was open. People have access to electronic documents at any time of the day and from almost any location (including the beach).
Vertical flow of organizational information	Horizontal flow of organizational information	Centralized files and reporting systems were designed to filter information, and reduce its volume, as it moved up the organizational hierarchy. Electronic document systems promote "organizational information democracy" by permitting direct access to a wider range of information sources.

Into this vortex goes the archivist, often the only person in an organization concerned about long-term storage of and access to information.[5] The archivist's challenge is not only the records, but the organizations that are changing as well.

DEFINITION OF RECORD

In previous chapters of this book, identifying records seemed very straightforward. Since information was expensive to record (and duplicate) manually, organizations controlled what was recorded and were concerned about the information once it was committed to writing. With computers so plentiful, there is much more organizational flotsam and jetsam for the archivist to sift. We can no longer assume that, just because something is recorded, the value of the information is reflected by the cost of recording.

There is even more confusion because terms like "document," "data," and "information" are used differently in various information professions. For the archivist, these terms have a very clear relationship to one another as outlined in Figure 10.2.

Figure 10.2 From Data to Archives

Term	Meaning
Data	Content
Information	Data communicated or received
Document	Information in context
Record	Document preserved
Archives	Document preserved for enduring value

In both electronic and paper environments, a *record* has three characteristics:

- *Content*. That which conveys information (text, data, symbols, numerals, images, sound, and vision).
- *Structure*. The appearance and arrangement of the content (relationships between fields, entities, language, style, fonts, page and paragraph breaks, links, and other editorial devices).
- *Context*. The background information that enhances understanding of technical and business environments to

which the records relate (application software, link to function or activity, provenance information).[6]

An *archival* record is one preserved because of its enduring value. In preserving electronic records, the archivist must make certain that context and structure—as well as content—are accessible over time. Content alone is virtually useless.

This discussion of what is or is not a record in the electronic environment may seem esoteric. In fact, it has very practical applications—just ask Oliver North and Manuel Noriega. One of the central issues in a recent court case, *Armstrong* v. *Executive Office of the President* (nicknamed the "PROFS Case" after the Professional Office System that was in use) is whether or not electronic mail from the Reagan and Bush administrations is a federal record.[7] Documents from this e-mail system were used in the investigations of the Iran-Contra affair and Manuel Noriega.

In August 1993, the U.S. Court of Appeals ruled that electronic mail records were not the equivalent of extra copies of paper records. Furthermore, printouts of e-mail records are not sufficient for preservation unless the context and structure, as well as the content, are preserved.[8]

So, when do we have a record in the electronic environment? David Bearman defines a record as a document created to *conduct a transaction*, deliberately preserved as evidence of that transaction. A transaction can be between two people, between one person and a source of data (like a database), or between two sources of data. Furthermore, the organization, not individual employees, determines what should be preserved.[9]

The changing nature of records has led to a new role that archivists are only now beginning to assume. The job description for this new archivist includes the following responsibilities:

- being involved in the design of electronic systems
- making sure investments in records and information systems are worthwhile
- ensuring that organizations maintain accountability through the protection of their evidence captured in transactional records
- focusing on the organizationally created information that gives evidence of the organization's activities
- Helping creators of electronic records to maintain them, rather than taking custody of all records.

The last point, in particular, is somewhat controversial. The traditional archival approach to records on any medium is to take custody of the records in order to guarantee their preservation and access. Some archival repositories, notably the U.S. National Archives and Records Administration, are using this approach with electronic records—they will take custody of and responsibility for electronic records of enduring value. Other archival repositories, including the Australian Archives, have taken another approach. They are working with the creators of electronic records to assure preservation and access over time in the agencies themselves. In this case, the archives does not take custody of the electronic records. David Bearman and Margaret Hedstrom have labeled this shift in thinking a change from a "rowing mentality" to a "steering mentality."[10] So, the definition of not just record—but also the definition of the record keeper—is changing.

STORAGE MEDIA

Archivists are quite concerned about storage media for electronic records. Will information, once captured, last as long as needed? Is there anything archivists can do to address the fragility of storage media?

A recent study by the National Media Laboratory (NML) in St. Paul, Minnesota, highlighted the problems with magnetic tape used for audio and video recording as well as for electronic records.[11] NML's best projection, based on current research, is that physical lifetimes for digital magnetic tapes are at least 10 to 20 years, "a value commensurate with the practical life of the digital recording technology."

The study pointed out, however, that media life expectancies are like miles per gallon ratings on automobiles—your actual results may vary. In particular, life expectancy is highly dependent on media storage conditions. Controlled temperature and humidity will increase media life expectancies. A National Institute of Standards and Technology (NIST) publication recommended that magnetic tape be stored at 65 degrees Fahrenheit (plus or minus 3 degrees) and 40 percent relative humidity (plus or minus 5 percent).[12]

Optical media are another storage option. There are erasable and nonerasable optical disk sizes up to 14 inches. To date, however, optical media have not been subjected to the same independent testing as magnetic media. As a result, there is no way to prove or disprove manufacturers' claims for life expectancy. It clearly is a case of *caveat emptor*.

Optical media, particularly CD-ROMs, *are* being used as a *transfer medium* for electronic records, if not a preservation medium. The U.S. National Archives, for example, will accept electronic records on CD-ROM; NARA then transfers the information to magnetic media for storage and preservation.

SYSTEM DEPENDENCE

A bigger problem than the longevity of the physical media is the dependence on hardware and software that soon will be obsolete; technological obsolescence of digital recording systems is a greater concern than medium longevity. Scientists at the NML have concluded that "technological obsolescence of digital recording systems is a challenge for those individuals tasked with preserving digital archives. Digital archives should be transcribed every 10 to 20 years to ensure that they will not become technologically obsolete. To realize lifetimes greater than this, one would be required to archive the recording system, system software, operating system, computer hardware, operations manuals, and ample spare parts along with the recorded media."[13] According to NML, the physical life of digital magnetic media may well exceed the lifetime of the recording technology.

A "problem, of course, is that electronic data can't be retrieved without the appropriate machine. And as new equipment replaces old, the capacity to review information that was stored in some outdated system may be lost. The only remaining machine in the United States that can read some census data from the early 1960s is literally a museum piece; it has been retied to the Smithsonian Institution."—*Newsday,* March 11, 1985.

An example of the problem is the 1960 U.S. federal census. In 1975 the National Archives learned that the Census Bureau still had 7,297 reels of tape readable only on a Univac II-A tape drive. The staff of the National Archives reviewed the files and determined that seven series, on 642 reels of tape, had enduring value. By this time, however, the Univac II-A drives were obsolete, thus presenting a major engineering challenge. The Census Bureau ultimately was successful in copying the tapes, though it took four years and a great deal of effort to do so.[14]

INTEGRITY OF RECORDS OVER TIME

A third issue to consider with electronic records is how will we know that the electronic records we use in the future have not been altered in some way? Archivists are concerned about this question since they are likely to be the individuals accountable for the integrity of the records over time.

"A conflict between a New York State prison regulation requiring that inmates be photographed clean-shaven and a religious belief that a man's beard must not be touched was resolved in Federal court yesterday through the latest computer technology.

"For the first time, New York State accepted a computer-generated image of what an inmate, in this case [a rabbi], would look like without a beard instead of making him shave for a conventional photograph. The state requires that a bearded inmate be photographed shaven so that he can be more easily identified if he escapes and shaves off his beard."
—*New York Times,* December 29, 1994.

Captain James T. Kirk faced this issue on the starship *Enterprise*. In an episode called "The Court Martial," Kirk is on trial for causing the death of a crew member, Ben Finney—who also happens to be the ship's records officer. The principal evidence against Kirk is the log of the *Enterprise,* an electronic record including full-motion images and sound. After the damning evidence is played in court, Kirk exclaims, "But that's not the way it happened!" The rest of the episode involves testing the integrity of the electronic records system, with some surprising results.[15]

Researchers using archival records were concerned about integrity long before there were electronic records. Researchers talk of two kinds of validity:

- *External validity.* Is this what it purports to be?
- *Internal validity.* Is the information accurate?

The famous Hitler diaries of a few years ago were tested for external validity, with experts concluding that they may have belonged to Joe or Jim Hitler, but certainly not Adolf. Questionable internal validity means that a record is what it purports to be (a Civil War diary, for example) but the specific information (on the course of a battle) is just plain wrong as verified from other sources.

How will we test internal and external validity of electronic records? Researchers are working on encryption and other devices to reassure anxious customers and clients. If these approaches prove successful, the archivist will inherit yet another layer of complexity in preserving records. Not only must we preserve hardware and software, but we must also preserve the encryption scheme (and the ability to read it) indefinitely. During the 1960s, a popular phrase was "You're either part of the solution or part of the problem." In the world of electronic records, a solution can become part of another problem.[16]

OUTLINE OF A SOLUTION

How are archivists reacting to all of the challenges outlined above? As noted earlier in this chapter, promising solutions are only now being developed and tested. Unlike other archival areas discussed in this book—arrangement, for example—where methods have been tested for decades and even centuries, dealing with electronic records is a work-in-progress. At the moment, the following two approaches seem to hold the greatest potential:

- formulating policy
- identifying system design requirements

FORMULATING POLICY

Policy statements were discussed earlier in this book—as part of acquisitions and reference services. In these cases, policy statements were part of building a consensus and offering consistent services. This also is true of electronic records.

With electronic records, however, policy statements are even more important. Without a policy defining electronic records and authorizing the archivist to intervene, it is extremely difficult for an archivist to have an impact on the electronic records of the organization; there are just too many other sources of power within the organization for the archivist to do battle alone.

In general, electronic records policies should

- be generalizable to the range of departments and problems being addressed
- pose clear alternatives with sufficient basis to support judgments
- be implementable, flexible, and cost effective

David Bearman outlines the issues associated with electronic records that require policy formulation and determination; these issues, and brief explanations, are summarized in Figure 10.3.

Figure 10.3 Policy Issues Associated with Electronic Records[17]	
Policy Issue	**Requirement**
Defining record and nonrecord	Define these concepts clearly enough so they can be implemented by people and systems.
Assigning responsibility	Identify which organizational entities have what specific responsibilities for management of electronic records.
Adjusting to cultural change	Accommodate shifting behaviors and attitudes, as well as changing technologies.
Assuring legality	Require the organization to take actions that will safeguard the legality of the electronic record.
Scheduling for disposition	Ensure the retention of records for only as long as required by law, organizational objectives, and research needs.
Appraising for enduring value	Be able to identify and preserve archival electronic records.
Integrating access	Require actions that prevent different formats of records from being a serious barrier to access.
Documenting	Require consistent methods of describing records from their creation to their destruction, for intellectual control and documentation purposes.
Storing	State who will have physical custody of archival electronic records.
Preserving media	Establish standards for care and storage of electronic records, and address the basis upon which storage media decisions are to be made.
Preserving functionality	Define to what extent original functionality is to be replicated or documented when migration of data and systems are necessary to ensure continuing access.
Ensuring security	Protect electronic information and preserve the rights of individuals and the confidentiality required of the organization.
Providing for use	Dictate how the organization and others entitled to access will be enabled to use electronic records.
Controlling costs	Address how the organization will avoid unnecessary costs and target essential expenditures in the management of electronic records.

To show how policies are formed, let's return to North Fork University. Since NFU is a progressive institution, it has begun to address the policy issues identified by Bearman. A particularly contentious issue was assigning responsibilities in the area of electronic records. After much debate, the NFU electronic records policy assigned responsibilities to staff in the three major areas shown in Figure 10.4.

Figure 10.4 North Fork University Staff Responsibliities for Electronic Records[18]	
Functional Area	**Responsibilities**
NFU Archivist	• Participate in planning for information systems and in reviewing their implementation to ensure that all electronic records are appraised and scheduled. • Review existing information systems to ensure that disposition of records in the system has been authorized. • Oversee implementation of disposition instructions.
Department heads, managers, and supervisors	• Determine what information is needed to support the program or administrative function. • Identify the applications supported by automated systems by describing their purposes, informational content, and the main stages through which the data flow. • Work with the NFU Archivist to formulate retention periods for their electronic records.
Information systems manager	• Identify all program and administrative activities that use or need electronic records systems. • Ensure that information in electronic form is protected, preserved, and accessible for its full retention period. • Implement authorized disposition instructions for electronic records maintained centrally.

There are numerous other examples of policies for various types of electronic records. Many of these policies are available on the World Wide Web:

- The Department of Defense, interim policy for electronic records management: http://www.dtic.dla.mil/c3i/recmgmt.html
- National Institute of Standards and Technology, digital signature standard: http://csrc.ncsl.nist.gov/fips/fips186.txt
- State of Florida, electronic mail policy: http://florida3.dos.state.fl.us/sos/divisions/dlis/barm/email.htm

- Australian Archives, "Keeping Electronic Records: Policy for Electronic Recordkeeping in the Commonwealth Government": http://www.aa.gov.au/AA_WWW_/Issues/KER/keepinger.html
- Commonwealth of Pennsylvania, "Electronic Records Management": Management Directive No. 210.10 Commonwealth of Pennsylvania, Governor's Office, issued November 15, 1994.
- State of Texas, "Standards and Procedures for Electronic Records of State Agencies," Administrative Rules of the Texas State Library and Archives Commission: Texas Administrative Code, Title 13, Chapter 6
- U.S. National Archives and Records Administration, various policies on electronic records and electronic mail: http://www.nara.gov

One thing these policies have in common is a requirement to use national and international *standards* as part of electronic records systems. For example, the management directive issued by the Commonwealth of Pennsylvania requires that electronic records systems "provide a standard interchange format, when necessary, to permit the exchange of documents on electronic media using different software/operating systems and allow for the conversion or migration of documents on electronic media from one system to another."

Archivists have been among the leading advocates for standard approaches rather than proprietary vendor solutions. The long-term nature of the archival enterprise gives the profession a much different view from that held by those enamored with the latest software or hardware product. In the words of Carol King and Gerry Goffin, archivists always are asking an electronic records system "Will you still love me tomorrow?"

The reason archivists advocate standards is that standards promote *interoperability* and *portability*. Interoperability means that different information systems can function together as a cohesive unit. Portability means that information can be carried to and used on different hardware and software platforms.

Standards develop in two ways. In some cases, a standard-setting organization—such as the American National Standards Institute (ANSI) in the United States or the International Organization for Standardization (ISO)—establishes criteria to which manufacturers and system designers adhere. These are called *de jure* standards. In other cases, a vendor product controls such a large market share that it becomes a *de facto* standard—Microsoft Windows, for instance.

While the list of applicable standards is growing all the time, archivists should be particularly aware of the following standards:

- *ASCII* (American Standard Code for Information Interchange). Used for text files.
- *JPEG* (Joint Photographics Expert Group). A standard for still image compression.
- *OSI* (Open Systems Interconnect). Networking standards for computer communication.
- *SGML* (Standard Generalized Markup Language). A system of tags used for electronic publishing.
- *SQL* (Structured Query Language). The most common database language.
- *TCP/IP* (Transmission Control Protocol/Internet Protocol). The communications standard that is the backbone of the Internet.
- *TIFF* (Tag Image File Format). A standard for graphic files, especially in desktop publishing programs.

Requiring that these and other standards be incorporated into electronic records systems is the best guarantee of interoperability and portability over time.[19]

IDENTIFYING SYSTEM DESIGN REQUIREMENTS

While policy statements and standards are *necessary* for an electronic records program, they are not *sufficient* to assure the preservation of electronic records of enduring value. Archivists are trying to find ways to fulfill the responsibility of being involved in the design of electronic records systems.

One of the more promising approaches is being developed at the University of Pittsburgh School of Information Sciences under the direction of Richard Cox. The Pittsburgh project is funded by the National Historical Publications and Records Commission (NHPRC), a division of the National Archives and Records Administration.

The goal of the project is to develop "recordkeeping functional requirements" that can be used to evaluate the recordkeeping aspects of electronic records systems. These requirements can either be integrated into software design or prescribed via organizational policy or government legislation.[20]

The concept of a "recordkeeping system" is critical to the research. Such systems do not just contain reusable data; rather they link the information contained in the system to the transactions documented. As defined by the Pittsburgh project, recordkeeping systems capture, maintain, and access evidence of transactions over time as required by the jurisdiction of implementation and according to common organizational practices. Recordkeeping systems support functions of the organization. These functions require records of transactions in order to continue daily operations, satisfy administrative and legal requirements, and maintain accountability. The functional requirements define records as a portion of all information sources. They provide strategies to control—through definition, policy, regulation, and technical applications—the flood of electronic information.

As noted above, recordkeeping systems must function in three broad areas: capture records, maintain records, and access records. These broad areas are similar to statements about the record "life cycle" discussed earlier in this book. With electronic records, archivists can no longer wait until the near end of the life cycle to address retention considerations; this must be done even before "capture"—at the system design stage.

The functional requirements are summarized in Figure 10.5.

Based on these functional requirements, the University of Pittsburgh project staff developed two other documents:

- *Production rules.* Borrowing a technique from the field of artificial intelligence, the staff developed formal language so that each requirement would be recognizable when implemented and testable as part of a system. The production rules are designed to be unambiguous, precise, consistent, and measurable.
- *Metadata specifications.* Metadata are defined as "data about data"; they provide information about system context, structure, and context. Metadata created and captured in a standardized way will facilitate the identification and migration of records over time.

These functional requirements are already being tested under subsequent NHPRC grants to Indiana University and the City of Philadelphia.

Indiana University

Indiana University is attempting to determine what works and what does not in the context of a large university system. They are also looking to see what additions, if any, must be made to the functional requirements and metadata specifications. The project is a collaboration among the Indiana University Archives, University Computing Services, Financial Management Services, and other administrative areas of the university. The project is divided into six stages:

Figure 10.5 Functional Requirements for Evidence in Recordkeeping Developed at the University of Pittsburgh[21]

Main Category	Subcategory	Explanation
Conscientious organization	1. Compliant	Organizations must comply with the legal and administrative requirements for recordkeeping within the jurisdictions in which they operate, and they must demonstrate awareness of best practices for the industry or business sector to which they belong and the business functions in which they are engaged.
Accountable recordkeeping system	2. Responsible	Recordkeeping systems must have accurately documented policies, assigned responsibilities, and formal methodologies for their management.
Accountable recordkeeping system	3. Implemented	Recordkeeping systems must be employed at all times in the normal course of business.
Accountable recordkeeping system	4. Consistent	Recordkeeping systems must process information in a fashion that assures that the records they create are credible.
Captured records	5. Comprehensive	Records must be created for all business transactions.
Captured records	6. Identifiable	Records must be bounded by linkage to a transaction that uses all the data in the record and only that data.
Captured records	7. Complete	Records must contain the content, structure, and context generated by the transaction they document.
	7a. Accurate	The content of records must be quality controlled at input to ensure that information in the system correctly reflects what was communicated in the transaction.
	7b. Understandable	The relationship between elements of information content must be represented in a way that supports their intended meaning.
	7c. Meaningful	The contextual linkages of records must carry information necessary to understand correctly the transactions that created and used them.

Figure 10.5 (cont.)

Main Category	Subcategory	Explanation
Captured records	8. Authorized	An authorized records creator must have originated all records.
Maintained records	9. Preserved	Records must continue to reflect content, structure, and context within any systems by which the records are retained over time.
	9a. Inviolate	Records are protected from accidental or intended damage or destruction and from any modification.
	9b. Coherent	The information content and structure of records must be retained in reconstructible relations.
	9c. Auditable	Record context represents all processes in which records participated.
Maintained records	10. Removable	Records content and structure supporting the meaning of content must be deletable.
Usable records	11. Exportable	It must be possible to transmit records to other systems without loss of information.
Usable records	12. Accessible	It must be possible to output record content, structure, and context.
	12a. Available	Records must be available.
	12b. Renderable	Records must display, print, or be abstractly represented as they originally appeared at the time of creation and initial receipt.
	12c. Evidential	Record's representations must reflect the context of the creation and use of the records.
Usable records	13. Redactable	Records must be masked when it is necessary to deliver censored copies, and the version as released must be documented in a linked transaction.

- goal setting, orientation, and training
- functional analysis and appraisal
- identification and analysis of existing record systems
- incorporation of functional requirements into the metadata repository
- implementing "accountable systems"
- evaluation

The project staff plans to produce the following products: a repository information model, record policy statements, retention schedules for financial and student information resources, specifications for new datasets or other digital objects, design specifications for capturing financial and student records, procedures for assessing and preserving financial and student records over time, and a metadata repository system incorporating archival requirements and linked to the records.[22]

City of Philadelphia

The Philadelphia Department of Records is testing the applicability of the Pittsburgh metadata requirements to the design of several large-scale municipal information systems. To carry out the project, the city formed a cross-disciplinary Electronic Records Group (ERG) drawn from the Records Management Division of the Department of Records, the Mayor's Office of Information Services, and Management Information Systems personnel from municipal government agencies now developing new, electronic information systems. The prototype application will be the Human Resources Information System being developed by the city's Personnel Department. Once refined, metadata elements will be incorporated into additional information systems.[23]

SUGGESTIONS FOR THE PRACTICAL ARCHIVIST

While there is much research in progress on electronic records, what is the practical archivist to do in the meantime? Following are some suggestions for the archivist who must begin to deal with electronic records *now*.

SUGGESTIONS FOR ORGANIZATIONS

An organization interested in improving the management and preservation of electronic records should do the following:

- Issue a policy that defines electronic records and gives the archivist responsibility for their preservation.
- Establish rules for naming files and labeling disks and other digital media.
- Assemble system documentation and plan for its preservation.
- Let software and hardware vendors know that the management of electronic documents is important. Take this into account when choosing potential vendors and products.

SUGGESTIONS FOR INDIVIDUALS

Archivists who raise the consciousness of individuals are often asked to provide specific guidance to employees. The following are suggestions that an archivist can propose to individuals within the organization:

- Attach meaningful descriptions to documents, if permitted by the software. At a minimum, fill in author and subject matter.
- Record information about each document created. This record will make it easier to match electronic and paper documents.
- Back up document storage media regularly, preferably storing one copy off-site.
- If documents are stored in compressed format, retain the software required to expand documents to their original formats. Ensure that later versions of the compression software can still expand documents stored previously. The same considerations apply to encrypted documents.
- Only use password protection on documents when it is really necessary, and ensure that there is always someone else who knows the password.
- Be particularly careful when storing compound documents (documents that incorporate information in different formats such as spreadsheets, databases, and images). All applications required to recreate the document must be maintained.
- As a last resort, print out paper copies of historically valuable documents and add them to regular files.[24]

STEPS FOR THE ARCHIVIST TO FOLLOW

Once an archivist is asked to assist a department with managing electronic records, what steps should be followed? Is there a proven strategy for identifying electronic records of value and designing systems to assure their preservation?

The following methodology was drawn from several sources and reflects best practices at the moment:

- *Conduct a preliminary investigation.* Profile the purpose of the department, its structure, the legal and regulatory environment, and any critical factors associated with recordkeeping.
- *Analyze business functions and activities.* Identify each business function, activity, or transaction. Establish a hierarchy of business functions, document the flow of business processes, and the transactions that they comprise.
- *Identify recordkeeping requirements.* Determine requirements for evidence, records retention, and other factors that will have an impact on recordkeeping systems.
- *Review existing recordkeeping systems.* Use interviews and analyze system documentation to determine the systems used and the records produced that support each business function.
- *Design improvements to recordkeeping systems.* Working with information systems professionals and endusers, determine how the three elements of the record (content, structure, and context) will be captured and retained over time.
- *Implement improvements to recordkeeping systems.* Make the improvements, keeping in mind the underlying business processes that create the records.
- *Review and evaluate.* Monitor the performance of the recordkeeping system to be certain it is functioning as planned.[25]

CONCLUSION

System design has always been *important* for recordkeeping systems. With electronic records, it has become *essential*. A partnership between records creators and archivists is the only thing that makes it *possible*. Like it or not, archivists of the future will have to spend as much time on this partnership as they spend on appraisal, arrangement, and other archival functions.

This book began with a letter from Clyde Champion Barrow praising one technology, the Model T, and ends with an international perspective on another technology, the computer. Archivists should keep this link in mind as they approach the preservation of records, especially those in electronic form. Until Henry Ford standardized automobile production in the Model T, both manufacturers and consumers were involved in a pioneering effort. Today, we near the threshold when digital records will have standardized content, structure, and context—embedded in metadata—that enable their low-cost capture and preservation. Barrow praised the Model T because of its "sustained speed and freedom from trouble." Isn't this also our hope for a practical system to preserve digital archives?

NOTES

1. Computer records have played central roles in other fictional works. For example, Michael Crichton's *Rising Sun* hinges on the alteration of a digital video image. Also, Tom Clancy's *Debt of Honor* includes an attack on the world financial order through its computer system.

2. Peter G. Neumann, *Computer Related Risks* (New York: Addison-Wesley, 1995). Neumann collected the anecdotes as moderator of an Internet newsgroup, the "Forum on Risks to the Public in the Use of Computers and Related Systems."

3. The National Historical Publications and Records Commission has funded major electronic records research projects at the University of Pittsburgh, the New York State Archives and Records Administration, Indiana University, the City of Philadelphia, and other institutions. Research on electronic media is taking place at the Image Permanence Institute (Rochester Institute of Technology) and the National Media Laboratory in St. Paul, Minnesota.

For a summary of the archival literature, see Nancy McGovern and Tom Ruller, compilers, "Electronic Records Bibliography," available from the University of Michigan's Web site: http://www.si.umich.

4. This information is summarized from Charles M. Dollar, *Archival Theory and Information Technologies: The Impact of Information Technologies on Archival Principles and Methods* (Macerata, Italy: University of Macerata, 1992).

5. Long-term is, of course, a relative term. Information systems professionals believe they are addressing long-term needs when they plan information storage for a year or two.

6. This information is taken from "Keeping Electronic Records: Policy for Electronic Recordkeeping in the Commonwealth Government," published by the Australian Archives and available from their World Wide Web site: http://www.aa.gov.au/.

7. The best discussion of the archival issues in this case is David Bearman, "The Implications of *Armstrong v. the Executive Office of the President* for the Archival Management of Electronic Records," *American Archivist* 56 (fall 1993): 674–689.

8. For an interesting perspective on the case, see Tom Blanton, ed., *White House E-Mail: The Top Secret Computer Messages the Reagan/Bush White House Tried to Destroy* (New York: Free Press, 1995).

9. The issue is likely to remain alive for a couple of hundred more years. In an episode of *Star Trek: The Next Generation,* Captain Jean-Luc Picard receives a transmission from another starship captain informing him of a suspected conspiracy within the Federation. The transmission is made using Star Fleet's most secure channel and the computer is instructed not to make a record of it. The episode, "Conspiracy," was first aired the week of May 8, 1988.

10. David Bearman and Margaret Hedstrom, "Reinventing Archives for Electronic Records: Alternative Service Delivery Options," in Margaret Hedstrom, ed., *Electronic Records Management Program Strategies* (Pittsburgh: Archives and Museum Informatics, 1993), 82–98.

11. John W. C. Van Bogart, *Magnetic Tape Storage and Handling: A Guide for Libraries and Archives* (Washington, D.C.: Commission on Preservation and Access, 1995).

12. Taken from a John Van Bogart letter to the editor of *Scientific American* written in response to an article in the January 1995 issue (Jeff Rothenberg, "Ensuring the Longevity of Digital Documents") which indicated that the physical lifetime of magnetic tape was only one to two years.

13. Van Bogart letter to *Scientific American.*

14. Narrative written by Margaret O. Adams of the National Archives and Records Administration, posted to the Electronic Records Listserv (ERECS-L) on April 15, 1996.

15. The episode was first aired on February 2, 1967.

16. For more on the challenges of electronic records, see "Archival Issues Raised by Information Stored in Electronic Form," a position statement issued by the Society of American Archivists in 1995; David Bearman, ed., *Archival Management of Electronic Records* (Pittsburgh, Pa.: Archives and Museum Informatics, 1991); "Archives and Electronic Records," a special issue of the *Bulletin of the American Society for Information Science* 20 (October/ November 1993): 9–26; and Paul Conway, *Preservation in the Digital World* (Washington, D.C.: Commission on Preservation and Access, 1996).

17. David Bearman, "Electronic Records Guidelines: A Manual for Policy Development and Implementation," in Bearman, *Electronic Evidence,* 72–116. Reprinted with permission.

18. Adapted from *Managing Electronic Records* (Washington, D.C.: National Archives and Records Administration, 1990).

19. For more on standards see Bearman, *Electronic Evidence*, 210–220.

20. This summary is based on an interim report that Richard Cox and other members of the team presented at the 1994 annual meeting of the Society of American Archivists (available from Richard Cox). See also "Functional Requirements for Recordkeeping," in Bearman, *Electronic Evidence,* 294–304.

21. The latest version of the functional requirements can be found on the University of Pittsburgh's Web site: http://www.sis.pitt.edu/~nhprc. Reprinted with permission.

22. See the Indiana University Web site: http://www.indiana.edu/~libarche/.

23. Mark Giguere, "Philadelphia Electronic Records Project: Phase I Update," *The Philadelphia Record* (fall 1995), 9–10. Another NHPRC-funded project was conducted at the New York State Archives and Records Administration. Called "Building Partnerships," the final report and working papers can be found at: http://www. sara.nysed.gov/pubs/build.htm. Archivists also should monitor research on digital libraries funded by the National Science Foundation and other sources. A starting point is the Web site of the University of Michigan's School of Information Studies: http://http2.si.umich.edu.

24. These hints are adapted from Commonwealth of Australia, "Draft Guidelines for Managing Electronic Documents in Australian Government Agencies," prepared by the Electronic Data

Management Subcommittee of the Information Exchange Steering Committee, February 1995, http://www.adfa.oz.au/.

25. Australian Archives, "Keeping Electronic Records: Policy for Electronic Recordkeeping in the Commonwealth Government," http://www.aa.gov.au/. See also Indiana University Web site: http://www.indiana.edu/~libarche/. For a report on a test that followed a similar methodology, see William E. Landis and Robert Royce, "Recommendations for an Electronic Records Management System: A Case Study of a Small Business," *Archival Issues* 20 (1995), 7–21.

APPENDIX A
NORTH FORK UNIVERSITY: INSTITUTIONAL BACKGROUND

INTRODUCTION

North Fork University (NFU) is a private institution founded in 1892. It is located on the rural North Fork of Long Island approximately 15 miles west of the Orient Point lighthouse. It is the only institution of higher education on the entire North Fork.

THE AREA

The North Fork of Long Island is known for its tranquil country environment and New England-like lifestyle. Once an area dominated by large farms growing potatoes and other vegetables, it is now on the verge of potentially major changes. In place of the potato farms are an increasing number of world-class vineyards, drawn by the similarity of the North Fork's climate to that of the wine-growing regions of France. In recent years another traditional industry, fishing, has been hurt by the pollution of local waterways.

While much of the North Fork remains undeveloped, there is increasing pressure to speed the pace of change. On one side of the debate are developers and their allies, who see great opportunities for profit in the broad expanses of the North Fork. On the other side are environmentalists and long-term residents who fear that the North Fork will become as crowded as the South Fork, sacrificing its distinctive lifestyle and culture in the process.

In spite of, or perhaps because of, these challenges, the North Fork retains a strong sense of history. A friendly rivalry exists between Southold (on the North Fork) and Southampton (on the South Fork) over which town was settled earlier (ca. 1640). The North Fork has several small local historical societies, but no one institution preserves the overall history of the area. There also is a strong community of genealogists living on the North Fork.

THE INSTITUTION

North Fork University is located on 200 acres bordering the Long Island Sound. It is a resident campus with an enrollment of over 3,000 full- and part-time students.

In addition to undergraduate programs, NFU offers masters degrees in public administration, social work, journalism, and environmental studies. Most of the North Fork's leaders in these four areas are graduates of NFU. In addition, NFU's graduates hold positions of national and international importance, especially in the area of environmental studies.

NFU is known for its involvement with the local community. Faculty and administrators have provided expertise and support to local groups concerned with environmental issues. The School of Social Work runs a nationally renowned program of assistance to migrant workers who toil on the farms and vineyards of the island. This program is also known for the active participation of both graduate and undergraduate students.

As one might expect, the university's two major intercollegiate sports are crew and sailing. These programs attract student athletes from across the nation.

ARCHIVES AND MANUSCRIPTS AT NFU

North Fork University has a Department of Archives and Special Collections located within the library. The archives was founded two years ago, largely through the initiative of the new president, Dr. Mary Swanson, who was appointed at that time. Dr. Swanson was born and raised on the North Fork, studied at Harvard and Cambridge, and had a distinguished career as a political scientist at the University of North Carolina before returning to Long Island.

The archives is located on the second floor of the library. In addition to areas for work and research, the archives has shelving that can accommodate approximately 500 cubic feet of records. Half of the shelving is now full.

As a recently established department, the archives has a considerable backlog of materials awaiting processing. The shelves contain both archival records (materials generated or received by the parent institution in the normal course of business) and special collections (records generated by other institutions, or papers generated by individuals and families).

The Department of Archives and Special Collections has been receiving favorable publicity, both on campus and off. Both the student newspaper and alumni quarterly have carried articles about the archives. In addition, *Newsday*, the local newspaper, featured the archives on the cover of Part II and the local cable television channel had an extensive report on "News 12 Long Island." Much of this interest was generated by the anniversary celebrations held by Southold and Southampton to commemorate their 1640 foundings.

As a result of all this publicity, the archives has been inundated with offers to donate materials. On-campus offices as well as alumni from across the country, have contacted the archives about donating NFU records. The campus has never had a records management program, so there is a considerable volume of inactive records taking up valuable space in the various offices. Many campus officials, eyeing the empty shelves in the archives, see this as a solution to their space problems. The alumni, in turn, care deeply about NFU and its history. Some have been holding materials, particularly records of the student organizations in which they were involved, since they left the university—until two years ago, the university itself never seemed committed to its history. Several former faculty members also have inquired about donating their papers to the archives.

The local community seems to have been energized by the formation of the archives. A wide variety of organizations and institutions (fraternal, business, social welfare, environmental) have said that they now see NFU as the logical place to donate their records. The same is true of several prominent individuals who live on the North Fork.

While most of the community is supporting NFU's efforts in archives and special collections, the university has heard some grumbling from the local historical societies and their supporters, who feel left out of the process to date and fear NFU's competition for local history collections.

The Department of Archives and Special Collections has two full-time professional archivists, one clerical assistant, and the possibility for student assistants. The department has a reasonable though modest budget for supplies and equipment. The department does use personal computers for preparing archival finding aids.

You recently have been appointed University Archivist and department head, replacing the person who established the archives. Your predecessor was just hired as archivist at Temple University and has relocated to Philadelphia.

In addition to the above points, you note that the department does not have a mission statement or collecting policy. In your experience, this is a common occurrence: new archivists are often so busy dealing with day-to-day concerns that they do not step back to set overall goals for the program. You resolve to correct this problem as soon as possible.

You also determine that your immediate focus will have to be on the area of appraisal. You will have to assess the value of the various materials being offered to the department from both internal and external sources. You also want to look carefully at the materials already on the shelves: you suspect that "extra" shelf space over the past two years may have led to the acquisition of some materials of questionable value.

You also decide that you will try to mend fences with the local historical societies. You hope to convince them that cooperation, not competition, will mark your tenure at NFU. Your underlying assumption is that no single institution, even one like NFU, can document all aspects of local life and culture.

Once you have determined what you will and will not gather, you will have to turn your attention to other aspects of the archival program. How long will it take to process your existing holdings? How will you balance processing time against the increasing volume of reference requests? What are the preservation needs of the collection and how will you meet these needs within the university's tight budget? How will you deal with the emerging problem of electronic records and their long-term preservation and use?

You have just returned from a meeting with President Swanson and the University Librarian (your boss). At this meeting you presented your preliminary findings and short-term priorities, receiving a generally favorable response. You leave the president's office on a positive note and return to your department to begin work in earnest. It is time to put the archival theory you have learned into practice.

APPENDIX B
CODE OF ETHICS FOR ARCHIVISTS

Archivists select, preserve, and make available documentary materials of long-term value that have lasting value to the organization or public that the archivist serves. Archivists perform their responsibilities in accordance with statutory authorization or institutional policy. They subscribe to a code of ethics based on sound archival principles and promote institutional and professional observance of these ethical and archival standards.

Archivists arrange transfers of records and acquire documentary materials of long-term value in accordance with their institutions' purposes, stated policies, and resources. They do not compete for acquisitions when competition would endanger the integrity or safety of documentary materials of long-term value, or solicit the records of an institution that has an established archives. They cooperate to ensure the preservation of materials in repositories where they will be adequately processed and effectively utilized.

Archivists negotiating with transferring officials or owners of documentary materials of long-term value seek fair decisions based on full consideration of authority to transfer, donate, or sell; financial arrangements and benefits; copyright; plans for processing; and conditions of access. Archivists discourage unreasonable restrictions on access or use, but may accept as a condition of acquisition clearly stated restrictions of limited duration and may occasionally suggest such restrictions to protect privacy. Archivists observe faithfully all agreements made at the time of transfer or acquisition.

Archivists establish intellectual control over their holdings by describing them in finding aids and guides to facilitate internal controls and access by users of the archives.

Archivists appraise documentary materials of long-term value with impartial judgment based on thorough knowledge of their institutions' administrative requirements or acquisitions policies. They maintain and protect the arrangement of documents and information transferred to their custody to protect its authenticity. Archivists protect the integrity of documentary materials of long-term value in their custody, guarding them against defacement, alteration, theft, and physical damage, and ensure that their evidentiary value is not impaired in the archival work of arrangement, description, preservation, and use. They cooperate with other archivists and law enforcement agencies in the apprehension and prosecution of thieves.

Archivists respect the privacy of individuals who created, or are the subjects of, documentary materials of long-term value, especially those who had no voice in the disposition of the materials. They neither reveal nor profit from information gained through work with restricted holdings.

Archivists answer courteously and with a spirit of helpfulness all reasonable inquiries about their holdings, and encourage use of them to the greatest extent compatible with institutional policies, preservation of holdings, legal considerations, individual rights, donor agreements, and judicious use of archival resources. They explain pertinent restrictions to potential users, and apply them equitably.

Archivists endeavor to inform users of parallel research by others using the same materials, and, if the individuals concerned agree, supply each name to the other party.

As members of a community of scholars, archivists may engage in research, publication, and review of the writings of other scholars. If archivists use their institutions' holdings for personal research and publication, such practices should be approved by their employers and made known to others using the same holdings. Archivists who buy and sell manuscripts personally should not compete for acquisitions with their own repositories, should inform their employers of their collecting activities, and should preserve complete records of personal acquisitions and sales.

Archivists avoid irresponsible criticism of other archivists or institutions and address complaints about professional or ethical conduct to the individual or institution concerned, or to a professional archival organization.

Archivists share knowledge and experience with other archivists through professional associations and cooperative activities and assist the professional growth of others with less training or experience. They are obligated by professional ethics to keep informed about standards of good practice and to follow the highest level possible in the administration of their institutions and collections. They have a professional responsibility to recognize the need for cooperative efforts and support the development and dissemination of professional standards and practices.

Archivists work for the best interests of their institutions and their profession and endeavor to reconcile any conflicts by encouraging adherence to archival standards and ethics.

CODE OF ETHICS FOR ARCHIVISTS AND COMMENTARY

The code is a summary of guidelines in the principal areas of professional conduct. A longer Commentary explains the reasons for some of the statements and provides a basis for discussion of the points raised. The Code of Ethics is in italic bold face; the Commentary is in modern type.

I. THE PURPOSE OF THE CODE OF ETHICS

The Society of American Archivists recognizes that ethical decisions are made by individuals, professionals, institutions, and societies. Some of the greatest ethical problems in modern life arise from conflicts between personal codes based on moral teachings, professional practices, regulations based on employment status, institutional policies and state and federal laws. In adopting a formal code of professional ethics for the Society, we are dealing with only one aspect of the archivist's ethical involvement.

Codes of ethics in all professions have several purposes in common, including a statement of concern with the most serious problems of professional conduct, the resolution of problems arising from conflicts of interest, and the guarantee that the special expertise of the members of a profession will be used in the public interest.

The archival profession needs a code of ethics for several reasons: (1) to inform new members of the profession of the high standards of conduct in the most sensitive areas of archival work; (2) to remind experienced archivists of their responsibilities, challenging them to maintain high standards of conduct in their own work and to promulgate those standards to others; and (3) to educate people who have some contact with archives, such as donors of material, dealers, researchers, and administrators, about the work of archivists and to encourage them to expect high standards.

A code of ethics implies moral and legal responsibilities. It presumes that archivists obey the laws and are especially familiar with the laws that affect their special areas of knowledge; it also presumes that they act in accord with sound moral principles. In addition to the moral and legal responsibilities of archivists, there are special professional concerns, and it is the purpose of a code of ethics to state those concerns and give some guidelines for archivists. The code identifies areas where there are or may be conflicts of interest, and indicates ways in which these conflicting interests may be balanced; the code urges the highest standards of professional conduct and excellence of work in every area of archives administration.

This code is compiled for archivists, individually and collectively. Institutional policies should assist archivists in their efforts to conduct themselves according to this code; indeed, institutions, with the assistance of their archivists, should deliberately adopt policies that comply with the principles of the code.

II. INTRODUCTION TO THE CODE

Archivists select, preserve, and make available documentary materials of long-term value that have lasting value to the organization or public that the archivist serves. Archivists perform their responsibilities in accordance with statutory authorization or institutional policy. They subscribe to a code of ethics based on sound archival principles and promote institutional and professional observance of these ethical and archival standards.

Commentary: The introduction states the principal functions of archivists. Because the code speaks to people in a variety of fields—archivists, curators of manuscripts, records managers—the reader should be aware that not every statement in the code will be pertinent to every worker. Because the code intends to inform and protect non-archivists, an explanation of the basic role of archivists is necessary. The term 'documentary materials of long-term value' is intended to cover archival records and papers without regard to the physical format in which they are recorded.

III. COLLECTING POLICIES

Archivists arrange transfers of records and acquire documentary materials of long-term value in accordance with their institutions' purposes, stated policies, and resources. They do not compete for acquisitions when competition would endanger the integrity or safety of documentary materials of long-term value, or solicit the records of an institution that has an established archives. They cooperate to ensure the preservation of materials in repositories where they will be adequately processed and effectively utilized.

Commentary: Among archivists generally there seems to be agreement that one of the most difficult areas is that of policies of collection and the resultant practices. Transfers and acquisitions should be made in accordance with a written policy statement, supported by adequate resources and consistent with the mission of the archives. Because personal papers document the whole career of a person, archivists encourage donors to deposit the entire body of materials in a single archival institution. This section of the code calls for cooperation rather than wasteful competition, as an important element in the solution of this kind of problem.

Institutions are independent and there will always be room for legitimate competition. However, if a donor offers materials that are not within the scope of the collecting policies of an institution, the archivist should tell the donor of a more appropriate institution. When two or more institutions are competing for materials that are appropriate for any one of their collections, the archivists must not unjustly disparage the facilities or intentions of others. As stated later, legitimate complaints about an institution or an archivist may be made through proper channels, but giving false information to potential donors or in any way casting aspersions on other institutions or other archivists is unprofessional conduct.

It is sometimes hard to determine whether competition is wasteful. Because owners are free to offer collections to several institutions, there will be duplication of effort. This kind of competition is unavoidable. Archivists cannot always avoid the increased labor and expense of such transactions.

IV. RELATIONS WITH DONORS, AND RESTRICTIONS

Archivists negotiating with transferring officials or owners of documentary materials of long-term value seek fair decisions based on full consideration of authority to transfer, donate, or sell; financial arrangements and benefits; copyright; plans for processing; and conditions of access. Archivists discourage unreasonable restrictions on access or use, but may accept as a condition of acquisition clearly stated restrictions of limited duration and may occasionally suggest such restrictions to protect privacy. Archivists observe faithfully all agreements made at the time of transfer or acquisition.

Commentary: Many potential donors are not familiar with archival practices and do not have even a general knowledge of copyright, provision of access, tax laws, and other factors that affect the donation and use of archival materials. Archivists have the responsibility for being informed on these matters and passing all pertinent and helpful information to potential donors. Archivists usually discourage donors from imposing conditions on gifts or restricting access to collections, but they are aware of sensitive material and do, when necessary, recommend that donors make provision for protecting the privacy and other rights of the donors themselves, their families, their correspondents, and associates.

In accordance with regulations of the Internal Revenue Service and the guidelines accepted by the Association of College and Research Libraries, archivists should not appraise, for tax purposes, donations to their own institutions.

Some archivists are qualified appraisers and may appraise records given to other institutions.

It is especially important that archivists be aware of the provisions of the copyright act and that they inform potential donors of any provision pertinent to the anticipated gift.

Archivists should be aware of problems of ownership and should not accept gifts without being certain that the donors have the right to make the transfer of ownership.

Archivists realize that there are many projects, especially for editing and publication, that seem to require reservation for exclusive use. Archivists should discourage this practice. When it is not possible to avoid it entirely, archivists should try to limit such restrictions; there should be a definite expiration date, and other users should be given access to the materials as they are prepared for publication. This can be done without encouraging other publication projects that might not conform to the standards for historical editing.

V. DESCRIPTION

Archivists establish intellectual control over their holdings by describing them in finding aids and guides to facilitate internal controls and access by users of the archives.

Commentary:Description is a primary responsibility and the appropriate level of intellectual control should be established over all archival holdings. A general descriptive inventory should be prepared when the records are accessioned. Detailed processing can be time-consuming and should be completed according to a priority based on the significance of the material, user demand and the availability of staff time. It is not sufficient for archivists to hold and preserve materials; they also facilitate the use of their collections and make them known. Finding aids, repository guides, and reports in the appropriate publications permit and encourage users in the institution and outside researchers.

VI. APPRAISAL, PROTECTION AND ARRANGEMENT

Archivists appraise documentary materials of long-term value with impartial judgment based on thorough knowledge of their institutions' administrative requirements or acquisitions policies. They maintain and protect the arrangement of documents and information transferred to their custody to protect its authenticity. Archivists protect the integrity of documentary materials of long-term value in their custody, guarding them against defacement, alteration, theft, and physical damage, and ensure that their evidentiary value is not impaired in the archival work of arrangement, description, preservation, and use. They cooperate with other archivists and law enforcement agencies in the apprehension and prosecution of thieves.

Commentary: Archivists obtain material for use and must insure that their collections are carefully preserved and therefore available. They are concerned not only with the physical preservation of materials but even more with the retention of the information in the collections. Excessive delay in processing materials and making them available for use would cast doubt on the wisdom of the decision of a certain institution to acquire materials, though it sometimes happens that materials are acquired with the expectation that there soon will be resources for processing them.

Some archival institutions are required by law to accept materials even when they do not have the resources to process those materials or store them properly. In such cases archivists must exercise their judgment as to the best use of scarce resources, while seeking changes in acquisitions policies or increases in support that will enable them to perform their professional duties according to accepted standards.

VII. PRIVACY AND RESTRICTED INFORMATION

Archivists respect the privacy of individuals who created, or are the subjects of, documentary materials of long-term value, especially those who had no voice in the disposition of the materials. They neither reveal nor profit from information gained through work with restricted holdings.

Commentary: In the ordinary course of work, archivists encounter sensitive materials and have access to restricted information. In accordance with their institutions' policies, they should not reveal this restricted information, they should not give any researchers special access to it, and they should not use specifically restricted information in their own research. Subject to applicable laws and regulations, they weigh the need for openness and the need to respect privacy rights to determine whether the release of records or information from records would constitute an invasion of privacy.

VIII. USE AND RESTRICTIONS

Archivists answer courteously and with a spirit of helpfulness all reasonable inquiries about their holdings, and encourage use of them to the greatest extent compatible with institutional policies, preservation of holdings, legal considerations, individual rights, donor agreements, and judicious use of archival resources. They explain pertinent restrictions to potential users, and apply them equitably.

Commentary: Archival materials should be made available for use (whether administrative or research) as soon as possible. To facilitate such use, archivists should discourage the imposition of restrictions by donors.

Once conditions of use have been established, archivists should see that all researchers are informed of the materials that are available, and are treated fairly. If some materials are reserved temporarily for use in a special project, other researchers should be informed of these special conditions.

IX. INFORMATION ABOUT RESEARCHERS

Archivists endeavor to inform users of parallel research by others using the same materials, and, if the individuals concerned agree, supply each name to the other party.

Commentary: Archivists make materials available for research because they want the information on their holdings to be known as much as possible. Information about parallel research interests may enable researchers to conduct their investigations more effectively. Such information should consist of the previous researcher's name and address and general research topic and be provided in accordance with institutional policy and applicable laws. Where there is any question, the consent of the previous researcher should be obtained. Archivists do not reveal the details of one researcher's work to others or prevent a researcher from using the same materials that others have used. Archivists are also sensitive to the needs of confidential research, such as research in support of litigation, and in such cases do not approach the user regarding parallel research.

X. RESEARCH BY ARCHIVISTS

As members of a community of scholars, archivists may engage in research, publication, and review of the writings of other scholars. If archivists use their institutions' holdings for personal research and publication, such practices should be approved by their employers and made known to others using the same hold-

ings. Archivists who buy and sell manuscripts personally should not compete for acquisitions with their own repositories, should inform their employers of their collecting activities, and should preserve complete records of personal acquisitions and sales.

Commentary: If archivists do research in their own institutions, there are possibilities of serious conflicts of interest—an archivist might be reluctant to show to other researchers material from which he or she hopes to write something for publication. On the other hand, the archivist might be the person best qualified to research an area represented in institutional holdings. The best way to resolve these conflicts is to clarify and publicize the role of the archivist as researcher.

At the time of their employment, or before undertaking research, archivists should have a clear understanding with their supervisors about the right to research and to publish. The fact that archivists are doing research in their institutional archives should be made known to patrons, and archivists should not reserve materials for their own use. Because it increases their familiarity with their own collections, this kind of research should make it possible for archivists to be more helpful to other researchers. Archivists are not obliged, any more than other researchers are, to reveal the details of their work or the fruits of their research. The agreement reached with the employers should include in each instance a statement as to whether the archivists may or may not receive payment for research done as part of the duties of their positions.

XI. COMPLAINTS ABOUT OTHER INSTITUTIONS

Archivists avoid irresponsible criticism of other archivists or institutions and address complaints about professional or ethical conduct to the individual or institution concerned, or to a professional archival organization.

Commentary: Disparagement of other institutions or of other archivists seems to be a problem particularly when two or more institutions are seeking the same materials, but it can also occur in other areas of archival work. Distinctions must be made between defects due to lack of funds, and improper handling of materials resulting from unprofessional conduct.

XII. PROFESSIONAL ACTIVITIES

Archivists share knowledge and experience with other archivists through professional associations and cooperative activities and assist the professional growth of others with less training or ex-

perience. They are obligated by professional ethics to keep informed about standards of good practice and to follow the highest level possible in the administration of their institutions and collections. They have a professional responsibility to recognize the need for cooperative efforts and support the development and dissemination of professional standards and practices.

Commentary:Archivists may choose to join or not to join local, state, regional, and national professional organizations, but they must be well-informed about changes in archival functions and they must have some contact with their colleagues. They should share their expertise by participation in professional meetings and by publishing. By such activities, in the field of archives, in related fields, and in their own special interests, they continue to grow professionally.

XIII. CONCLUSION

Archivists work for the best interests of their institutions and their profession and endeavor to reconcile any conflicts by encouraging adherence to archival standards and ethics.

Commentary:The code has stated the "best interest" of the archival profession—such as proper use of archives, exchange of information, and careful use of scarce resources. The final statement urges archivists to pursue these goals. When there are apparent conflicts between such goals and either the policies of some institutions or the practices of some archivists, all interested parties should refer to this code of ethics and the judgment of experienced archivists.

BIBLIOGRAPHY

GENERAL

Alegbeleye, G. B. O. "Archives Administration and Records Management in Nigeria: Up the Decades from Amalgamation." *ARMA Records Management Quarterly* 22 (July 1988): 26–31.

Allen, Barbara. "Story in Oral History: Clues to Historical Consciousness." *Journal of American History* 79 (September 1992): 606–611.

Andrews, Patricia A., and Bettye J. Grier, compilers. *Writings on Archives, Historical Manuscripts, and Current Records, 1979–82.* Washington, D.C.: National Archives and Records Service, 1985.

Andrews, Patricia A., compiler. "Writings on Archives, Historical Manuscripts, and Current Records: 1983." *American Archivist* 49 (summer 1986): 277–303.

Archival Forms Manual. Chicago: Society of American Archivists, 1981.

Archives Journals: A Study of Their Coverage by Primary and Secondary Sources. Paris: UNESCO, 1981.

Barritt, Marjorie Rabe, and Nancy Bartlett, eds. "European Archives in an Era of Change." Special issue of *American Archivist* 55 (winter 1992): 4–223.

Baumann, Roland M., ed. *A Manual of Archival Techniques.* Rev. ed. Harrisburg, Pa.: Pennsylvania Historical and Museum Commission, 1982.

Bellardo, Lewis J., and Lynn Lady Bellardo. *A Glossary for Archivists, Manuscript Curators, and Records Managers.* Chicago: Society of American Archivists, 1992.

Benedict, Karen M., ed. *A Select Bibliography on Business Archives and Records Management.* Chicago: Society of American Archivists, 1981.

Berner, Richard C. "Archival Management and Librarianship: An Exploration of Prospects for their Integration." *Advances in Librarianship* 14 (1986): 253–283.

Boccaccio, Mary, ed. *Constitutional Issues and Archives.* New York: Mid-Atlantic Regional Archives Conference, 1988.

Bordin, Ruth B., and Robert M. Warner. *The Modern Manuscript Library.* New York: Scarecrow Press, 1966.

Bradsher, James Gregory. "A Brief History of the Growth of Federal Government Records, Archives, and Information, 1789–1985." *Government Publications Review* 13 (July/August 1986): 491–505.

Brichford, Maynard J. "Academic Archives: *Uberlieferungsbildung.*" *American Archivist* 43 (fall 1980): 449–460.

———. "Seven Sinful Thoughts." *American Archivist* 43 (winter 1980): 13–16.

Bridges, Edwin C. "Can State Archives Meet the Challenges of the Eighties? Four Recent Views on the Condition of American State Archives." *ARMA Records Management Quarterly* 20 (April 1986): 15, 21, 52.

Bridges, Edwin C., et al. "Historians and Archivists: A Rationale for Cooperation." *Journal of American History* 80 (June 1993): 179–186.

Brooks, Philip C. *Research in Archives: The Use of Unpublished Primary Sources.* Chicago: University of Chicago Press, 1969.

Burckel, Nicholas C., and J. Frank Cook. "A Profile of College and University Archives in the United States." *American Archivist* 45 (fall 1982): 410–428.

Burke, Frank G. "The Future Course of Archival Theory in the United States." *American Archivist* 44 (winter 1981): 40–46.

———. "Letting Sleeping Dogmas Lie." *American Archivist* 55 (fall 1992): 530–537.

Carmicheal, David W. "Involving Volunteers in Archives." *Mid-Atlantic Regional Archives Conference Technical Leaflet No. 6.* Mid-Atlantic Regional Archives Conference, 1990.

Child, Margaret S. "Reflections on Cooperation Among Professions." *American Archivist* 46 (summer 1983): 286–292.

Cole, Arthur H. "Business Manuscripts: Collection, Handling, and Cataloging." *Library Quarterly* 8 (January 1938): 93–114.

College and University Archives: Selected Readings. Chicago: Society of American Archivists, 1979.

College and University Guidelines. Chicago: Society of American Archivists, 1979.

Conway, Paul. "Perspectives on Archival Resources: The 1985 Census of Archival Institutions." *American Archivist* 50 (spring 1987): 174–191.

Cook, Michael. *The Management of Information from Archives.* Brookfield, Vt.: Gower, 1986.

Cox, Richard J. "American Archival History: Its Development, Needs, and Opportunities." *American Archivist* 46 (winter 1983): 31–41.

———. "An Annotated Bibliography of Basic Readings on Archives and Manuscripts." *Technical Leaflet No. 130.* Nashville, Tenn.: American Association for State and Local History, 1980.

————. "Archivists and Public Historians in the United States." *Public Historian* 8 (summer 1986): 29–45.

————. *Managing Institutional Archives: Foundational Principles and Practices.* New York: Greenwood Press, 1992.

————. "On the Value of Archival History in the United States." *Libraries and Culture* 23 (spring 1988): 135–51.

————, compiler. *Archives and Manuscript Administration: A Basic Annotated Bibliography.* Nashville, Tenn.: American Association for State and Local History, 1990.

Crew, Spencer R., and John A. Fleckner. "Archival Sources for Business History at the National Museum of American History." *Business History Review* 60 (autumn 1986): 474–486.

Daniels, Maygene F., and Timothy Walch, eds. *A Modern Archives Reader: Basic Readings on Archival Theory and Practice.* Chicago: Society of American Archivists, 1984.

Dearstyne, Bruce W. *The Archival Enterprise: Modern Archival Principles, Practices, and Management Techniques.* Chicago: American Library Association, 1993.

Deiss, William A. *Museum Archives: An Introduction.* Chicago: Society of American Archivists, 1983.

Dellheim, Charles. "Business in Time: The Historian and Corporate Culture." *Public Historian* 8 (spring 1986): 9–22.

Duchein, Michel. "The History of European Archives and the Development of the Archival Profession in Europe." *American Archivist* 55 (winter 1992): 14–25.

Duckett, Kenneth W. *Modern Manuscripts: A Practical Manual for Their Management, Care and Use.* Nashville, Tenn.: American Association for State and Local History, 1975.

Duffy, Mark J. "The Archival Bridge: History, Administration, and the Building of Church Tradition." *Historical Magazine of the Protestant Episcopal Church* 55 (December 1986): 275–287.

Duranti, Luciana. "The Odyssey of Records Managers: Part I." *ARMA Records Management Quarterly* 23 (July 1989): 3–11.

————. "The Odyssey of Records Managers: Part II." *ARMA Records Management Quarterly* 23 (October 1989): 3–11.

Edgerly, Linda. "The Present and Future of Corporate Archives: A Golden Age?" *Business and Economic History,* 2d series. 15 (1986): 197–203.

Ellis, Judith, ed. *Keeping Archives.* 2d ed. Port Melbourne, Australia: D. W. Thorpe, 1993.

Eulenberg, Julia Neibuhr. "The Corporate Archives: Management Tool and Historical Resource." *Public Historian* 6 (winter 1984): 21–37.

Evans, Frank B., et al. *A Basic Glossary for Archivists, Manu-*

script Curators, and Records Managers. Chicago: Society of American Archivists, 1974.

—————. *Modern Archives and Manuscripts: A Select Bibliography.* Chicago: Society of American Archivists, 1975.

—————. "Promoting Archives and Research: A Study in International Cooperation." *American Archivist* 50 (winter 1987): 48–65.

—————. *Writings on Archives Published by and with the Assistance of UNESCO: A RAMP Study.* Paris: UNESCO, 1983.

Fleckner, John A. "Archives and Museums." *Midwestern Archivist* 15 (1990): 67–76.

Foote, Kenneth E. "To Remember and Forget: Archives, Memory, and Culture." *American Archivist* 53 (summer 1990): 378–393.

Gracy, David B., II. "Archives and Society: The First Archival Revolution." *American Archivist* 47 (winter 1984): 7–10.

—————. *An Introduction to Archives and Manuscripts.* New York: Special Libraries Association, 1981.

Grimsted, Patricia Kennedy. "*Glasnost* in the Archives? Recent Developments on the Soviet Archival Scene." *American Archivist* 52 (spring 1989): 214–236.

Guidelines for Archives and Manuscript Repositories. New York: Mid-Atlantic Regional Archives Conference, 1983.

Hackman, Larry J. "From Assessment to Action: Toward a Usable Past in the Empire State." *Public Historian* 7 (summer 1985): 23–34.

—————. "A Perspective on American Archives." *Public Historian* 8 (summer 1986): 10–28.

—————. "State Government and Statewide Archival Affairs: New York as a Case Study." *American Archivist* 55 (fall 1992): 578–599.

—————. "Toward the Year 2000." *Public Historian* 8 (summer 1986): 92–98.

Hackman, Larry J., et al. "Case Studies in Archives Program Development." *American Archivist* 53 (fall 1990): 548–561.

Ham, F. Gerald. "Archival Choices: Managing the Historical Record in an Age of Abundance." *American Archivist* 47 (winter 1984): 11–22.

—————. "The Archival Edge." *American Archivist* 38 (January 1975): 5–13.

—————. "Archival Strategies for the Post-Custodial Era. *American Archivist* 44 (summer 1981): 207–216.

Hamer, Philip M. *A Guide to Archives and Manuscripts.* New Haven, Conn.: Yale University Press, 1961.

Haury, David A. "The Research Potential of Religious Archives: The Mennonite Experience." *Midwestern Archivist* 11 (1986): 135–140.

Hedlin, Edie. *Business Archives: An Introduction.* Chicago: Society of American Archivists, 1978.

———. *"Chinatown* Revisited: The Status and Prospects of Government Records in America." *Public Historian* 8 (summer 1986): 46–59.

Hesselager, Lise. "Fringe or Grey Literature in the National Library: On 'Papyrolatry' and the Growing Similarity Between the Materials in Libraries and Archives." *American Archivist* 47 (summer 1984): 255–270.

Hildebrand, Suzanne, ed. *Women's Collections: Libraries, Archives, and Consciousness.* New York: Haworth Press, 1986.

Hives, Christopher L. "Business Archives: Historical Developments and Future Prospects." M.A. thesis, University of British Columbia, 1985.

Hodson, J. H. *The Administration of Archives.* Oxford: Pergamon Press, 1972.

Holmes, Oliver Wendell. "The Evaluation and Preservation of Business Archives." *American Archivist* 1 (1938): 171–185.

———. "Some Reflections on Business Archives in the United States." *American Archivist* 17 (October 1954): 291–304.

Hunter, Gregory S. "Archival Management: The 1980's and Beyond." *Records and Retrieval Report* 2 (October 1986): 9–12.

———. "Thinking Small to Think Big: Archives, Micrographics and the Life Cycle of Records." *American Archivist* 49 (summer 1986): 315–320.

International Council on Archives, Committee on Business Archives. *Business Archives: Studies on International Practices.* New York: K. G. Saur, 1983.

Jenkinson, Hilary. *Archives in the Ancient World.* Cambridge, Mass.: Harvard University Press, 1972.

———. *A Manual of Archive Administration.* London: Percy Lund, Humphries and Co., 1965.

Jones, H. G. *The Records of a Nation: Their Management, Preservation and Use.* New York: Atheneum, 1969.

Kane, Lucille. *A Guide to the Care and Administration of Manuscripts.* 2d ed. Nashville, Tenn.: American Association for State and Local History, 1966.

Kantrow, Alan M., ed. "Why History Matters to Managers." *Harvard Business Review* 64 (January–February 1986).

Ketelaar, Eric. *Archival and Records Management Legislation and Regulations: A RAMP Study with Guidelines.* Paris: UNESCO, 1985.

Kousser, J. Morgan. "Ignoble Intentions and Noble Dreams: On Relativism and History with a Purpose [Litigation Support]." *Public Historian* 15 (summer 1993): 15–28.

Ladeira, Caroline Durant, and Maryellen Trautman, compilers. "Writings on Archives, Historical Manuscripts, and Current Records: 1984." *American Archivist* 49 (fall 1986): 425–454.

Lowell, Howard P. "Elements of a State Archives and Records Management Program." *ARMA Records Management Quarterly* 21 (October 1987): 3–14.

———. "The Quiet Crisis in State Archives." *ARMA Records Management Quarterly* 22 (April 1988): 23–27.

Managing Audiovisual Records. Washington, D.C.: National Archives and Records Administration, 1990.

Managing Cartographic and Architectural Records. Washington, D.C.: National Archives and Records Administration, 1989.

Maher, William J. *The Management of College and University Archives*. Chicago: Society of American Archivists and Scarecrow Press, 1992.

Mayer, Dale C. "The New Social History: Implications for Archivists." *American Archivist* 48 (fall 1985): 388–399.

McCrank, Lawrence, ed. *Archives and Library Administration: Divergent Traditions and Common Concerns*. New York: Haworth Press, 1986.

McDowall, Duncan. " 'Wonderful Things': History, Business, and Archives Look to the Future." *American Archivist* 56 (spring 1993): 348–357.

Merz, Nancy M. "Archives and the One World of Records." *Inform* 2 (April 1988): 30–36.

Mitchell, Thornton W., ed. *Norton on Archives: The Writings of Margaret Cross Norton*. Chicago: Society of American Archivists, 1975.

Muller, Samuel, John A. Feith, and Robert Fruin. *Manual for the Arrangement and Description of Archives*. 2d ed. New York: H. W. Wilson, 1940.

Ogawa, Chiyoko. "Archives in Japan: The State of the Art." *American Archivist* 54 (fall 1991): 546–555.

O'Toole, James M. "On the Idea of Uniqueness." *American Archivist* 57 (fall 1994): 632–659.

———. "The Symbolic Significance of Archives." *American Archivist* 56 (1993): 234–255.

———. *Understanding Archives and Manuscripts*. Chicago: Society of American Archivists, 1992.

Pacifico, Michelle F. "Founding Mothers: Women in the Society of American Archivists, 1936–72." *American Archivist* 50 (summer 1987): 370–389.

Peace, Nancy E., and Nancy Fisher Chudacoff. "Archivists and Librarians: A Common Mission, a Common Education." *American Archivist* 42 (October 1979): 456–462.

Peterson, Gary M., and Trudy Huskamp Peterson. *Archives and Manuscripts: Law.* Chicago: Society of American Archivists, 1985.

Peterson, Trudy Huskamp. "An Archival Bestiary." *American Archivist* 54 (spring 1991): 192–205.

_____. "The National Archives and the Archival Theorist Revisited, 1954–1984." *American Archivist* 49 (spring 1986): 125–133.

Pomeroy, Robert W., ed. "Business and History." Special issue of the *Public Historian* 3 (summer 1981). 6–159.

Posner, Ernst. *American State Archives.* Chicago: University of Chicago Press, 1964.

Preservation Needs in State Archives. Albany, N.Y.: National Association of Government Archives and Records Administrators, 1986.

Proffitt, Kevin. "The Archival Bridge." *Midwestern Archivist* 16 (1991): 115–120.

Rhoads, James B. *The Applicability of UNISIST Guidelines and ISO International Standards to Archives Administration and Records Management: A Records and Archives Management Program (UNESCO) Study.* Paris: UNESCO, 1982.

_____. *The Role of Archives and Records Management in National Information Systems: A RAMP Study.* Paris: UNESCO, 1983.

Roberts, John W. "Archival Theory: Much Ado About Shelving." *American Archivist* 50 (winter 1987): 66–74.

_____. "Archival Theory: Myth or Banality." *American Archivist* 53 (winter 1990): 110–120.

Russell, Mattie U. "The Influence of Historians on the Archival Profession in the United States." *American Archivist* 46 (summer 1983): 277–285.

Sanders, Robert L. "Archivists and Records Managers: Another Marriage in Trouble?" *ARMA Records Management Quarterly* 23 (April 1989): 12–20.

Schellenberg, Theodore R. *The Management of Archives.* New York: Columbia University Press, 1965.

_____. *Modern Archives: Principles and Techniques.* Chicago: University of Chicago Press, 1956.

Seton, Rosemary E. *The Preservation and Administration of Private Archives: A RAMP Study.* Paris: UNESCO, 1984.

Shkolnik, Leon. "The Role of the Archive in the Corporate Structure." *ARMA Records Management Quarterly* 24 (October 1990): 18–25.

Simmons, Joseph M. "The Special Librarian as Company Archivist." *Special Libraries* 56 (1965): 647–650.

Skemer, Don C., and Geoffrey P. Williams. "Managing the Records of Higher Education: The State of Records Management in American Colleges and Universities." *American Archivist* 53 (fall 1990): 532–547.

Smith, David R. "An Historical Look at Business Archives." *American Archivist* 45 (summer 1982): 273–278.

Smith, George David. "Dusting Off the Cobwebs: Turning the Business Archives Into a Managerial Tool," *American Archivist* 45 (summer 1982): 287–290.

Stark, Marie Charlotte. *Development of Records Management and Archives Services Within United Nations Agencies: A RAMP Study.* Paris: UNESCO, 1983.

Stielow, Frederick J. *The Management of Oral History Sound Archives.* Westport, Conn.: Greenwood Press, 1986.

Strengthening New York's Historical Records Programs: A Self-Study Guide. Albany, N.Y.: State Archives and Records Administration, 1989.

Suelflow, August. *Religious Archives: An Introduction.* Chicago: Society of American Archivists, 1980.

Taylor, Priscilla S., ed. *Manuscripts: The First Twenty Years.* Westport, Conn.: Greenwood Press, 1984.

Trevelen, Dale. "Oral History and the Archival Community: Common Concerns About Documenting Twentieth-Century Life." *International Journal of Oral History* 10 (February 1989): 50–58.

Vaughn, Stephen, ed. *The Vital Past: Writings on the Uses of History.* Athens, Ga.: University of Georgia Press, 1985.

Walch, Timothy, ed. *Guardian of Heritage: Essays on the History of the National Archives.* Washington, D.C.: National Archives and Records Administration, 1985.

Walker, Bill. "Records Managers and Archivists: A Survey of Roles." *ARMA Records Management Quarterly* 23 (January 1989): 18–21.

Weinstein, Robert A., and Larry Booth. *Collection, Use, and Care of Historical Photographs.* Nashville, Tenn.: American Association for State and Local History, 1977.

Weldon, Edward. "Archives and the Challenge of Change." *American Archivist* 46 (spring 1983): 125–134.

Wilsted, Thomas, and William Nolte. *Managing Archival and Manuscript Repositories.* Chicago: Society of American Archivists, 1991.

Wosh, Peter J. "Bibles, Benevolence, and Bureaucracy: The Changing Nature of Nineteenth Century Religious Records." *American Archivist* 52 (spring 1989): 166–178.

Yates, JoAnne. "From Press Book and Pigeonhole to Vertical Filing: Revolution in Storage and Access Systems for Correspondence." *Journal of Business Communication* 19 (summer 1982): 5–26.

CONDUCTING A SURVEY AND STARTING AN ARCHIVES PROGRAM

Baumann, Roland M. "Oberlin College and the Movement to Establish an Archives, 1920–1966." *Midwestern Archivist* 13 (1988): 27–38.

Christian, John F., and Shonnie Finnegan. "On Planning an Archives." *American Archivist* 37 (1974): 573–578.

Eddy, Henry H. "Surveying for Archives Buildings." *American Archivist* 24 (1961): 75–79.

Evans, Frank B., and Eric Ketelaar. *A Guide for Surveying Archival and Records Management Systems and Services: A RAMP Study.* Paris: UNESCO, 1983.

Fleckner, John. *Archives and Manuscripts: Surveys.* Chicago: Society of American Archivists, 1977.

———, ed. "Records Surveys: A Multi-Purpose Tool for the Archivist." *American Archivist* 42 (July 1979): 293–311.

Frye, Dorothy T. "Linking Institutional Missions to University and College Archives Programs: The Land-Grant Model." *American Archivist* 56 (winter 1993): 36–53.

Gracy David B., II. "Starting an Archives." *Georgia Archive* 1 (1972): 20–29.

Gross, John W. "Inventorying and Scheduling Records." *ARMA Records Management Quarterly* 7 (1973): 28–31.

Henry, Linda J. "Archival Advisory Committees: Why?" *American Archivist* 48 (summer 1985): 315–319.

Koplowitz, Bradford. "The Oklahoma Historical Records Survey." *American Archivist* 54 (winter 1991): 62–68.

Somers, Dale A., et al. "Surveying the Records of a City: The History of Atlanta Project." *American Archivist* 36 (July 1973): 353–359.

Starting an Archives. Problems in Archives Kit No. 3. Chicago: Society of American Archivists, 1980.

Thomson, Robert P. "The Business Records Survey in Wisconsin." *American Archivist* 14 (July 1951): 249–255.

Yakel, Elizabeth. "Institutionalizing an Archives: Developing Historical Records Programs in Organizations." *American Archivist* 52 (spring 1989): 202–207.

Zitmore, Irving. "Planning a Records Management Survey." *American Archivist* 18 (April 1955): 133–140.

SELECTION, APPRAISAL, ACQUISITIONS, AND ACCESSIONING

Abraham, Terry. "Collection Policy or Documentation Strategy: Theory and Practice." *American Archivist* 54 (winter 1991): 44–53.

Alexander, Philip N., and Helen W. Samuels. "The Roots of 128: A Hypothetical Documentation Strategy." *American Archivist* 50 (fall 1987): 518–531.

Allen, Marie B., and Roland M. Baumann. "Evolving Appraisal and Accessioning Policies of Soviet Archives." *American Archivist* 54 (winter 1991): 96–111.

Anderson, R. Joseph. "Managing Change and Chance: Collecting Policies in Social History Archives." *American Archivist* 48 (summer 1985): 296–303.

Barritt, Marjorie Rabe. "The Appraisal of Personally Identifiable Student Records." *American Archivist* 49 (summer 1986): 263–275.

Bassett, T. D. Seymour. "Documenting Recreation and Tourism in New England." *American Archivist* 50 (fall 1987): 550–569.

Bauer, G. Philip. *The Appraisal of Current and Recent Records.* Staff Information Circular 13. Washington, D.C.: National Archives, 1946.

Becker, Ronald L. "On Deposit: A Handshake and a Lawsuit." *American Archivist* 56 (winter 1993): 320–329.

Benedict, Karen. "Invitation to a Bonfire: Reappraisal and Deaccessioning of Records as Collection Management Tools in an Archives: A Reply to Leonard Rapport." *American Archivist* 47 (winter 1984): 43–50.

Blouin, Francis X., Jr. "A New Perspective on the Appraisal of Business Records: A Review." *American Archivist* 42 (July 1979): 312–320.

Boles, Frank. *Archival Appraisal.* New York: Neal-Schuman, 1991.

———. "Mix Two Parts Interest to One Part Information and Appraise Until Done: Understanding Contemporary Record Selection Processes." *American Archivist* 50 (summer 1987): 356–368.

———. "Sampling in Archives." *American Archivist* 44 (spring 1981): 125–130.

Boles, Frank, and Julia Marks Young. "Exploring the Black Box: The Appraisal of University Administrative Records." *American Archivist* 48 (spring 1985): 121–140.

Bodem, Dennis R. "The Use of Forms in the Control of Archives at the Accessioning and Processing Level." *American Archivist* 31 (October 1968): 365–369.

Booms, Hans. "Society and the Formation of a Documentary Heritage: Issues in the Appraisal of Archival Sources." *Archivaria* 24 (summer 1987): 69–107.

Bradsher, James Gregory. "The FBI Records Appraisal." *Midwestern Archivist* 13 (1988): 51–66.

Breton, Arthur J. "The Critical First Step: *In Situ* Handling of Large Collections." *American Archivist* 49 (fall 1986): 455–458.

Brichford, Maynard. *Archives and Manuscripts: Appraisal and Accessioning.* Chicago: Society of American Archivists, 1977.

Brooks, Philip C. "The Selection of Records for Preservation." *American Archivist* 3 (October 1940): 221–234.

Burton, Shirley J. "Documentation of the United States at War in the Twentieth Century: An Archivist's Reflection on Sources, Themes, and Access." *Midwestern Archivist* 13 (1988): 17–26.

Carleton, Don E. " 'McCarthyism Was More than McCarthy': Documenting the Red Scare at the State and Local Level." *Midwestern Archivist* 12 (1987): 13–19.

Chestnut, Paul I. "Appraising the Papers of State Legislators." *American Archivist* 48 (spring 1985): 159–172.

Coker, Kathy Roe. "Records Appraisal: Practice and Procedure." *American Archivist* 48 (fall 1985): 417–421.

Colman, Gould P. "Documenting Agriculture and Rural Life." *Midwestern Archivist* 12 (1987): 21–27.

Cox, Richard J. "A Documentation Strategy Case Study: Western New York." *American Archivist* 52 (spring 1989): 192–200.

Cox, Richard J., and Helen W. Samuels. "The Archivist's First Responsibility: A Research Agenda to Improve the Identification and Retention of Records of Enduring Value." *American Archivist* 51 (winter/spring 1988): 28–51.

Crawford, Miriam I. *A Model for Donor Organizations and Institutional Repository Relationships in the Transfer of Organizational Archives.* Philadelphia: National Federation of Abstracting and Information Services, 1987.

Davis, Richard Carter. "Getting the Lead Out: The Appraisal of Silver-Lead Mining Records at the University of Idaho." *American Archivist* 55 (summer 1992): 454–463.

Day, Deborah Cozort. "Appraisal Guidelines for Reprint Collections." *American Archivist* 48 (winter 1985): 56–63.

Disposition of Federal Records: A Records Management Handbook. Washington, D.C.: National Archives and Records Administration, 1992.

Duranti, Luciana. "The Concept of Appraisal and Archival Theory." *American Archivist* 57 (spring 1994): 328–344.

Elzy, Martin I. "Scholarship vs. Economy: Records Appraisal at the National Archives." *Prologue* 6 (1974): 183–188.

Endelman, Judith E. "Looking Backward to Plan for the Future: Collection Analysis for Manuscript Repositories." *American Archivist* 50 (summer 1987): 340–355.

Evans, Max J. "The Visible Hand: Creating a Practical Mechanism for Cooperative Appraisal." *Midwestern Archivist* 11 (1986): 7–13.

Fishbein, Meyer. "Appraisal of Twentieth Century Records for Historical Use." *Illinois Libraries* 52 (1970): 154–162.

———. "Reflections on Appraising Statistical Records." *American Archivist* 50 (spring 1987): 226–234.

Gilfoyle, Timothy J. "Prostitutes in the Archives: Problems and Possibilities in Documenting the History of Sexuality." *American Archivist* 57 (summer 1994): 514–527.

Gray, David P. "A Technique for Manuscript Collection Development Analysis." *Midwestern Archivist* 12 (1987): 91–104.

Greene, Mark. "Store Wars: Some Thoughts on the Strategy and Tactics of Documenting Small Business." *Midwestern Archivist* 16 (1991): 95–104.

Haas, Joan K., Helen Willa Samuels, and Barbara Trippel Simmons. "The MIT Appraisal Project and Its Broader Applications." *American Archivist* 49 (summer 1986): 310–314.

Hackman, Larry J., and Joan Warnow-Blewett. "The Documentation Strategy Process: A Model and a Case Study." *American Archivist* 50 (winter 1987): 12–47.

Ham, F. Gerald. *Selecting and Appraising Archives and Manuscripts.* Chicago: Society of American Archivists, 1993.

Henry, Linda J. "Collecting Policies of Special-Subject Repositories." *American Archivist* 43 (winter 1980): 57–63.

Hinding, Andrea. "Inventing a Concept of Documentation." *Journal of American History* 80 (June 1993): 168–178.

Hite, Richard W and Daniel J. Linke. "A Statistical Summary of Appraisal During Processing: A Case Study With Manuscript Collections." *Archival Issues* 17 (1992): 23–30.

Hull, Felix. *The Use of Sampling Techniques in the Retention of Records: A RAMP Study with Guidelines.* Paris: UNESCO, 1981.

Intrinsic Value. Staff Information Paper 21. Washington, D.C.: National Archives and Records Service, 1982.

Janzen, Mary E. "Pruning the Groves of Academe: Appraisal, Arrangement and Description of Faculty Papers." *Georgia Archive* 9 (fall 1981): 31–41.

Jung, Maureen A. "Documenting Nineteenth-Century Quartz Mining in Northern California." *American Archivist* 53 (summer 1990): 406–419.

Kemp, Edward C. *Manuscript Solicitation for Libraries, Special Collections, Museums, and Archives*. Littleton, Co.: Libraries Unlimited, 1978.

Kepley, David R. "Sampling in Archives: A Review." *American Archivist* 47 (summer 1984): 237–242.

Klaassen, David J. "Achieving Balanced Documentation: Social Services from a Consumer Perspective." *Midwestern Archivist* 11 (1986): 111–124.

Kolsrud, Ole. "The Evolution of Basic Appraisal Principles: Some Comparative Observations." *American Archivist* 55 (winter 1992): 26–39.

Krizack, Joan D. "Hospital Documentation Planning: The Concept and the Context." *American Archivist* 56 (winter 1993): 16–35.

Kula, Sam. *The Archival Appraisal of Moving Images: A RAMP Study with Guidelines*. Paris: UNESCO, 1983.

Leary, William H. *The Archival Appraisal of Photographs: A RAMP Study with Guidelines*. Paris: UNESCO, 1985.

Lewinson, Paul. "Archival Sampling." *American Archivist* 20 (October 1957): 291–312.

———. "Toward Accessioning and Standards: Research Records." *American Archivist* 23 (July 1960): 297–309.

Lockwood, Elizabeth. " 'Imponderable Matters': The Influence of New Trends in History on Appraisal at the National Archives." *American Archivist* 53 (summer 1990): 394–405.

Lutzker, Michael A. "Max Weber and the Analysis of Modern Bureaucratic Organization: Notes Toward a Theory of Appraisal." *American Archivist* 45 (spring 1982): 119–130.

Mattern, Carolyn J. "Documenting the Vietnam Soldier: A Case Study in Collection Development." *Midwestern Archivist* 15 (1990): 99–107.

McCree, Mary Lynn. "Good Sense and Good Judgment: Defining Collections and Collecting." *Drexel Library Quarterly* 2 (1975): 21–32.

McReynolds, Samuel A. "Rural Life in New England." *American Archivist* 50 (fall 1987): 532–548.

Menne-Haritz, Angelika. "Appraisal or Documentation: Can We

Appraise Archives by Selecting Content?" *American Archivist* 57 (summer 1994): 528–543.

Miller, Fredric M. "Social History and Archival Practice." *American Archivist* 44 (spring 1981): 113–124.

———. "Use, Appraisal, and Research: A Case Study of Social History." *American Archivist* 49 (fall 1986): 371–392.

Mills, Thomas E. "Appraisal of Social Welfare Case Files." *Technical Leaflet No. 1.* New York: Mid-Atlantic Regional Archives Conference, 1982.

O'Toole, James M. "On the Idea of Permanence." *American Archivist* 52 (winter 1989): 10–25.

———. "Things of the Spirit: Documenting Religion in New England." *American Archivist* 50 (fall 1987): 500–517.

Peace, Nancy A. *Archival Choices: Managing the Historical Record in an Age of Abundance.* Lexington, Mass.: Lexington Books, 1984.

Peterson, Trudy Huskamp. "The Gift and the Deed." *American Archivist* 42 (January 1979): 61–66.

Phillips, Faye. "Developing Collecting Policies for Manuscript Collections." *American Archivist* 47 (winter 1984): 30–42.

Pinkett, Harold T. "Accessioning Public Records: Anglo-American Practices and Possible Improvements." *American Archivist* 41 (October 1978): 413–421.

———. "Identification of Records of Continuing Value." *Indian Archives* 16 (January 1965): 54–61.

———. "Selective Preservation of General Correspondence." *American Archivist* 30 (January 1967): 33–43.

Rapport, Leonard. "In the Valley of Decision: What to Do About the Multitude of Files of Quasi Cases." *American Archivist* 48 (spring 1985): 173–189.

———. "No Grandfather Clause: Reappraising Accessioned Records." *American Archivist* 44 (spring 1981): 143–150.

Reed-Scott, Jutta. "Collection Management Strategies for Archivists." *American Archivist* 47 (winter 1984): 23–29.

Ruller, Thomas J. "Dissimilar Appraisal Documentation as an Impediment to Sharing Appraisal Data: A Survey of Appraisal Documentation in Government Archival Repositories." *Archival Issues* 17 (1992): 65–74.

Samuels, Helen Willa. *Varsity Letters: Documenting Modern Colleges and Universities.* Chicago: Society of American Archivists and Scarecrow Press, 1992.

———. "Who Controls the Past." *American Archivist* 49 (spring 1986): 109–124 [re: documentation strategies].

Sanders, Robert L. "Accessioning College and University Publications: A Case Study." *American Archivist* 49 (spring 1986): 180–183.

Schaeffer, Roy C. "Transcendent Concepts: Power, Appraisal, and the Archivist as 'Social Outcast.'" *American Archivist* 55 (fall 1992): 608–619.

Schellenberg, Theodore R. *The Appraisal of Modern Public Records*. Bulletin No. 8. Washington, D.C.: National Archives, 1956.

Schrock, Nancy Carlson. "Images of New England: Documenting the Built Environment." *American Archivist* 50 (fall 1987): 474–498.

Sink, Robert. "Appraisal: The Process of Choice. *American Archivist* 53 (summer 1990): 452–459.

Smith, Wilfred I. "Archival Selection: A Canadian View." *Society of Archivists Journal* 3 (1967): 275–280.

Steinwall, Susan D. "Appraisal and the FBI Case Files: For Whom Do Archivists Retain Records?" *American Archivist* 49 (winter 1986): 52–63.

Turnbaugh, Roy. "Plowing the Sea: Appraising Public Records in an Ahistorical Culture." *American Archivist* 53 (fall 1990): 562–565.

Wertheimer, Jack, Debra Bernhardt, and Julie Miller. "Toward the Documentation of Conservative Judaism." *American Archivist* 57 (spring 1994): 374–379.

Wrathall, John D. "Provenance as Text: Reading the Silences Around Sexuality in Manuscript Collections." *Journal of American History* 79 (June 1992): 165–178.

Yates, JoAnne. "Internal Communication Systems in American Business Structures: A Framework to Aid Appraisal." *American Archivist* 48 (spring 1985): 141–158.

Young, Julia Marks, compiler. "Annotated Bibliography on Appraisal." *American Archivist* 48 (spring 1985): 190–216.

ARRANGEMENT

Abraham, Terry. "Oliver W. Holmes Revisited: Levels of Arrangement and Description in Practice." *American Archivist* 54 (summer 1991): 370–377.

Berner, Richard C. "Arrangement and Description: Some Historical Observations." *American Archivist* 41 (April 1978): 169–181.

Boles, Frank. "Disrespecting Original Order." *American Archivist* 45 (winter 1982): 26–32.

Carmicheal, David W. *Organizing Archival Records: A Practical*

Method of Arrangement and Description for Small Archives. Harrisburg, Pa.: Pennsylvania Historical and Museum Commission, 1993.

Evans, Frank B. "Modern Methods of Arrangement of Archives in the United States." *American Archivist* 29 (April 1966): 241–263.

Evans, Max J. "Authority Control: An Alternative to the Record Group Concept." *American Archivist* 49 (summer 1986): 249–261.

Gracy, David B., II. *Archives and Manuscripts: Arrangement and Description.* Chicago: Society of American Archivists, 1977.

Haller, Uli. "Processing for Access." *American Archivist* 48 (fall 1985): 400–415.

———. "Variations in the Processing Rates on the Magnuson and Jackson Senatorial Papers." *American Archivist* 50 (winter 1987): 100–109.

Hite, Richard W., and Daniel J. Linke. "Teaming Up with Technology: Team Processing." *Midwestern Archivist* 15 (1990): 91–98.

Holmes, Oliver W. "Archival Arrangement: Five Different Operations at Five Different Levels." *American Archivist* 27 (January 1964): 21–41.

The Lone Arranger. Problems in Archives Kit. Chicago: Society of American Archivists, 1983.

Miller, Fredric M. *Arranging and Describing Archives and Manuscripts.* Chicago: Society of American Archivists, 1992.

Roe, Kathleen. *Guidelines for Arrangement and Description of Archives and Manuscripts.* New York: New York State Archives and Records Administration, 1991.

Slotkin, Helen W., and Karen T. Lynch. "An Analysis of Processing Procedures: The Adaptable Approach." *American Archivist* 45 (spring 1982): 155–163.

DESCRIPTION

Bearman, David. "Archives and Manuscript Control with Bibliographic Utilities: Opportunities and Challenges." *American Archivist* 52 (winter 1989): 26–39.

Berner, Richard C., and M. Gary Bettis. "Description of Manuscript Collections: A Single Network System." *College and Research Libraries* 30 (1969): 405–416.

Berner, Richard C., and Uli Haller. "Principles of Archival Inventory Construction." *American Archivist* 47 (spring 1984): 134–155.

Carson, James G. "The American Medical Association's Historical Health Fraud and Alternative Medicine Collection: An Integrated Approach to Automated Collection Description." *American Archivist* 54 (spring 1991): 184–191.

Cloud, Patricia. "RLIN, AMC, and Retrospective Conversion." *Midwestern Archivist* 11 (1986): 125–134.

Coombs, Leonard. "A New Access System for the Vatican Archives." *American Archivist* 52 (fall 1989): 538–546.

Davis, Richard Carter. "Adventures with MicroMARC: A Report on Idaho's Centennial Database." *American Archivist* 55 (fall 1992): 600–607.

Dooley, Jackie M. "Subject Indexing in Context." *American Archivist* 55 (spring 1992): 344–354.

Gracy, David B. "Finding Aids Are Like Streakers." *Georgia Archive* 4 (1976): 39–47.

Hensen, Steven, ed. *Archives, Personal Papers, and Manuscripts: A Cataloging Manual for Archival Repositories, Historical Societies, and Manuscript Libraries.* 2d ed. Chicago: Society of American Archivists, 1989.

———. "The Use of Standards in the Application of the AMC Format." *American Archivist* 49 (winter 1986): 31–40.

Hodges, Martha. "Using the MARC Format for Archives and Manuscripts Control to Catalog Published Microfilms of Manuscript Collections." *Microform Review* 18 (winter 1989): 29–35.

Holmes, William M., Jr.; Edie Hedlin; and Thomas E. Weir, Jr. "MARC and Life Cycle Tracking at the National Archives: Project Final Report." *American Archivist* 49 (summer 1986): 305–309.

Honhart, Frederick L. "MicroMARC:AMC: A Case Study in the Development of an Automated System." *American Archivist* 52 (winter 1989): 80–86.

Inventories and Registers: A Handbook of Techniques and Examples. Chicago: Society of American Archivists, 1976.

Lucas, Lydia. "Efficient Finding Aids: Developing a System for Control of Archives and Manuscripts." *American Archivist* 44 (winter 1981): 21–26.

MARC Format and Life Cycle Tracking at the National Archives: A Study. Washington, D.C.: National Archives and Records Administration, 1986.

Meissner, Dennis. "Online Archival Cataloging and Public Access at the Minnesota Historical Society." *Archival Issues* 17 (1992): 31–48.

Michelson, Avra. "Description and Reference in the Age of Automation." *American Archivist* 50 (spring 1987): 192–208.

Morton, Katharine D. "The MARC Formats: An Overview." *American Archivist* 49 (winter 1986): 21–30.

Preparation of Preliminary Inventories. Staff Information Circular 14. Washington, D.C.: National Archives, 1950.

Pugh, Mary Jo. "The Illusion of Omniscience: Subject Access and the Reference Archivist." *American Archivist* 45 (winter 1982): 33–44.

Sahli, Nancy. "Finding Aids: A Multi-Media, Systems Perspective." *American Archivist* 44 (winter 1981): 15–20.

———. "Interpretation and Application of the AMC Format." *American Archivist* 49 (winter 1986): 9–20.

Smiraglia, Richard, ed. *Describing Archival Materials: The Use of the MARC AMC Format.* New York: Haworth, 1990.

Spindler, Robert P., and Richard Pearce-Moses. "Does AMC Mean 'Archives Made Confusing'? Patron Understanding of USMARC AMC Catalog Records." *American Archivist* 56 (spring 1993): 330–341.

"Standards for Archival Description." Special issues of *American Archivist* 52 (fall 1989): 432–537 and 53 (winter 1990): 24–109.

Vargas, Mark A., and Janet Padway. "Catalog Them Again for the First Time." *Archival Issues* 17 (1992): 49–64.

Zboray, Ronald J. "dBase III Plus and the MARC AMC Format: Problems and Possibilities." *American Archivist* 50 (spring 1987): 210–225.

PRESERVATION

Allen, Barbara Ann. *A Guide to Bibliotherapy.* Chicago: Association of Specialized and Cooperative Library Agencies, 1982.

Appelbaum, Barbara. *Guide to Environmental Protection of Collections.* Madison, Conn.: Sound View Press, 1991.

"Archival Preservation of Motion Pictures: A Summary of Current Findings." *Technical Leaflet No. 126.* Nashville, Tenn.: American Association for State and Local History.

Banks, Paul N. *Preservation of Library Materials.* Chicago: Newberry Library, 1978.

———. *A Selective Bibliography on the Conservation of Research Library Materials.* Chicago: Newberry Library, 1981.

Book Longevity: Reports of the Committee on Production Guide-

lines for Book Longevity. Washington, D.C.: Council on Library Resources, 1982.

Brittle Books. Washington, D.C.: Council on Library Resources, 1986.

Calmes, Alan. "To Archive and Preserve: A Media Primer." *Inform* 1 (May 1987): 14–17, 33.

Carey, Kathryn M. "Preservation of Colonial Court Records: Treating a Vast Collection of Historic Documents." *Technology and Conservation* 6 (spring 1981): 42–45.

Clapp, Verner W. "The Story of Permanent/Durable Book-Paper, 1150–1970." *Restaurator* 3 (1972): 1–51.

Conway, Paul. *Preservation in the Digital World*. Washington, D.C.: Commision on Preservation and Access, 1996.

Cribbs, Margaret A. "Photographic Conservation: An Update." *ARMA Records Management Quarterly* 22 (July 1988): 17–19.

Cunha, George, and Dorothy Cunha. *Library and Archives Conservation: 1980's and Beyond*. 2 vols. Metuchen, N.J.: Scarecrow Press, 1983.

Cunningham, Veronica Colley. "The Preservation of Newspaper Clippings." *Special Libraries* (winter 1987): 41–46.

D'Arienzo, Daria, Anne Ostendarp, and Emily Silverman. "Preservation Microfilming: The Challenges of Saving a Collection at Risk." *American Archivist* 57 (summer 1994): 498–513.

Dimitroff, Michael, and James W. Lacksonen. "The Diffusion of Sulfur Dioxide in Air Through Stacked Layers of Paper." *Journal of the American Institute for Conservation* 25 (spring 1986): 31–37.

Eaton, George. *Conservation of Photographs*. Rochester, N.Y.: Eastman Kodak, 1985.

Environmental Controls Resource Packet. Albany, N.Y.: New York State Library, 1991.

Field, Jeffrey. "The NEH Office of Preservation, 1986–1988." *Microform Review* 17 (October 1988): 187–189.

Fox, Lisa L. "A Two Year Perspective on Library Preservation: An Annotated Bibliography." *Library Resources and Technical Services* 30 (July/September 1986): 290–318.

Grimard, Jacques. "Mass Deacidification: Universal Cure or Limited Solution?" *American Archivist* 57 (fall 1994): 674–679.

Gwinn, Nancy E. "The Fragility of Paper: Can Our Historical Records Be Saved?" *Public Historian* 13 (summer 1991): 33–54.

Haines, John H., and Stuart A. Kohler. "An Evaluation of Ortho-Phenyl as a Fumicidal Fumigant for Archives and Libraries." *Journal of the American Institute for Conservation* 25 (spring 1986): 49–55.

Hendriks, Klaus B. *The Preservation and Restoration of Photographic Materials in Archives and Libraries: A RAMP Study with Guidelines.* Paris: UNESCO, 1984.

Hunter, Gregory S. "Reprography." *World Encyclopedia of Library and Information Services.* 3d ed. Chicago: American Library Association, 1993.

Kaebnick, Gregory E. "Slow Fires: A National, NEH-Funded Microfilming Program Seeks to Rescue Civilization." *Inform* 3 (November 1989): 12–14.

Kaplan, Hilary A., Maria Holden, and Kathy Ludwig, compilers. "Archives Preservation Resource Review." *American Archivist* 54 (fall 1991): 502–545.

Kathpalia, Y. P. *Conservation and Preservation of Archives.* Paris: UNESCO 1973.

———. *A Model Curriculum for the Training of Specialists in Document Preservation and Restoration: A RAMP Study With Guidelines.* Paris: UNESCO, 1984.

Krasnow, Lawrence L. "Legal Aspects of Conservation: Basic Considerations of Contracts and Negligence." *Technology and Conservation* 7 (spring 1982): 38–40.

Lull, William P., with the assistance of Paul N. Banks. *Conservation Environment Guidelines for Libraries and Archives.* Albany, N.Y.: New York State Library, 1990.

Mathey, Robert. *Air Quality Criteria for Storage of Paper-Based Archival Records.* Washington, D.C.: National Bureau of Standards, 1983.

O'Toole, James M. "On the Idea of Permanence." *American Archivist* 52 (winter 1989): 10–25.

Petherbridge, Guy, ed. *Conservation of Library and Archive Materials and the Graphic Arts.* London: Butterworths, 1987.

Poole, Frazer G. "Some Aspects of the Conservation Problem in Archives." *American Archivist* 40 (April 1977): 163–171.

"Preservation." Special issue. *American Archivist* 53 (spring 1990): 184–369.

Preservation of Archival Materials: A Report of the Task Forces on Archival Selection to the Commission on Preservation and Access. Washington, D.C.: Commission on Preservation and Access, 1993.

Preservation of Historical Records. Washington, D.C.: National Research Council, 1986.

"Preservation: Old and New Technologies Save Books for Future Use." *Journal of Information and Image Management* 18 (November 1985): 22–27.

Preserving the Intellectual Heritage: A Report of the Bellagio Conference, June 7–10, 1993. Washington, D.C.: Commission on Preservation and Access, 1993.

Pursell, Carroll. "Preservation Technologies: As Answers Get Easier, Questions Remain Hard." *Public Historian* 13 (summer 1991): 113–116.

"Rare Book and Paper Repair Techniques." *Technical Leaflet No. 13.* Nashville, Tenn.: American Association for State and Local History.

Reilly, James M. *Care and Identification of Nineteenth-Century Photographic Prints.* Rochester, N.Y.: Eastman Kodak Company, 1986.

Reilly, James M., Douglas W. Nishimura, and Edward Zinn. *New Tools for Preservation: Assessing Long-Term Environmental Effects on Library and Archives Collections.* Washington, D.C.: Commission on Preservation and Access, 1995.

Ritzenthaler, Mary Lynn. *Archives and Manuscripts: Conservation.* Chicago: Society of American Archivists, 1983.

———. *Preserving Archives and Manuscripts.* Chicago: Society of American Archivists, 1993.

Schmidt, J. David. "Freeze-Drying of Historic/Cultural Properties: A Valuable Process in Restoration and Documentation." *Technology and Conservation* 9 (spring 1985): 20–26.

Schur, Susan E. "Conservation Profile: The Northeast Document Conservation Center." *Technology and Conservation* 7 (fall 1982): 32–39.

———. "Conservation Profile: The Preservation Office of the Library of Congress." *Technology and Conservation* 7 (summer 1982): 26–35.

Sebera, Donald K. *Isoperms: An Environmental Management Tool.* Washington, D.C.: Commission on Preservation and Access, 1994.

Story, Keith O. *Approaches to Pest Management in Museums.* Washington, D.C.: Conservation Analytical Laboratory, Smithsonian Institution, 1985.

Trinkaus-Randall, Gregor. *Protecting Your Collections: A Manual of Archival Security.* Chicago: Society of American Archivists, 1995.

Waegemann, C. Peter. "Preservation of Information." *Records and Retrieval Report* 2 (March 1986): 1–15.

Walker, Gay. "Advanced Preservation Planning at Yale." *Microform Review* 18 (winter 1989): 20–28.

———. "Storing Paper." *Records and Retrieval Report* 3 (September 1987): 1–12.

White, John R. "An Introduction to the Preservation of Information on Paper, Film, Magnetic, and Optical Media." Silver Spring, Md.: Association for Information and Image Management.

SECURITY AND DISASTER PLANNING

Anderson, Hazel. *Planning Manual for Disaster Control in Scottish Libraries and Records Offices*. Edinburgh: National Library of Scotland, 1985.

Archives and Records Centers. Leaflet 232AM. Quincy, Mass.: National Fire Protection Association, 1986.

Balon, Brett J., and H. Wayne Gardner. "Disaster Contingency Planning: The Basic Elements." *ARMA Records Management Quarterly* 21 (January 1987): 14–16.

Barton, John P., and Johanna G. Wellheiser, eds. *An Ounce of Prevention: A Handbook on Disaster Contingency Planning for Archives, Libraries, and Records Centers*. Toronto: Toronto Area Archivists, 1986.

Bohem, Hilda. *Disaster Prevention and Disaster Preparedness*. Berkeley, Calif.: University of California, 1978.

Buchanan, Sally. "Disaster: Prevention, Preparedness and Action." *Library Trends* (fall 1981): 241–252.

———. *Resource Materials for Disaster Planning in New York Institutions*. Albany, N.Y.: New York State Library, 1988.

Bulgawicz, Susan, and Charles E. Nolan. "Disaster Planning and Recovery: A Regional Approach." *ARMA Records Management Quarterly* 21 (January 1987): 18–20, 44.

Disaster Planning Kit. Andover, Mass.: Northeast Document Conservation Center, 1982.

Disaster Prevention and Preparedness. Problems in Archives Kit. Chicago: Society of American Archivists, 1982.

Eulenberg, Julia N. *Handbook for the Recovery of Water Damaged Business Records*. Prairie Village, Kans.: Association of Records Managers and Administrators, 1986.

Fortson, Judith. *Disaster Planning and Recovery*. New York: Neal-Schuman, 1992.

Fuss, Eugene L. "Security in Cultural Institutions: Advances in Electronic Protection Techniques." *Technology and Conservation* 4 (winter 1979): 34–37.

Galvin, Theresa. "The Boston Case of Charles Merrill Mount: The Archivist's Arch Enemy." *American Archivist* 53 (summer 1990): 442–451.

Griffith, J. W. "After the Disaster: Restoring Library Service." *Wilson Library Bulletin* 58 (December 1983): 258–265.

Hell and High Water: A Disaster Information Sourcebook. New York: New York Metropolitan Reference and Research Library Agency (METRO): 1988.

Hendriks, Klaus B., and Brian Lesser. "Disaster Preparedness and

Recovery: Photographic Materials." *American Archivist* 46 (winter 1983): 52–68.

Hoffman, Annie, and Bryan Baumann. "Disaster Recovery: A Prevention Plan for Northwestern National Life Insurance." *ARMA Records Management Quarterly* 20 (April 1986): 40–44.

Hunter, John E. "Museum Disaster Planning." *Museums, Archives, and Library Security.* Woburn, Mass.: Butterworth Publishers, 1983.

Kemp, Toby. "Disaster Assistance Bibliography: Selected References for Cultural/ Historic Facilities." *Technology and Conservation* 8 (summer 1983): 25–27.

Mathieson, David F. "Hurricane Preparedness: Establishing Workable Policies for Dealing with Storm Threats." *Technology and Conservation* 8 (summer 1983): 28–29.

Morris, John. *The Library Disaster Preparedness Handbook.* Chicago: American Library Association, 1986

Murray, Toby. "Bibliography on Disasters, Disaster Preparedness and Disaster Recovery," *ARMA Records Management Quarterly* 21 (April 1987): 18–30, 41.

———. "Don't Get Caught with Your Plans Down." *ARMA Records Management Quarterly* 21 (April 1987): 12–17.

O'Connell, Mildred. "Disaster Planning: Writing and Implementing Plans for Collections-Holding Institutions." *Technology and Conservation* 8 (summer 1983): 18–24.

Protection of Records. Leaflet 232. Quincy, Mass.: National Fire Protection Association, 1986.

Tiszkus, Alphonse T., and E. G. Dressler. "Fire Protection Planning for Cultural Institutions: Blending Risk Management, Loss Prevention, and Physical Safeguards." *Technology and Conservation* 5 (summer 1980): 18–23.

Totka, Vincent A., Jr. "Preventing Patron Theft in the Archives: Legal Perspectives and Problems." *American Archivist* 56 (fall 1993): 664–673.

Trinkaus-Randall, Gregor. *Protecting Your Collections: A Manual of Archival Security.* Chicago: Society of American Archivists, 1995.

Vital Records. Prairie Village, Kans.: Association of Records Managers and Administrators, 1984.

Vossler, Janet L. "The Human Element of Disaster Recovery." *ARMA Records Management Quarterly* 21 (January 1987): 10–12.

Waegemann, C. Peter. "Disaster Prevention and Recovery." *Records and Retrieval Report* 1 (March 1985).

Walch, Timothy. *Archives and Manuscripts: Security.* Chicago: Society of American Archivists, 1977.

Waters, Peter. *Procedures for Salvage of Water-Damaged Library Materials*. Washington, D.C., Library of Congress, 1975.

Wolff, Richard E. "Snap, Crackle and Pop." *ARMA Records Management Quarterly* 19 (April 1985): 3–7.

Zeidberg, David S. "We Have Met the Enemy: Collection Security in Libraries." *Rare Book and Manuscript Librarianship* 2 (spring 1987): 19–26.

ACCESS, REFERENCE, AND OUTREACH

Aubitz, Shawn, and Gail F. Stern. "Developing Archival Exhibitions." *Mid-Atlantic Regional Archives Conference Technical Leaflet No. 5*. Mid-Atlantic Regional Archives Conference, 1990.

Baumann, Roland M. "The Administration of Access to Confidential Records in State Archives: Common Practices and the Need for a Model Law." *American Archivist* 49 (fall 1986): 349–369.

Blouin, Francis X., Jr. "A Case for Bridging the Gap: The Significance of the Vatican Archives Project for International Archival Information Exchange." *American Archivist* 55 (winter 1992): 182–191.

Bradsher, James Gregory. "Researchers, Archivists, and the Access Challenge of the FBI Records in the National Archives." *Midwestern Archivist* 11 (1986): 95–110.

Brauer, Carl M. "Researcher Evaluation of Reference Services." *American Archivist* 43 (winter 1980): 77–79.

Bruemmer, Bruce H. "Access to Oral History: A National Agenda." *American Archivist* 54 (fall 1991): 494–501.

Casterline, Gail Farr. *Archives and Manuscripts: Exhibits*. Chicago: Society of American Archivists, 1980.

Conway, Paul. "Facts and Frameworks: An Approach to Studying the Users of Archives." *American Archivist* 49 (fall 1986): 393–408.

———. "Research in Presidential Libraries: A User Survey." *Midwestern Archivist* 11 (1986): 35–56.

Crawford, Michael J. "Copyright, Unpublished Manuscript Records, and the Archivist." *American Archivist* 46 (spring 1983): 135–147.

Danielson, Elena S. "The Ethics of Access." *American Archivist* 52 (winter 1989): 52–62.

Dearstyne, Bruce W. "What is the *Use* of Archives? A Challenge for the Profession." *American Archivist* 50 (winter 1987): 76–87.

Delgado, David J. "The Archivist and Public Relations." *American Archivist* 30 (October 1967): 557–564.

DeWitt, Donald L. "The Impact of the MARC AMC Format on Archival Education and Employment During the 1980s." *Midwestern Archivist* 16 (1991): 73–86.

Diamond, Sigmund. "Archival Adventure Along the Freedom of Information Trail: What Archival Records Reveal About the FBI and the Universities in the McCarthy Period." *Midwestern Archivist* 12 (1987): 29–42.

Dowler, Lawrence. "The Role of Use in Defining Archival Practice and Principles: A Research Agenda for the Availability and Use of Records." *American Archivist* 51 (winter/spring 1988): 74–95.

Duchein, Michel. *Obstacles to the Access, Use, and Transfer of Information from Archives: A RAMP Study*. Paris: UNESCO, 1983.

Ericksen, Paul A. "Letting the World in: Anticipating the Use of Religious Archives for the Study of Nonreligious Subjects." *Midwestern Archivist* 12 (1987): 83–90.

Finch, Elsie Freeman, ed. *Advocating Archives: An Introduction to Public Relations for Archivists*. Metuchen, N.J.: Society of American Archivists and Scarecrow Press, 1994.

Finch, Elsie Freeman. "Making Sure They Want It: Managing Successful Public Programs." *American Archivist* 56 (winter 1993): 70–75.

Freedom and Equality of Access to Information: A Report to the American Library Association. Chicago: American Library Association, 1986.

Freeman, Elsie T. "In the Eye of the Beholder: Archives Administration from the User's Point of View." *American Archivist* 47 (spring 1984): 111–123.

_____. "Soap and Education: Archival Training, Public Service, and the Profession: An Essay." *Midwestern Archivist* 16 (1991): 87–94.

Freivogel, Elsie Freeman. "Education Programs: Outreach as an Administrative Function." *American Archivist* 41 (April 1978): 147–153.

Geselbracht, Raymond H. "The Origins of Restrictions on Access to Personal Papers at the Library of Congress and the National Archives." *American Archivist* 49 (spring 1986): 142–162.

Gilardi, Ronald L. "The Archival Setting and People with Disabilities: A Legal Analysis." *American Archivist* 56 (fall 1993): 704–713.

Gilliland-Swetland, Anne J., and Carol Hughes. "Enhancing Archival Description for Public Computer Conferences of Historical Value: An Exploratory Study." *American Archivist 55* (spring 1992): 316–330.

Goerler, Raimund E. "Play It Again, Sam: Historical Slide Presentations in Archivists' Public Programming." *American Archivist 54* (summer 1991): 378–388.

Goggin, Jacqueline. "The Indirect Approach: A Study of Scholarly Users of Black and Women's Organizational Records in the Library of Congress Manuscript Division." *Midwestern Archivist 11* (1986): 57–67.

Gray, Edward. "Copyright and the Right to Copy: Thoughts on the Betamax Case." *Journal of Information and Image Management 17* (December 1984): 48–49.

Harris, Verne, and Christopher Merrett. "Toward a Culture of Transparency: Public Rights of Access to Official Records in South Africa." *American Archivist 57* (fall 1994): 680–693.

Herzstein, Robert Edwin. "The Recently Opened United Nations War Crime Archives: A Researcher's Comments." *American Archivist 52* (spring 1989): 208–213.

Hodson, Sara S. "Freeing the Dead Sea Scrolls: A Question of Access." *American Archivist 56* (fall 1993): 690–703.

Hoff-Wilson, Joan. "Access to Restricted Collections: The Responsibility of Professional Historical Organizations." *American Archivist 46* (fall 1983): 441–447.

Holbert, Sue E. *Archives and Manuscripts: Reference and Access.* Chicago: Society of American Archivists, 1977.

Jacobsen, Phebe R. " 'The World Turned Upside Down': Reference Priorities and the State Archives." *American Archivist 44* (fall 1981): 341–345.

Jordan, Philip D. "The Scholar and the Archivist: A Partnership." *American Archivist 31* (January 1968): 57–65.

Joyce, William L. "Archivists and Research Use." *American Archivist 47* (spring 1984): 124–133.

Kepley, Brenda Beasley. "Archives: Accessibility for the Disabled." *American Archivist 46* (winter 1983): 42–51.

Klaassen, David J. "Achieving Balanced Documentation: Social Services from a Consumer Perspective." *Midwestern Archivist 11* (1986): 111–124.

Lathrop, Alan K. "Copyright of Architectural Records: A Legal Perspective." *American Archivist 49* (fall 1986): 409–423.

Library Reproduction of Copyrighted Works (17 U.S.C. 108): Report of the Register of Copyrights. Washington, D.C.: Library of Congress, 1988.

Long, Linda J. "Question Negotiation in the Archival Setting: The

Use of Interpersonal Communication Techniques in the Reference Interview." *American Archivist* 52 (winter 1989): 40–51.

Looking to the Past, Teaching for the Future: Recommendations for the Improvement of Teaching Using Historical Records. Albany, N.Y.: New York State Council for the Social Studies, 1989.

Maher, William J. "The Use of User Studies." *Midwestern Archivist* 11 (1986): 15–26.

Martin, Lyn M. "Viewing the Field: A Literature Review and Survey of the Use of U.S. MARC AMC in U.S. Academic Archives." *American Archivist* 57 (summer 1994): 482–497.

McAdam, Rhona. "AIDS and Confidentiality: The Records Manager's Dilemma." *ARMA Records Management Quarterly* 23 (July 1989): 12–16, 28.

Miller, Fredric. "Use, Appraisal, and Research: A Case Study of Social History." *American Archivist* 49 (fall 1986): 371–392.

Miller, Harold L. "Will Access Restrictions Hold Up in Court? The FBI's Attempt to Use the Braden Papers at the State Historical Society of Wisconsin." *American Archivist* 52 (spring 1989): 180–190.

Miller, Page Putnam. "Archival Issues and Problems: The Central Role of Advocacy." *Public Historian* 8 (summer 1986): 60–73.

Montgomery, Bruce P. "Nixon's Legal Legacy: White House Papers and the Constitution." *American Archivist* 56 (fall 1993): 586–613.

Nixon, Diane S. "Providing Access to Controversial Public Records: The Case of the Robert F. Kennedy Assassination Files." *Public Historian* 11 (summer 1989): 29–44.

Orbach, Barbara C. "The View from the Researcher's Desk: Historians' Perceptions of Research and Repositories." *American Archivist* 54 (winter 1991): 28–43.

Patry, William F. *The Fair Use Privilege in Copyright Law.* Washington, D.C.: Bureau of National Affairs, 1985.

Pedersen, Ann E., and Gail Farr Casterline. *Archives and Manuscripts: Public Programs.* Chicago: Society of American Archivists, 1980.

Peterson, Trudy Huskamp. "After Five Years: An Assessment of the Amended U.S. Freedom of Information Act." *American Archivist* 43 (spring 1980): 161–168.

————. "Reading, 'Riting, and 'Rithmetic: Speculations on Change in Research Processes." *American Archivist* 55 (summer 1992): 414–419.

Preston, Jean. "Problems in the Use of Manuscripts." *American Archivist* 28 (July 1965): 367–380.

Pugh, Mary Jo. *Providing Reference Services for Archives and Manuscripts.* Chicago: Society of American Archivists, 1992.

Ress, Imre. "The Effects of Democratization on Archival Administration and Use in Eastern Middle Europe." *American Archivist* 55 (winter 1992): 86–93.

Robbin, Alice. "State Archives and Issues of Personal Privacy: Policies and Practices." *American Archivist* 49 (spring 1986): 163–175.

Schwarz, Judith. "The Archivist's Balancing Act: Helping Researchers While Protecting Individual Privacy." *Journal of American History* 79 (June 1992): 179–189.

Speakman, Mary N. "The User Talks Back." *American Archivist* 47 (spring 1984): 164–171.

Stewart, Virginia R. "Problems of Confidentiality in the Administration of Personal Case Records." *American Archivist* 37 (July 1974): 387–398.

Synnott, Marcia G. "*The Half-Opened Door*: Researching Admissions Discrimination at Harvard, Yale, and Princeton." *American Archivist* 45 (spring 1982): 175–187.

Taylor, Hugh A. *Archival Services and the Concept of the User: A RAMP Study.* Paris: UNESCO, 1984.

———. "Clio in the Raw: Archival Materials and the Teaching of History." *American Archivist* 35 (July/October 1972): 317–330.

Tibbo, Helen R. "The Epic Struggle: Subject Retrieval from Large Bibliographic Databases." *American Archivist* 57 (spring 1994). 310–326

Turnbaugh, Roy C. "Archival Mission and User Studies." *Midwestern Archivist* 11 (1986): 27–33.

Van Camp, Anne. "Access Policies for Corporate Archives." *American Archivist* 45 (summer 1982): 296–298.

Warnow-Blewett, Joan. "Work to Internationalize Access to the Archives and Manuscripts of Physics and Allied Sciences." *American Archivist* 55 (summer 1992): 484–489.

Weinberg, David M. "The Other Side of the Human Experience: Providing Access to Social Service Case Study Files." *American Archivist* 53 (winter 1990): 122–129.

Whalen, Lucille, and Bill Katz, eds. *Reference Services in Archives.* New York: Haworth Press, 1986.

Yakel, Elizabeth. "Pushing MARC AMC to Its Limits: The Vatican Archives Project." *American Archivist* 55 (winter 1992): 192–201.

Yakel, Elizabeth, and Laura L. Bost. "Understanding Administrative Use and Users in University Archives." *American Archivist* 57 (fall 1994): 596–615.

ELECTRONIC RECORDS

"Archival Issues Raised by Information Stored in Electronic Form." Position statement issued by Society of American Archivists, 1995.

Bearman, David. "Diplomatics, Weberian Bureaucracy, and the Management of Electronic Records in Europe and America." *American Archivist* 55 (winter 1992): 168–181.

———. "The Implications of *Armstrong v. Executive Office of the President* for the Archival Management of Electronic Records." *American Archivist* 56 (fall 1993): 674–689.

———, ed. "Archival Management of Electronic Records." *Archives and Museum Informatics Technical Report No. 13.* Pittsburgh: Archives and Museum Informatics, 1991.

———. *Electronic Evidence.* Pittsburgh, Pa.: Archives and Museum Informatics, 1995.

Bikson, Tora K. "Organizational Trends and Electronic Media: Work in Progress." *American Archivist* 57 (winter 1994): 48–69.

Brown, Thomas Elton. "The Society of American Archivists Confronts the Computer." *American Archivist* 47 (fall 1984): 366–382.

Chamberlin, Brewster, Marilyn Courtot, and Lawrence F. Karr. "Holocaust Memorial Museum: New Approaches for an All-in-One Resource Center." *Journal of Information and Image Management* 19 (July 1986): 35–40.

Cloud, Patricia. "RLIN, AMC, and Retrospective Conversion." *Midwestern Archivist* 11 (1986): 125–134.

Cook, Michael. *Archives and the Computer.* 2d ed. Boston: Butterworth, 1986.

———. *Information Management and Archival Data.* London: Library Association Publishing, 1993.

Dollar, Charles M. "Appraising Machine-Readable Records." *American Archivist* 41 (October 1978): 423–430.

———. *Archival Theory and Information Technologies.* Macerata, Italy: University of Macerata Press, 1992.

Dollar, Charles M., and Carolyn L. Geda, eds. "Archivists, Archives, and Computers: A Starting Point." *American Archivist* 42 (April 1979): 149–193.

Durr, W. Theodore. "Some Thoughts and Designs about Archives and Automation, 1984." *American Archivist* 47 (summer 1984): 271–289.

Effects of Electronic Recordkeeping on the Historical Record of the U.S. Government. Washington, D.C.: National Academy of Public Administration, 1989.

Florian, Doris. "The Impact of Artificial Intelligence on Information Management: Questions and Answers." *International Information Management Congress Journal* 24 (1988): 18–21.

Forsyth, Richard. *Machine Learning: Applications in Expert Systems and Information Retrieval.* New York: Halsted, 1986.

Geda, Carolyn, Eric W. Austin, and Francis X. Blouin, Jr. *Archives and Machine-Readable Records.* Chicago: Society of American Archivists, 1980.

Gildemeister, Glen A. "Automation, Reference, and the Small Repository, 1967–1997." *Midwestern Archivist* 13 (1988): 5–16.

Goerler, Raimund E. "Towards 2001: Electronic Workstations and the Future of Academic Archives." *Archival Issues* 17 (1992): 11–22.

Greenstein, Shane. "Tape Story Tapestry: Historical Research with Inaccessible Digital Information Technologies." *Midwestern Archivist* 15 (1990): 77–85.

Harrison, Donald F., ed. *Automation in Archives.* Washington, D.C.: Mid-Atlantic Regional Archives Conference, 1993.

Hedstrom, Margaret L. *Archives and Manuscripts: Machine-Readable Records.* Chicago, Society of American Archivists: 1984.

———. "Understanding Electronic Incunabula: A Framework for Research on Electronic Records." *American Archivist* 54 (summer 1991): 334–354.

———, ed. *Electronic Records Management Program Strategies.* Pittsburgh, Pa.: Archives and Museum Informatics, 1993.

Hendley, Tony. *The Archival Storage Potential of Microfilm, Magnetic Media, and Optical Data Disks.* Hertford, England: National Reprographic Centre for Documentation, 1983.

Hensen, Steven L. "The Use of Standards in the Application of the AMC Format." *American Archivist* 49 (winter 1986): 31–40.

Hickerson, Thomas H. *Archives and Manuscripts: An Introduction to Automated Access.* Chicago: Society of American Archivists, 1980.

Hodges, Martha. "Using the MARC Format for Archives and Manuscripts Control to Catalog Published Microfilms of Manuscript Collections." *Microform Review* 18 (winter 1989): 29–35.

Holmes, William M., Jr.; Edie Hedlin; and Thomas E. Weir, Jr. "MARC and Life Cycle Tracking at the National Archives: Project Final Report." *American Archivist* 49 (summer 1986): 305–309.

Honhart, Frederick L. "MicroMARC:AMC: A Case Study in the Development of an Automated System." *American Archivist* 52 (winter 1989): 80–86.

Hopkins, Mark. "Computerizing a Government Records Archives: The FEDDOCS [Federal Archives Division of the Public Archives of Canada] Experience." *ARMA Records Management Quarterly* 20 (July 1986): 36–39.

Jordahl, Gregory. "NARA Takes Steps to Protect the [Electronic] Historical Record." *Inform* 4 (July/August 1990): 10–11.

Katz, Richard N., and Victoria A. Davis. "The Impact of Automation on Our Corporate Memory." *ARMA Records Management Quarterly* 20 (January 1986): 10–14.

Kaufhold, Penny. "The Rough Edges of the Learning Curve." *ARMA Records Management Quarterly* 21 (April 1987): 33–34, 39.

Kesner, Richard. *Automation for Archivists and Records Managers: Planning and Implementation Strategies.* Chicago: Society of American Archivists, 1984.

———. "Computers, Archival Administration, and the Challenges of the 1980's." *Georgia Archive,* 9 (fall 1981): 1–18.

———. *Information Management, Machine-Readable Records, and Administration: An Annotated Bibliography.* Chicago: Society of American Archivists, 1983.

———. *Information Systems: A Strategic Approach to Planning and Implementation.* Chicago: American Library Association, 1988.

———. "Microcomputer Archives and Records Management Systems: Guidelines for Future Development." *American Archivist* 45 (summer 1982): 299–311.

Landis, William E., and Robert Royce. "Recommendations for an Electronic Records Management System: A Case Study of a Small Business." *Archival Issues* 20 (1995): 7–21.

Maher, William J. "Administering Archival Automation: Development of In-House Systems." *American Archivist* 47 (fall 1984): 405–417.

Mallinson, John C. "On the Preservation of Human and Machine-Readable Records." *Information Technologies and Libraries* 7 (March 1988): 19–22.

Managing Electronic Records. Washington, D.C.: National Archives and Records Administration, 1990.

MARC Format and Life Cycle Tracking at the National Archives: A Study. Washington, D.C.: National Archives and Records Administration, 1986.

Michelson, Avra. "Description and Reference in the Age of Automation." *American Archivist* 50 (spring 1987): 192–208.

Michelson, Avra, and Jeff Rothenberg. "Scholarly Communication and Information Technology: Exploring the Impact of Changes in the Research Process on Archives." *American Archivist* 55 (spring 1992): 236–315.

Mohlhenrich, Janice, ed. *Preservation of Electronic Formats and Electronic Formats for Preservation*. Fort Atkinson, Wis.: Highsmith Press, 1993.

Morton, Katharine D. "The MARC Formats: An Overview." *American Archivist* 49 (winter 1986): 21–30.

Motz, Arlene. "Applying Records Management Principles to Magnetic Media." *ARMA Records Management Quarterly* 20 (April 1986): 22–26.

Neumann, Peter G. *Computer Related Risks*. New York: Addison-Wesley, 1995.

Nowicke, Carole Elizabeth. "Managing Tomorrow's Records Today: An Experiment in Archival Preservation of Electronic Mail." *Midwestern Archivist* 13 (1988): 67–76.

Paton, Christopher Ann. "Annotated Selected Bibliography of Works Relating to Sound Recordings and Magnetic and Optical Media." *Midwestern Archivist* 16 (1991): 31–48. [Issue contains other articles on audio preservation.]

Peterson, Trudy Huskamp. "Archival Principles and Records of the New Technology." *American Archivist* 47 (fall 1984): 383–393.

Prietto, Carole. "Automating the Archives: A Case Study." *American Archivist* 57 (spring 1994): 364–373.

"Reviews: Computer Applications Programs." *Midwestern Archivist* 11 (1986): 69–83.

Rhodes, Steven B. "Archival and Records Management Automation." *ARMA Records Management Quarterly* 25 (April 1991): 12–17.

Rothenberg, Jeff. "Ensuring the Longevity of Digital Documents." *Scientific American* (January 1995). 42–47.

Saffady, William. *Managing Electronic Records*. Prairie Village, Kans.: Association of Records Managers and Administrators, 1992.

Sahli, Nancy A. "Interpretation and Application of the AMC Format." *American Archivist* 49 (winter 1986): 9–20.

Sanders, Robert M. "The Company Index: Information Retrieval Thesauri for Organizations and Institutions." *ARMA Records Management Quarterly* 20 (April 1986): 3–14.

———. "While Waiting for the Real Computerization of Your Archives: A Lo-Tech Recipe." *ARMA Records Management Quarterly* 18 (October 1984): 5–11.

Skillman, Juanita, and April Dmytrenko. "A Comparison of PC Based Records Management Software." *ARMA Records Management Quarterly* 23 (April 1989): 21–33.

Skupsky, Donald S. "Establishing Retention Periods for Electronic Records." *ARMA Records Management Quarterly* 27 (April 1993): 40–43.

Smither, Roger. "Formats and Standards: A Film Archive Perspective on Exchanging Computerized Data." *American Archivist* 50 (summer 1987): 324–337.

Sprehe, J. Timothy. "Archiving Electronic Databases: The NAPA [National Academy of Public Administration] Report." *Inform* 6 (March 1992): 28–31.

Stielow, Frederick J. "Archival Theory and the Preservation of Electronic Media: Opportunities and Standards Below the Cutting Edge." *American Archivist* 55 (spring 1992): 332–343.

———. "The Impact of Information Technology on Archival Theory: A Discourse on the Automation Pedagogy." *Journal of Education for Library and Information Science* 34 (winter 1993): 48–65.

Stout, Leon J., and Donald A. Baird. "Automation in North American College and University Archives: A Survey." *American Archivist* 47 (fall 1984): 394–404.

Taylor, Hugh. "Information Ecology and the Archives in the 1980's." *Archivaria* 18 (summer 1984): 25–37.

———. " 'My Very Act and Deed': Some Reflections on the Role of Textual Records in the Conduct of Affairs." *American Archivist* 51 (fall 1988): 456–469.

Van Bogart, John. *Magnetic Tape Storage and Handling: A Guide for Libraries and Archives.* Washington, D.C.: Commission on Preservation and Access, 1995.

Weber, Lisa. "Electronic Records: Too Ephemeral?" *Inform* 6 (February 1992): 32–36.

Weissman, Ronald F. E. "Archives and the New Information Architecture of the Late 1990s." *American Archivist* 57 (winter 1994): 20–35.

Whaley, John H., Jr. "Digitizing History." *American Archivist* 57 (fall 1994): 660–674.

Wheaton, Bruce R. "A Computer Database System to Store and Display Archival Data on Correspondence of Historical Significance." *American Archivist* 45 (fall 1982): 455–466.

Williams, Robert F. "Electronic Document Management: The Coming Revolution in Records Management." *International Information Management Congress Journal* 21 (fourth Quarter 1985): 33–37.

Yen, David, and Huang-Lian Tang. "Future Trends of Computer-Based Information Systems." *ARMA Records Management Quarterly* 22 (October 1988): 12–19.

Zboray, Ronald J. "dBase III Plus and the MARC AMC Format: Problems and Possibilities." *American Archivist* 50 (spring 1987): 210–225.

MANAGEMENT

Abraham, Terry, Stephen E. Balzarini, and Anne Frantilla. "What is Backlog is Prologue: A Measurement of Archival Processing." *American Archivist* 48 (winter 1985): 31–44.

Archival Processing Costs. Problems in Archives Kit. Chicago: Society of American Archivists, 1981.

Atherton, Jay. "Emphasizing the *Management* in Time Management." *ARMA Records Management Quarterly* 20 (October 1986): 26–29.

Bailey, Martha J. *The Special Librarian as Supervisor or Middle Manager.* New York: Special Libraries Association, 1977.

Bridges, Edwin C. "Can State Archives Meet the Challenges of the Eighties? Four Recent Views on the Condition of American State Archives." *ARMA Records Management Quarterly* 20 (April 1986): 15–21, 52.

Burke, Frank G. "Archival Cooperation." *American Archivist* 46 (summer 1983): 293–305.

Conway, Paul. "Perspectives on Archival Resources: The 1985 Census of Archival Institutions." *American Archivist* 50 (spring 1987): 174–191.

Davis, W. N., Jr. "Budgeting for Archival Processing." *American Archivist* 43 (spring 1980): 209–211.

Dearstyne, Bruce W. "Planning for Archival Programs: An Introduction." *Technical Leaflet No. 3.* New York: Mid-Atlantic Regional Archives Conference, 1983.

Evaluation of Archival Institutions: Services, Principles, and Guide to Self-Study. Chicago: Society of American Archivists, 1982.

Ewing, Susan E. "Using Volunteers for Special-Project Staffing at the National Air and Space Museum Archives." *American Archivist* 54 (spring 1991): 176–183.

Francis, James, Cynthia L. Sutton, and Bill Cox. "New Tools for the Information Manager [Quality Circles and Nominal Grouping Technique]." *ARMA Records Management Quarterly* 21 (April 1987): 3–8.

Grabowski, John J. "Keepers, Users, and Funders: Building an Awareness of Archival Value." *American Archivist* 55 (summer 1992): 464–472.

Hackman, Larry J. "Historical Documentation in the United States: Archivists—and Historians?" *Organization of American Historians Newsletter* (August 1985): 17–18.

Haller, Uli. "Variations in the Processing Rates on the Magnuson and Jackson Senatorial Papers." *American Archivist* 50 (winter 1987): 100–109.

Ham, F. Gerald. "Planning for the Archival Profession." *American Archivist* 48 (winter 1985): 26–30.

Hefner, Loretta L. "The Change Masters: Organizational Development in a State Archives." *American Archivist* 51 (fall 1988): 440–454.

Henry, Linda J. "Archival Advisory Committees: Why?" *American Archivist* 48 (summer 1985): 315–319.

Hunter, Gregory S. "Filling the GAP: Planning on the Local and Individual Levels." *American Archivist* 50 (winter 1987): 110–115.

Klein, Phyllis A. *Our Past Before Us: A Five-Year Regional Plan for METRO's Archives and Historical Records Program*. New York: New York Metropolitan Reference and Research Library Agency [METRO], 1989.

Long-Range Planning for Academic Archives. Problems in Archives Kit. Chicago: Society of American Archivists, 1983.

Maher, William J. "The Importance of Financial Analysis in Archival Programs." *Midwestern Archivist* 3 (1978): 3–24.

McCarthy, Paul H. "The Management of Archives: A Research Agenda." *American Archivist* 51 (winter/spring 1988): 52–73.

McShane, Stephen G. "Planning is Prologue: The Planning Process and the Archival Profession." *Midwestern Archivist* 15 (1990): 109–116.

Planning for the Archival Profession: A Report of the SAA Task Force on Goals and Priorities. Chicago: Society of American Archivists, 1986.

Strengthening New York's Historical Records Programs: A Self-Study Guide. New York: State Archives and Records Administration, 1989.

Virgo, Julie. *Principles of Strategic Planning in the Library Environment*. Chicago: Association of College and Research Libraries, 1984.

Waegemann, C. Peter. "Cost Management in Records Management." *Records and Retrieval Report* 1 (February 1985). 21–36.

Wilsted, Thomas. "Computing the Total Cost of Archival Processing." *Technical Leaflet No. 2*. New York: Mid-Atlantic Regional Archives Conference, 1982.

Wilsted, Thomas, and William Nolte. *Managing Archival and Manuscript Repositories*. Chicago: Society of American Archivists, 1991.

EDUCATION, PROFESSIONAL DEVELOPMENT, AND ETHICS

Albada, Joan Van. "The Identity of the American Archival Profession: A European Perspective." *American Archivist* 54 (summer 1991): 398–402.

Bearman, Toni Carbo. "The Education of Archivists: Future Challenges for Schools of Library and Information Science." *Journal of Education for Library and Information Science* 34 (winter 1993): 66–72.

Bennett, George E. *Librarians in Search of Science and Identity: The Elusive Profession.* Metuchen, N.J.: Scarecrow Press, 1988.

Brichford, Maynard. "Who Are the Archivists and What Do They Do?" *American Archivist* 51 (winter/spring 1988): 106–110.

Bridges, Edwin, et al. "Toward Better Documenting and Interpreting of the Past: What History Graduate Programs in the Twenty-First Century Should Teach About Archival Practices." *American Archivist* 56 (fall 1993): 730–749.

Brumm, Eugenia K. "Graduate Education in Records Management: The University of Texas Model." *Journal of Education for Library and Information Science* 33 (fall 1992): 333–337.

"A Code of Ethics for Archivists." *American Archivist* 43 (summer 1980): 414–418.

Conway, Paul. "Archival Education and the Need for Full-Time Faculty." *American Archivist* 51 (summer 1988): 254–265.

———. "Effective Continuing Education for Training the Archivist." *Journal of Education for Library and Information Science* 34 (winter 1993): 38–47.

Cook, Michael. *The Education and Training of Archivists: Status Report of Archival Training Programs and Assessment of Manpower Needs.* Paris: UNESCO, 1979.

———. *Guidelines for Curriculum Development in Records Management and the Administration of Modern Archives: A RAMP Study.* Paris: UNESCO, 1982.

Cox, Richard J. "American Archival Literature: Expanding Horizons and Continuing Needs, 1901–1987." *American Archivist* 50 (summer 1987): 306–323.

———. "Archivists and Public Historians in the United States." *Public Historian* 8 (summer 1986): 29–45.

———. "Our Disappearing Past." *Organization of American Historians Newsletter* 15 (February 1987): 8–9.

———. "Professionalism and Archivists in the United States." *American Archivist* 49 (summer 1986): 229–247.

BIBLIOGRAPHY **277**

————, ed. "Educating the American Archivist for the Twenty-First Century." *Journal of Education for Library and Information Science* special issue 34 (winter 1993).

Danielson, Elena S. "The Ethics of Access." *American Archivist* 52 (winter 1989): 52–62.

Davis, Susan E. "Continuing Education for Archivists." *Journal of Education for Library and Information Science* 34 (winter 1993): 79–81.

————. "Development of Managerial Training for Archivists." *American Archivist* 51 (summer 1988): 278–285.

Delmas, B. *The Training of Archivists: Analysis of the Study Programmes of Different Countries and Thoughts on the Possibilities of Harmonization.* Paris: UNESCO, 1979.

Duranti, Luciana. "The Archival Body of Knowledge: Archival Theory, Method, and Practice, and Graduate and Continuing Education." *Journal of Education for Library and Information Science* 34 (winter 1993): 8–24.

Eastwood, Terry. "Nurturing Archival Education in the University." *American Archivist* 51 (summer 1988): 228–252.

Endelman, Judith E., and Joel Wurl. "The NHPRC/Mellon Foundation Fellowship in Archives Administration: Structured Training on the Job." *American Archivist* 51 (summer 1988): 286–297.

Ericson, Timothy L. " 'Abolish the Recent': the Progress of Archival Education." *Journal of Education for Library and Information Science* 34 (winter 1993): 25–37.

————. "Professional Associations and Archival Education: A Different Role, or a Different Theater?" *American Archivist* 51 (summer 1988): 298–311.

Fleckner, John A. " 'Dear Mary Jane': Some Reflections on Being an Archivist." *American Archivist* 54 (winter 1991): 8–13.

Gabehart, Alan D. "Qualifications Desired by Employers for Entry-Level Archivists in the United States." *American Archivist* 55 (summer 1992): 420–439.

Gilliland-Swetland, Luke J. "The Provenance of a Profession: The Permanence of the Public Archives and Historical Manuscripts Tradition in American Archival History." *American Archivist* 54 (spring 1991): 160–175.

Gracy, David B., II "Archivists, You Are What People Think You Keep." *American Archivist* 52 (winter 1989): 72–78.

Ham, F. Gerald, et al. "Is the Past Still Prologue? History and Archival Education." *American Archivist* 56 (fall 1993): 718–729.

Helmuth, Ruth W. "Education for American Archivists: A View from the Trenches." *American Archivist* 44 (fall 1981): 295–303.

Horn, David E. "The Development of Ethics in Archival Practice." *American Archivist* 52 (winter 1989): 64–71.

Joyce, William L. "Archival Education: Two Fables." *American Archivist* 51 (winter/ spring 1988): 16–22.

Kigongo-Bukenya, I. M. N. "Education and Training of Archivists at the East African School of Librarianship in the 1990s and Beyond." *American Archivist* 56 (spring 1993): 358–365.

Lytle, Richard H. "Ethics of Information Management." *ARMA Records Management Quarterly* 4 (October 1970): 5–8.

MacNeil, Heather. *Without Consent: The Ethics of Disclosing Personal Information in Public Archives.* Chicago: Society of American Archivists and Scarecrow Press, 1992.

Maher, William J. "Contexts for Understanding Professional Certification: Opening Pandora's Box?" *American Archivist* 51 (fall 1988): 408–427.

———. "Cooperative Competitors: Local, State, and National Archival Associations." *Midwestern Archivist* 16 (1991): 105–114.

Martin, Robert Sidney. "The Development of Professional Education for Librarians and Archivists in the United States: A Comparative Essay." *American Archivist* 57 (summer 1994): 544–559.

McAdam, Rhona. "AIDS and Confidentiality: The Records Manager's Dilemma." *ARMA Records Management Quarterly* 23 (July 1989): 12–16, 28.

Menne-Haritz, Angelika. "Archival Training in Germany: A Balance Between Specialization in Historical Research and Administrative Needs." *American Archivist* 57 (spring 1994): 400–409.

Mirandi, Paul J., Jr. "Associationalism, Statism, and Professional Regulation: Public Accountants and the Reform of the Financial Markets, 1896–1940." *Business History Review* 60 (autumn 1986): 438–468.

Museum Ethics. Washington, D.C.: American Association of Museums, 1978.

O'Toole, James M. "Curriculum Development in Archival Education: A Proposal." *American Archivist* 53 (summer 1990): 460–466.

Rene-Bazis, Paule. "The Future of European Archival Education." *American Archivist* 55 (winter 1992): 58–65.

"Roundtable: Ethics and Public History." *The Public Historian* 8 (winter 1986): 5–68.

Ruth, Janice E. "Educating the Reference Archivist." *American Archivist* 51 (summer 1988): 266–276.

Skupsky, Donald S. "Legal Liability of the Records and Information Management Professional." *ARMA Records Management Quarterly* 21 (April 1987): 36–39.

Stielow, Frederick. "Archival Theory Redux and Redeemed: Definition and Context Toward a General Theory." *American Archivist* 54 (winter 1991): 14–26.

Taylor, Hugh A. "From Dust to Ashes: Burnout in the Archives." *Midwestern Archivist* 12 (1987): 73–82.

Waegemann, C. Peter. "Careers in Records Management." *Records and Retrieval Report* 2 (December 1986): 1–10.

Wallot, Jean-Pierre. "Free Trade in Archival Ideas: The Canadian Perspective on North American Archival Development." *American Archivist* 57 (spring 1994): 380–399.

Walters, Tyler O. "Possible Educations for Archivists: Integrating Graduate Archival Education with Public History Education Programs." *American Archivist* 54 (fall 1991): 484–492.

White, Brenda. *Directory of Audio-Visual Materials for Use in Records Management and Archives Administration Training.* Paris: UNESCO, 1982.

Wiegand, Wayne A. *The Politics of an Emerging Profession: The American Library Association, 1876–1917.* Westport, Conn.: Greenwood Press, 1986.

Wosh, Peter J., and Elizabeth Yakel. "Smaller Archives and Professional Development: Some New York Stories." *American Archivist* 55 (summer 1992): 474–482.

INDEX

ABOUT THE AUTHOR

Gregory S. Hunter is an Associate Professor in the Palmer School of Library and Information Science, Long Island University. He also is president of his own consulting firm, Hunter Information Management Services, Inc. He earned a doctorate in American History at New York University and is both a Certified Archivist and a Certified Records Manager. In 1989, Dr. Hunter was elected the first president of the Academy of Certified Archivists. He also has served as chair of the Society of American Archivists' Committee on Education and Professional Development and treasurer of the Mid-Atlantic Regional Archives Conference. He is a frequent author and lecturer on archives, records management, electronic imaging systems, electronic records, and organizational change issues.